Deciphering *Good*

ALSO OF INTEREST
AND FROM MCFARLAND

Death in Supernatural: Critical Essays (edited by
Amanda Taylor and Susan Nylander, 2019)

*Joss Whedon Versus the Corporation: Big Business Critiqued
in the Films and Television Programs* (Erin Giannini, 2017)

Deciphering *Good Omens*

Nice and Accurate Essays on the Novel and Television Series

Edited by ERIN GIANNINI *and* AMANDA TAYLOR

McFarland & Company, Inc., Publishers
Jefferson, North Carolina

This book has undergone peer review.

LIBRARY OF CONGRESS CATALOGUING-IN-PUBLICATION DATA

Names: Giannini, Erin, 1974– editor. | Taylor, Amanda, editor.
Title: Deciphering Good omens : nice and accurate essays on the novel and television series / edited by Erin Giannini and Amanda Taylor.
Description: Jefferson, North Carolina : McFarland & Company, Inc., Publishers, 2023. | Includes bibliographical references and index.
Identifiers: LCCN 2023034333 | ISBN 9781476681641 (paperback : acid free paper) ∞
ISBN 9781476649887 (ebook)
Subjects: LCSH: Good omens (Television program) | Gaiman, Neil. Good omens.
Classification: LCC PN1992.77.G648 D43 2023 | DDC 791.45/72—dc23/eng/20230801
LC record available at https://lccn.loc.gov/2023034333

BRITISH LIBRARY CATALOGUING DATA ARE AVAILABLE

ISBN (print) 978-1-4766-8164-1
ISBN (ebook) 978-1-4766-4988-7

© 2023 Erin Giannini and Amanda Taylor. All rights reserved

No part of this book may be reproduced or transmitted in any form or by any means, electronic or mechanical, including photocopying or recording, or by any information storage and retrieval system, without permission in writing from the publisher.

Front cover: (left to right) David Tennant and Michael Sheen in the 2019 season of *Good Omens* (Amazon Studios/Photofest)

Printed in the United States of America

McFarland & Company, Inc., Publishers
  Box 611, Jefferson, North Carolina 28640
  www.mcfarlandpub.com

Acknowledgments

This book took a bit of time to come into being, not the least of which the pandemic. We could not have done it without the assistance of some wonderful people in our lives, including John Taylor, Susan Nylander, Kristopher Woofter, and Carol Giannini, all of whom provided encouragement, support, and patience. Of course, we would be remiss if we didn't thank both Neil Gaiman and (the late) Terry Pratchett for their rich world-building, and our wonderful contributors for their efforts, thoughtfulness, and flexibility. An extra special thank-you is due to Layla Milholen, who was unfailingly patient and supportive from this book's conception to its publication. Finally, we ask the reader to proclaim a soft "Wahoo!" that this book has come to fruition. It has been a sweet temptation to accomplish.

Table of Contents

Acknowledgments   v

In the Beginning: Nice and Accurate Analyses of Good Omens
    ERIN GIANNINI *and* AMANDA TAYLOR   1

Good Omens and Adaptation

Avoiding a Contemporary Apocalypse: Examining the Effects of Shifting *Good Omens* from Its Cold War Context
    RHIAN WALLER   11

God Is a Woman: *Good Omens*, Voice-Over, and the Female Gaze
    JULIA VANESSA PAUSS   30

Ways of Mourning: Reading Grief as Friendship in Terry Pratchett and Neil Gaiman's *Good Omens* (1990)
    PAVAN MANO   46

Good Omens and Fan Culture

"Okay, Crowley, Junior": Subversions and Transformations of *Good Omens* in *Supernatural* and Its Fandom
    CAIT COKER   61

Fan Desire and Normative Masculinities in *Good Omens* Gift Exchanges
    MARY INGRAM-WATERS   74

The Theology of Good Omens

"In the beginning, it was a nice day": Aziraphale and the Subversive Miltonian Angelology of *Good Omens*
    MELISSA D. AARON   87

Eschatological Ambiguity in *Good Omens*: How Concerns
for Survival Blur the Lines Between Good and Evil
 Morgan Shipley 104

Sola Fide: Ineffability, *Good Omens,* and the Reformation
 Philip Goldfarb Styrt 120

"This Angel, who is now become a Devil, is my particular
friend": Romantic Satanism and Loving Opposition
in *Good Omens* (2019)
 Alex Tankard 133

Naming, Artifacts, and Texts in *Good Omens*

Adam's Task: Naming and Sub-creation in *Good Omens*
 Janet Brennan Croft 151

The Book as Character: Tracing Textual Elements of *Good Omens*
Across the Novel and Miniseries
 Tara Prescott-Johnson 163

"Welcome to the end times": A Conclusion
 Amanda Taylor *and* Erin Giannini 177

About the Contributors 179

Index 183

In the Beginning

Nice and Accurate Analyses of Good Omens

Erin Giannini *and* Amanda Taylor

At its core, *Good Omens* (both book and series) serves as a riff on Revelation, particularly John's Apocalypse. Using as a starting point the notion of biblical inerrancy—that is, that every word in the Bible is both true and divinely inspired—Terry Pratchett and Neil Gaiman created a book that could be considered, much as Milton's *Paradise Lost*, as Bible fanfiction, albeit with a satirical bent. Like its source material, the world of *Good Omens* features the Garden of Eden at the start of a world only 6,000 years old, with the innocent couple (Adam and Eve) tempted by a snake (soon introduced as the demon Crowley) into eating fruit from the Tree of Knowledge and being expelled from the Garden by the angel Aziraphale.

Suggested in the text but shown explicitly in the mini-series, *Good Omens*' version of these events finds the angel Aziraphale not only providing the couple with his sword out of concern for their survival outside the Garden, but questioning whether he, and Heaven, had done the right thing. Crowley's question to him, "It'd be funny if we both got it wrong, eh? If I did the good thing and you did the bad one?" ("In the Beginning"), suggests that in both the book and television versions of Gaiman and Pratchett's fanfiction, humans are not inherently sinful, angels are not necessarily paragons of virtue, and demons can care more about driving beautiful vintage cars than damning humanity.

The novel mainly focuses on three narrative strands: the roles of Crowley and Aziraphale in helping start, and end, the world; the prophecies of medieval witch Agnes Nutter and her descendants' interpretation of her work; and the adventures of Antichrist Adam Young and his friends in a small English village called Tadfield. These elements converge as the End of Days approach, with Adam initially unaware of his status as Satan's son, and Nutter descendant Anathema Device—paired with

Newton Pulsifer (whose ancestor burned hers at the stake)—and Crowley and Aziraphale attempting to prevent the world-ending cosmic war. Despite any number of setbacks, including incompetence and lack of communication, the Apocalypse is averted, and the main players go back to their (somewhat) normal lives.

Centering Crowley and Aziraphale

In creating the mini-series—a co-production of the BBC and Amazon Studios—Gaiman indicated he was fulfilling a promise to the late Terry Pratchett (Rodriguez 2019), who had wanted to see an adaptation of their collaborative work. For the adaptation, however, Gaiman elected to center two characters who, while not minor players in the novel, nonetheless did not occupy the narrative real estate they do in the adaptation: the angel Aziraphale (Michael Sheen) and the demon Crowley (David Tennant). Both are outliers in their respective cosmic settings. Aziraphale loves books and foods and humanity. Crowley interprets his job as demon as creating inconvenience rather than damnation for humans (e.g., the horrible design of the M25 roadway). The pair's relationship serves as the fulcrum of the series, with a far greater amount of screentime developing their story, interaction, and importance to the narrative than that of Adam Young, the young Antichrist set to bring about Armageddon.

There are multiple reasons why the focus on Aziraphale and Crowley is necessary. One, both were popular in *Good Omens* fandom before the miniseries aired. Known as the "Ineffable Husbands," their dynamic easily lends itself to being read as queer within the initial novel as well as in the miniseries, with the pairing significantly outpacing any other *Good Omens* pairing on the fanfiction site Archive of Our Own.[1] Building on this, Gaiman wrote a 30-minute-plus cold opening to the third episode ("Hard Times"), which traces the angel and demon's relationship from the Garden of Eden to 1960s Soho, London—scenes that do not exist in the source material. The final moments of the final episode are devoted not to the 11-year-old Antichrist Adam Young confined to his family's garden, but rather to Crowley and Aziraphale sharing a toast to humanity, suggesting it is primarily their story, rather than Adam's ("The Very Last Day of the Rest of Their Lives" 1.6). This foregrounding of the two underscore the miniseries' thematic suggestion that it is ultimately the relationship between the (seemingly) divine and (supposedly) diabolical that matters, particularly their shifting balance within each of us. As with Crowley and Aziraphale, we, too, are not solely "good" or "evil." Despite their cosmic roles, their relationship is one way to emphasize the source material's essential humanism.

It should be noted that there are also production level reasons for the couple's prominence in the adaptation. Given its status as a co-production between the BBC and Amazon Studios, there are restrictions on how many hours the actors playing Adam and the Them can work in both the U.S. ("Child Entertainment Laws as of...") and the UK ("England Performance Legislation"). One solution appears to be reflected in not only Tennant and Sheen's expanded roles, but the development of minor characters such as Gabriel (Jon Hamm) and Beelzebub (Anna Maxwell Martin). Finally, of the actors featured in the series, Tennant and Sheen's previous work is likely more internationally well-known. Sheen's starring role in U.S. cable network Showtime's *Masters of Sex*, as well as a featured role in the enormously profitable *Twilight* films introduced him to a broad audience. Tennant's comparatively long tenure as the Tenth Doctor[2] in *Doctor Who* is still considered a highlight of the rebooted series. This could account for the fact that both the actors and their characters are the most prominent in the publicity surrounding the series and the bonus features included on the DVD/Blu-ray release. Even the packaging of the physical media releases features an oversized Crowley and Aziraphale hovering over an Earth populated with significantly smaller pictures of the rest of the cast.

Our Project

Both book and miniseries offer numerous entry points for further examination. While both Gaiman and Pratchett's work has been well-canvassed in both academic and popular analyses (indeed, in 2019, Trinity College in Dublin launched the Terry Pratchett Project, a wide-ranging research project focused on Pratchett's collection at the library), their collaboration on *Good Omens* remains under-examined, even though the novel itself actually represents Gaiman's first. (The graphic novel *Sandman* had already been published, and Pratchett and Gaiman had been friends for nearly five years before deciding to collaborate on *Good Omens*.) This book, as well as a planned second volume following the airing of the unexpected second season, is an attempt to address that gap through the lenses of adaptation, theology, fandom, and the text itself.

Good Omens and Adaptation

The first part of the book examines the correspondences and differences in adapting the novel into the miniseries. Rhian Waller starts off by

4 Deciphering *Good Omens*

discussing what it means for the adaptation to jettison the explicitly Cold War setting of the novel and setting the miniseries in contemporary times. Referring to this shift as an "uneven time lift," Waller points out the ways in which the ecological critique and nuclear anxiety of the novel's late-1980s setting are muddled within the adaptation. Further, the novel's Cold War implications embodied in Crowley and Aziraphale's loyalty more to the "adversary" they are stationed with on Earth rather than the machinations of their superiors, renders the contemporary setting oddly dated despite its recent (2019) setting.

Julia Vanessa Pauss teases out the implications of the adaptation's decision not only to employ God as narrator and voiceover, but casting Frances McDormand as God. She touches on the controversy generated by the series' choice, with God being gendered only to the audience through the sound of McDormand's voice, rather than explicitly referred to within the diegesis. Despite this, the choice of a woman as the literal "voice of God," Pauss argues, does not function as an "empty gesture," but rather one that "challenges normative relations of power and control."

Finally, Pavan Mano brings to light the grief and reckoning with death that suffuses the adaptation, as opposed to the novel. That is, the novel itself was a collaborative work between two friends who enjoyed one another and the process of writing together. Pratchett's death from Alzheimer's complications in 2015, and Gaiman's sense of loss, is particularly embodied within the expanded (and expansive) relationship between Crowley and Aziraphale in the series, functioning as a meditation on grief and loss as much as on the Apocalypse.

Good Omens and Fan Culture

The second section situates book and series in dialogue with both fandom and other series. Cait Coker teases out the implications of the interplays between *Good Omens*—as novel and miniseries—and the recently ended *Supernatural*. *Supernatural* creator Eric Kripke was admittedly a fan of Gaiman's work, and references to a large spectrum of it appear through the series' 15-season run. However, it is both the interplay between heaven, hell, and humans apparently in *Good Omens* and *Supernatural*, as well as *Supernatural*'s subversion of particular elements of *Good Omens*' cosmic and relational stories that form the crux of her examination.

Mary Ingram-Waters turns a critical eye toward the effect of the 2019 series on both visual and textual portrayals of Aziraphale and Crowley in fanworks. While Sheen and Tennant's embodiments of the roles have influenced fan perceptions (e.g., Aziraphale, as played by Sheen, is more conventionally attractive than as described in the text), Waters argues that this is only accelerated how fanworks have conceptualized the pair to reflect more normative—and masculine—cultural portrayals, despite the supposed "subversion" of heteronormativity the pairing represents.

The Theology of *Good Omens*

Offering several different takes on thorny issues presented in both the text and adaptation, the third part focuses particularly on the intersection of theology and eschatology in *Good Omens*. Melissa D. Aaron views *Good Omens* through both its literary (*Paradise Lost*) and theological antecedents. Aaron traces the ways in which Milton's epic itself broke with traditional portrayals of angels and demons, leading into Pratchett and Gaiman's further subversion of Milton's subversions in the ways it upends common perceptions of the proper behavior of celestial beings and notions of free will.

Opening his article with his own students' take on notions of good and evil, Morgan Shipley also argues that *Good Omens*' take—in both the novel and series—does not offer black and white notions of morality and ethics. Rather, as in the conversation between Crowley, Aziraphale, and Adam near the end of the series, *Good Omens* is concerned less with "good" and "evil" and more with choice, free will, and agency.

Philip Goldfarb Styrt puts both the novel's and miniseries' theological elements within the context of the Protestant Reformation and its emphasis on an individual's faith and interpretation of biblical text, versus the pre-and Counter-Reformation's more "traditional practices and collective cultural consensus." In particular, the way characters and text embody these concepts (e.g., the angel Gabriel as traditionalist) as well as *Good Omens*' emphasis on personal interpretation of Agnes Nutter's prophecies suggests a Reformation impulse at the core of the novel, for both text and belief.

Finally, like Waller, Alex Tankard initially questions the adaptation's update from late–1980s Cold War politics to contemporary times but examines the ways in which the miniseries embraces the thread of Romantic Satanism present in the source material, further personalizing the moral and theological issues (the "barren" outcome of the cosmic battle, among other things) of the novel through Crowley and Aziraphale's interactions with heaven, hell, humanity, and one another.

Naming, Artifacts, and Texts in *Good Omens*

The final section offers two different approaches to the texts of both the novel and miniseries. Janet Brennan Croft addresses the importance of names and naming in *Good Omens*. While focusing primarily on Adam Young and his powers of bending reality through naming, or un-naming, the things in his world, she also makes a distinction between those who name—or rename—themselves and others and those who don't and the process and responsibilities of sub-creation.

Tara Prescott-Johnson focuses on the textual elements of both the book and the miniseries. Prescott-Johnson suggests that not only does both book and series "break apart" false and simplistic dichotomies of "good" and "evil," but the irrelevance of the similar dichotomies around "book" versus "movie" arguments. In essence, Prescott-Johnson argues, the miniseries is faithful to its source material, as well as being faithful to books more generally by having the printed word (novels, magazines, etc.) as vital elements to the plot.

How the Collection Came to Be

The genesis, if you will, of this collection was a series of messages between its editors, who, following the first episode, mutually agreed "there needs to be a book about this." After realizing how little had been written about the source material itself, despite other analyses of both Gaiman's and Pratchett's solo work, this morphed into: "We need to do a book about this." Despite the ordinary challenges of time (graduate school, teaching, and other work) and the unexpected ones (the Covid pandemic) in bringing this collection to completion, we hope the following represents the beginning of greater scholarly attention on both the novel and the series.

Notes

1. As of 2021, the Crowley/Aziraphale pairing has more than 40000 entries between book and miniseries versions; at a not-at-all close second is Anathema Device and Newton Pulsifer, with under 1000 entries.

2. Tennant (2005–2010) is second only to Tom Baker (1974–1981), who played the Fourth Doctor, in the length of his tenure in the role.

Works Cited

"Ambitious Terry Pratchett Project to Generate Exciting New Research Opportunities" [press release]. Trinity College, Dublin. https://www.tcd.ie/trinitylongroomhub/media/news/articles/2019-09-19-Pratchett-Project.php.

"Child Entertainment Laws as of January 20, 2021." U.S. Dept. of Labor, Wage and Hours Division. https://www.dol.gov/agencies/whd/state/child-labor/entertainment.

"England Performance Legislation." National Network for Children in Employment and Entertainment. https://www.nncee.org.uk/page/39/legislation-england.
"Hard Times." *Good Omens*, season 1, episode 3, written by Neil Gaiman, directed by Douglas Mackinnon, BBC Video, 2019.
"In the Beginning." *Good Omens*, season 1, episode 1, written by Neil Gaiman, directed by Douglas Mackinnon, BBC Video, 2019.
Rodriguez, Ashley. "Famed Author Neil Gaiman on the Emotional Making of Amazon's 'Good Omens' and Keeping the 'Promise I Made to My Friend Who Died.'" *Insider*. 29 May 2019. https://www.businessinsider.com/neil-gaiman-making-amazon-good-omens-series-2019-5.
"The Very Last Day of the Rest of Their Lives." *Good Omens*, season 1, episode 6, written by Neil Gaiman, directed by Douglas Mackinnon, BBC Video, 2019.

Good Omens and Adaptation

Avoiding a Contemporary Apocalypse

Examining the Effects of Shifting *Good Omens* from Its Cold War Context

RHIAN WALLER

> "There's only one thing we have to fear ... it's not global warming, and it's not nuclear Armageddon...."
> —Shadwell (2: 18.15)

Both the *Good Omens* television and novel open with a discussion that reveals, with playful pedantry, the most accurate calculation for the age of the universe is wrong by almost 15 minutes (Gaiman and Pratchett 23). Both versions derive urgency from a prophetic countdown which, like a primed bomb or the hand of the Doomsday Clock, begins ticking (Pratchett and Gaiman 61). Clearly, these texts share a preoccupation with time. It is odd, therefore, that the miniseries is updated without "much more than a cosmetic consideration of how changing the time frame would affect the story" (Kraiser). While the novel is couched firmly in a late Cold War context, lending a very particular resonance to various characterizations and plot points, the television show is set in 2019.

Recent television adaptations of Gaiman's work (*American Gods, Sandman*) have also been updated, suggesting an element of adaptational continuity (Gaiman himself has gone on record to say that changing things is "part of the fun" [CBC Radio]). However, a broader context of 1980s and early 1990s nostalgia in streamed television content and cinema indicates this direction is not a given. The successes of *Stranger Things* (2016–present), *IT* (2017), *GLOW* (2017–2019), and *Ready Player One* (2018) demonstrate an appetite for late 20th-century settings. Moreover, much of *Good Omens* takes place in earlier historic eras and ahistorical, supernatural spaces.

12 *Good Omens* and Adaptation

This shift to a post-millennial setting arguably dislocates key parts of the narrative. These elements may not be immediately obvious. The conflicts and culture of the last thirty years seem to have conspired to preserve the relevance of some plot points. Smartphones now enable the petty evil of cold calling on a great scale. Stage and screen revivals have cycled Queen and the *Sound of Music* back into the cultural conversation. The shift to a televisual format adds a fourth wall-breaking edge to Aziraphale's protest that Armageddon has become a show devised to be sold in as many territories as possible (Pratchett and Gaiman 54). Even the risk of nuclear war seems more credible thanks to the posturing of world leaders both on Twitter and in arenas of war, while concerns about nuclear safety firmly occupy space in public discourse and pop culture.

However, the uneven time-lift also strains elements of the story, from throw-away gags to core themes. The miniseries Elvis, working as a short-order cook, looks remarkably sprightly for 84, compared to 55, as in the book. Anathema's New Age preoccupations, and by extension Adam's manifestations of Atlantis, Tibetan Monks, and their discussions of *X-Files*-style government cover ups, seem dated in the context of contemporary conspiracies, which range from Holocaust denial and anti-vaccination fears to Flat Earth theory. Admittedly, these are quibbles, and it is notable the original text contains anachronism. "That went down like a lead balloon," quips Crowley, several thousand years before balloons are invented (Pratchett and Gaiman 15). However, the anachronisms introduced into the television series pose greater problems.

Among those elements of *Good Omens* that suffer most in transition, two are of key and interlinked concern here: the nuclear and ecological features. To investigate the effects of both the time-lift and the retention of certain aspects of the original late–1980s[1] novel on these themes, it is necessary to analyze the texts through the useful and related standpoints of nuclear criticism and ecocriticism.

Daniel Cordle argues nuclear criticism, which focuses on texts that utilize atomic tropes, blends two strands: the "straightforwardly ethical" and the aesthetic and theoretical debate prefaced by Derrida's declaration that the unrealized concept of nuclear obliteration, is "fabulously textual," as it is constructed in the imaginations of readers and audiences of nuclear texts. Daniel Zins outlines the early goal of nuclear criticism "to deconstruct these texts and to demystify the discourses which legitimize the nuclear national security state," which hints at the incorporation of both aesthetics and ethics.

Ecocriticism, like nuclear criticism, is less a theoretical framework and more a broad and flexible series of thematic positions from which texts can be scrutinized and their underlying concerns critiqued and articulated. It is "a study of human-nature relations in literature, film and other cultural expressions" (Bracke and Corporaal 709). Ecocriticism takes an "environmental" or "earth centred" critical approach, exploring "the relationship between the human and the nonhuman" (Marland 846–847). Pippa Marland points out ecocriticism "frequently extends from the perspective of anxieties around humanity's destructive impact on the biosphere" (846).

One of the most pressing of the many intertwined issues drawn into ecocritical discourse is climate change. Driven by industrial activity, anthropogenic climate change is a phenomenon wherein global temperatures alter more drastically and swiftly than would occur without human intervention. The effects of this, Adam Trexler warns, have the potential to rival nuclear radiation and fallout in terms of scope, as he predicts increased "droughts, tropical cyclones, heat waves, crop failures, forest diebacks and fires, floods, and erosion" (6). My hope in this essay is to continue the work carried out by ecocritics who reconcile an "interest in the relationship between literature and the physical environment with narratology's focus on the literary structures and devices by which writers compose narratives" (James xv), while employing nuclear criticism to provide both parallel and counterpoint positions.

It is unsurprising that *Good Omens* is suffused with nuclear anxiety, given Terry Pratchett's early role as a press officer for a nuclear power company (Pratchett). The novel's characters live within a "state of suspense" (Cordle) experienced by those anticipating secular nuclear destruction or a biblical apocalypse, and this lends the story much of its tension. As it repeatedly employs nuclear motifs, riffing on anxieties about the industrial use of radioactive materials in power generation and shaping the climax of the story around the threat of nuclear war, it arguably finds a home in the emerging canon of nuclear texts. While these are varied in form and content, all give over a significant portion of the narrative to consideration of nuclear potential, power, or weaponry.

Nuclear texts are sometimes bitterly comical, from the black humor of German Nuclear-Age Fiction (Lueckel) to satires like *Dr. Strangelove* (Hendershot). While *Good Omens* could be dismissed as a lightweight supernatural comedy, like other popular culture artifacts, it provides opportunities to explore "theoretical concepts [and] dilemmas of foreign policy," (Nexon and Neumann 12) and to "comment on the way readers understand their place in history" (Clemens).

I argue, however, despite the presence of environmental themes, the novel's status as an ecological text is doubtful. This is understandable, as McCright and Dunlap argue climate change was broadly recognized as a pressing problem in the mid-1990s, after its publication. But, by shifting into the present day, the television adaptation both misses an opportunity to enact a more-than-cosmetic update to incorporate pressing contemporary environmental issues. Moreover, this time shift damages the integral nuclear analogy by pulling the narrative away from the historical moment that shaped it.

The Biblical Borrowing of Ecocriticism and Nuclear Criticism

Nuclear criticism and ecocriticism deal with unease about the eventual fate of the world as a consequence of human activity. Both corpuses of criticism, which have the potential to compete with and complement each other, exhibit internal tension between a focus on aesthetic and formalist approaches and the drive for "'real world' impact" (Marland 849) and material political change (Zins). Interestingly, both reveal that focal ecocritical and nuclear texts tend to borrow from religious discourse. Such borrowing offers opportunities for the organic integration of nuclear and ecological themes into narratives that, like *Good Omens*, draw on Abrahamic religious dogma.

According to Franklin, the word "Armageddon" was attached to proto-doomsday device narratives more than a century ago (120), and Smetak bluntly asserts: "Nuclear War literature is Apocalyptic" (43). Both authors explore how the language of the Book of Revelation is deployed to examine the threat of apocalypse and the notion that, in creating nuclear weapons, mankind has seized godlike destructive power. The nuclear physicist is imagined as "Satan" (Doherty 191), while Warrick links the creation of nuclear weaponry to the banishment from Eden: "we had been expelled from the garden of simplicity where we lived before the fall of the bomb" (10). Smetak argues nuclear war literature "replaced God with a thermonuclear device" (45), noting in either case, "death comes from the sky." The word "holocaust," deployed as a key signifier of historic and sometimes religiously motivated genocides, particularly the murder and mass immolation of millions of people under the Nazi regime, is also sometimes used to describe the effects of the Hiroshima and Nagasaki bombings. It is not coincidental that the word is derived from a term for a Christian sacrifice by fire (Rowland). The scale of nuclear war, in popular and critical imaginations, is, in other words, biblical.

Similar patterns of discourse are evident in ecological texts. Johns Putra refers to post-climate change narratives as "postapocalyptic" literature, implying catastrophic climate breakdown occupies a similar status to nuclear obliteration, both in popular and critical imaginations. Erin and

Morel likewise note in their introduction to *Ecocriticism and Narrative Theory* a preoccupation with the apocalypse among their critics. Although critical of the philosophical underpinnings and ends of climate-focused ecocriticism, Aravamudan's work suggests climate change anxiety inherits the language and framework of nuclear narratives, displacing a focus on nuclear risk, and notes early biblical references in nuclear criticism, including a pivotal essay by Derrida, in which the critic links the motif of seven missiles to the seven seals of St John of Patmos' prophecy. This text, incidentally, features in Aziraphale's collection of esoteric writing. While the appropriation of eschatological language to articulate fears around superweaponry is nothing new, *Good Omens* flips this phenomenon by utilizing nuclear discourse to give shape to a divine war. As a result, the characters find themselves embroiled in a cold war that is rapidly warming up.

Agents of the Apocalypse and the Atomic Antichrist

The demon Crowley and the principality Aziraphale are ostensibly agents for their respective and opposing states: Hell and Heaven. Like the "stay behind units" of the Cold War powers (see Ganser), both remain in disputed territory (Earth), awaiting the moment one side or another gains the upper hand. Although nominally enemies engaged in a mixture of low-key "active measures," surveillance, intelligence-gathering, counter-espionage and obfuscation, they form a mutually beneficial arrangement, finding they have more in common with each other than with their eternally warring masters.

The antithetical positions of Heaven and Hell very closely mirror the Cold War powers. Angels and demons, like the USA, the USSR, and their allies, are engaged in a proxy war, recruiting and exploiting earthly agents (the Satanic nuns, Shadwell) in lieu of direct conflict. The abridged biblical narrative of *Good Omens* echoes the Cold War timeline: it is triggered by the end of a devastating war (World War II/the Rebellion and Fall) and spans a period of fluctuating tension which lasts until a point of symbolic resolution, whether destructive (apocalypse/nuclear war) or restorative (averting the apocalypse/the fall of the Berlin Wall in 1989). The massing angelic and demonic armies, more visible in the TV adaptation, and the growing power of the Antichrist, reflect the brinkmanship of the nuclear arms race. It is unlikely to be a coincidence that the miniseries portrays Hell as a space that looks uncannily like a concrete bunker. While there is no clear indication the impending celestial war will bring about the end of both Heaven and Hell, Pratchett and Gaiman are explicit that life on Earth will perish in the conflict, in line with the worst prognosis of Mutually Assured Destruction (MAD).

This conflict echoes the pattern of "transacting animosities among enemy powers locked in a struggle unto death" (Aravamudan). The God and Satan of the novel are largely unseen governing forces, and, like the East and Western bloc war-leaders, they plan and declare the war from remote positions. In contrast, humans and the ecosphere are regarded as acceptable collateral damage. The instigators of war are those most insulated from it, while those unwillingly involved in the conflict are most likely to perish. In this respect, *Good Omens* see-saws between allegory and satire.

In all of this, Crowley and Aziraphale's alliance is used to critique the hollowness of the ideological division between Heaven and Hell, East and West. While more overtly affectionate in the television series, their relationship within the novel is fueled by a kind of world-weary cynicism: they develop a policy of "tacit non-interference," with each other which ensures that, while neither win, they can demonstrate their loyalty and usefulness to their respective sides (Pratchett and Gaiman 53).

They meet in St. James' Park, which, in both the novel and the miniseries, is used so often as a contact point by secret agents that resident ducks can differentiate the breadcrumbs offered by international operatives. This setting makes perfect sense as a satire on Cold War dead drops and clandestine meetings, but, in a post-millennial world of cyber-interference, shifting Russian/U.S. relations and new, rising superpowers, the particular mention of the Russian cultural attaché in the narration (1: 26.58), and the significance an American diplomat becoming a surrogate to the cuckoo Antichrist become less pointed. Within a Cold War narrative, these minor characters function as reminders of historical and political context. Beyond the Cold War, they are relics—appendices to a story that has evolved to a point where their function is unclear.

Pratchett and Gaiman avoid assigning clear ancillary identities to their warring powers, although, in the novel, Shadwell briefly speculates Aziraphale is a Russian spy (the update removes this; instead, Crowley is suspected to be Mafia). Aside from the political issues that would arise from declaring one world power the counterpart of Heaven and the other of Hell, it becomes increasingly clear as the narrative progresses that Heaven and Hell are, in all the ways that truly matter, materially the same. While the subjects of the miniseries equivocate over this, somewhat, introducing a character arc of gradual realization for Aziraphale, it uses visual motifs to hammer the point home. For example, when Aziraphale and Crowley visit their respective headquarters, they do so simultaneously. While one travels up and the other down, the movement is synchronized and symmetrical, and the angel and demon enter through the same entrance (1: 37.21). In the novel, Crowley asks why they should continue referring to the concepts of good an evil, arguing, "They're just names for sides" (Pratchett and Gaiman 67).

Neither side, it emerges, is concerned with the ethics of Armageddon, the good of mankind, or the planet. That Aziraphale blithely declares guns, "lend weight to moral argument[s]" (Pratchett and Gaiman 110), strongly implies the hosts of Heaven not only believe the ends justify the means, but the means, however brutal, *lend credence* to the ends. In this system of thought, the victors decide what is righteous and just—might makes right. "Wars are to be won," says Michael (1: 38.26). The acceleration toward nuclear war is simply the logical conclusion of this reasoning. It is Crowley, the demon, who recognizes, in this scenario, everybody loses (111).

Speculating on how "it" will happen, Crowley comments that thermonuclear extinction is a consistently popular option (118). Thus, in God's Great Plan, the atomic age is tied to biblical time. Predestined from the start, and predicted in the 1600s by precognitive witch Agnes Nutter, the distinctly modern threat of nuclear annihilation is pulled into a mythologizing framework. This is not uncommon in the early nuclear fiction of the 1950s and 1960s, including alien invasion and monster movies like *Earth vs. the Flying Saucers*, and *20,000 Miles to Earth*. As Hendershot notes: "This tension between the apparent novelty of nuclear weapons and their apparent connection to continuous, ahistorical forces is one that is equally present in fictional works." Hendershot argues this is symptomatic of a "paranoiac response" to the atomic threat.

The *Good Omens* novel, which links the nuclear threat to divine forces, flirts with nuclear paranoia, while the miniseries delves further into conspiracy by revealing the extent of the self-serving "back door" politicking of high-ranking angels and demons. However, by deploying bathos and comic pedantry and by exposing angelic and demonic incompetence and pettiness, Pratchett and Gaiman's texts work to de-mythologize Judeo-Christian mythology, pulling Armageddon into the arena of bully-boy Cold War conflict, and ascribing human ego and failings to superhuman forces.

Unlike the "paranoiac" narratives of "mythic battles between good and evil" (Hendershot), Hell and Heaven are ruthless, but also hypocritical and fallible. There is no "good" side engaging in, as Hofstadter, discussing U.S. cultural paranoia, puts it, "an all-out crusade" (29). Their agents and soldiers buy into paranoid mythologizing and binary narratives, sometimes for reasons of tradition or inadequate imagination, but Crowley and Aziraphale do not. Crowley in particular exhibits a nuanced view of the conflict and devises a middle-way, attempting to delay the apocalypse and win Earth a few more years (67).

This conflict between Heaven and Hell, it is heavily hinted, is borne of historical inertia and political expediency. It is a state of Orwellian perma-war, conducted in the name of or against an absent God, which ensures the survival of the current celestial hegemony. The quiet alliance of Crowley and Aziraphale is not simple treason. It is a radical challenge to an established order propped up by the threat of the Other.

This critique, highly relevant in the early 1990s, would be fresh in the minds primed for nuclear risk-awareness by a decade of high-profile pre- and post-apocalyptic films and novels, including *Mad Max*, *When the Wind Blows* (Briggs), *War Games*, and *The Terminator*. However, in the interim, Aravamudan argues, cultural awareness of nuclear risk has grown stale. A revisit to the subject, in a modernized setting, may well be timely: nuclear weapons have not gone away. However, seismic geopolitical shifts over the last 30 years, including the dissolution of the USSR, the erosion of Western bloc economies, the rise of new world powers such as India and China, and nuclear anti-proliferation efforts complicate the current landscape of nuclear conflict. As Debs and Monteiro point out, the majority of states with nuclear arsenals are friendly or neutral toward the USA. The duolithic model of Cold War antagonism no longer applies, and so the allegory breaks down. Rather than providing parallel and mutually reinforcing critiques of religion and recent politics, as the novel does, the miniseries deploys a historic and obsolete political model to highlight the logical fallacies of Revelation. The sharp edge of satire is aimed away from earthly politics and at a hierarchy which, in the context of the story's ontology, exists independently of humanity.

Crowley and Aziraphale's roles as parodic Cold War agents are effectively dismantled by the time-lift. The decision to move the story to a contemporary setting, as well as an additional scene in which they covertly meet in a Victorian version of St James' Park, underscores this; their "arrangement" and roles extend far beyond the Cold War era. This has the effect of dragging the blended nuclear and biblical apocalypse into an undefined and ahistorical *now and forever*, linking back to paranoiac mythologizing and the notion of the Apocalypse as a moment continually deferred. Crowley and Aziraphale become agents without a Cold War. The Bomb, however, still overshadows the narrative.

Adam Young, a composite-parody of the child–Antichrist in *The Omen* and of William Brown (Crompton), is the nuclear center around whom all other elements of the novel revolve, although he is a lesser presence in the miniseries. He is simultaneously a naughty but ultimately good-hearted eleven-year-old and the son of Satan, Lord of Hell and the harbinger of the endtimes (Pratchett and Gaiman 52). Together with a gang known as The Them, consisting of Pepper,[2] Brian, and Wensleydale, whose personalities and habits mark them as reflections and foils of the Horsemen, he lives an idyllic and elegiac existence in the small village of Tadfield.

To all intents, the Antichrist operates as an *Adam bomb*. He is, both literally and figuratively, a Little Boy, analogous to the first atom bomb ever used in warfare. Pratchett and Gaiman are not the first writers to make this linguistic connection. In the seminal nuclear narrative *Riddley Walker*, Hoban's characters conflate Christianity with atomic science, and interpret an image of "the Crucified Saviour" as the "Littl shynin man the Addom" (30), whose "splitting" triggers a catastrophe. The Adam of *Good Omens* is split, too, caught in a push-pull between his supernatural nature and the nurturing of his upbringing. This is the crisis of the entire narrative; for as God-as-narrator reminds us at the climax, in a moment, the missiles will launch, the armies of hell and heaven are prepared to go to war and, at the center of it all is Adam (6: 7.08).

In a narrative where many characters are locked into prophecy and lack agency, Adam exercises his will. Unlike the massing armies of Heaven and Hell, he deliberately and permanently relinquishes power, as if engaging in a spiritual version of nuclear disarmament. The celestial powers lack the empathy toward mankind identified by Fey, Poppe, and Rauch as one of the "pillars" of the nuclear taboo, but Adam is capable of compassion. By advocating setting aside violent mastery in favor of a smaller, human existence, Gaiman and Pratchett seem to equate nuclear arms with a vision of monstrosity at odds with the survival of humanity, in all senses of the world.

At the climax, Adam, like a missile, has launched. He rises into the air, primed and ready to destroy the world. It takes The Them to avert Adam's disastrous rise to power. Their arguments crudely echo the discourse of ecological and anti-nuclear campaigns, Pepper reminding him that millions of people will die and generations will be wiped out (5: 42.08).[3] His friends' protests, in the face of their own annihilation, force Adam to realize the extent of what will be lost, and he performs a literal de-escalation, returning to the ground.

As "human incarnate" (Pratchett and Gaiman 370), Adam defies the dichotomy of atomic age "saviour or Antichrist" (Dowling). Simultaneously the weapon and its wielder, Adam's position within the novel suggests nuclear weapons do not possess a mythical ontology, inexplicable, ahistorical and divorced from their human origins. They are, the authors insist, the result of human ingenuity and humans are culpable for both their creation, use and prevention. Much like the Artificial Intelligence in

Wargames, Adam decides the only way to win is not to play. This is a useful, if well-worn message. However, the updated setting of the TV show, and tweaks to the script, transforms the previously effective religio–Cold War analogy into an anachronism, but as will be discussed, the framework of that analogy persists within the adaptation. In doing so, its crumbling remains prevent a similarly effective, updated and ecological vision of the apocalypse from taking root.

Satan's Son and the Four Horsemen of the Environmental Apocalypse

The framing of climate change and environmental issues within the *Good Omens* television show is complicated somewhat by the adaptational time-shift and by several subtle amendments to the original text. Both narratives incorporate themes that chime with ecocritical concerns. Adam is a key figure in this respect; both versions of *Good Omens* link his awakening as the Antichrist to ecological concerns.

In the lead-up to Adam's awakening, he is introduced to a series of environmental and ethical problems that shape his unconscious manifestations of power. The witch Anathema Device exposes him to an amorphous blend of New Age mysticism and ecology, which Adam treats as revelatory. The time lift, again, makes these story elements seem anachronistic. While this is somewhat credible in a 1990s narrative, the idea of an eleven-year-old who has not encountered the concepts of Bigfoot, Atlantis, genetic modification, and climate change in 2019 stretches credulity, especially as Pepper and Adam's dialogue suggests the internet has penetrated the nostalgia-bubble of Tadfield. The latter are still framed as things not taught at school, which is patently no longer the case. As an opportunity for the miniseries to explore accelerating ecological threats, this is a wasted opportunity. "Don't get me started on Global Warming," Anathema warns—and she never does (3: 37.40).

These revelations inform Adam's first actions as Antichrist, and he twists the prophecies of Revelation into something that resembles Gaia's revenge rather than Satanic chaos. In a scene excised from the adaptation, Adam unconsciously revives part of the Amazonian rainforest which, aided by a friendly janitor, destroys a mall, a symbol of the "grass materialism" [sic] (221) fuzzily conceptualized by The Them. The rise of the Kraken heralds the destruction of a whaling fleet rather than the marine apocalypse imagined by Aziraphale and Crowley. In the diametric opposite of a nuclear meltdown, Adam warps reality so a power station is able, miraculously, to produce completely clean power without a reactor core.

Behind all of this is Adam's new awareness of anthropogenic activity. The turning-point of the story is not Adam's confrontation with the Horsemen; by then he is resolved on a course of action that will save the world. The true crux is when he comes into his power and is confronted with the choice of whether to embrace it and destroy Creation, or to de-escalate and relinquish his power. Adam's philosophy mirrors eco-fascism, wherein humans are viewed not as part of nature, but as something inimical to it that must be removed (Aravamudan). Fatalistically, Adam declares that nuclear annihilation is a chance to wipe the slate clean and start again (4: 42.02). When his gang questions him, it is environmental degradation, not biblical sin, that emerges as the locus of this view: "What's going to be left when we grow up.... Everything's being killed or used up." (4: 33.00) Adam's lament clumsily articulates frustration at denialism and inaction in the face of environmental collapse, which may be "our time's lasting legacy on earth" (Trexler 1). His nihilistic response is not to address these issues as mutable and soluble problems, but to destroy everything. In contrast, Brian supports restorative ecological intervention. He argues that burning everything because of the mistakes of previous generations is not the way; that this is, instead, a "reason to fix it, not destroy it" (5: 34.00). In light of this, and of contemporary geopolitics and ecocide, Adam's subsequent decision to retain his humanity falls rather flat. His abdication from power is also an abdication from a position where he may be able to "fix" things, particularly as one of the earliest manifestations of his power is the ability to stabilize climate: he freezes his village in an artificial and paradoxical "bountiful present" and a "vanished past" (Garrard 42), shielding it from development and modern progress.

The problematic aspects of Adam's choice are underscored in the aftermath of the final confrontation, when Anathema points out Adam's potential to help, only for Adam to walk off with his friends (376). Thirty years on from first publication and, in light of global inaction following the 2007 "bombshell" dropped by the Intergovernmental Panel on Climate Change (IPCC), which calls for urgent remedial environmental action (Aravamudan), Anathema's ignored plea rings with greater desperation. It is clear that the ills represented by the Horsemen—including environmental degradation—remain part of the *Good Omens* universe.

The Horsemen, past and present, reflect cultural anxieties, but they also echo the miseries predicted by environmental scientists, including "regional conflicts" over strained resources (War), "inadequate water supplies [and] malnutrition" (Famine) and "diarrheal disease, and infectious diseases" (Pestilence) (Trexler 2). Climate change itself is, of course, driven by Pollution and its consequence, Trexler warns, is Death. Pratchett and Gaiman are unequivocal about the importance of Pollution in their re-imagined vision of Revelation. Pestilence, we are told, retired in 1936 after the discovery of penicillin. The television adaptation notes Pollution had a hand in creating the internal combustion engine, plastics, and weed killers, and is responsible for as many deaths as Famine and War (4: 11.10).

Pollution is one of the most effective Horsemen, creating a series of computer viruses that lock human operators out of the nuclear defense systems, enabling War to wield a missile system like a sword that encloses the world (345). This is thematically appropriate as fallout and radiation are simply persistent forms of pollution. However, in crucial ways, the miniseries version of Pollution seems time-locked into the 1980s. While War's introduction is updated and relocated, and Famine's first scene plays on post-millennial molecular gastronomy and sensory dining, we meet Pollution beside a rubbish-clogged river in Britain.

The sludgy, foaming Uck (196) recalls the "gruesome" rivers and streams of the 1950s to the mid–1980s (Sutcliffe). These blighted waterways, where "fish dare not swim" (Taylor), were well within recent memory in the early 1990s. Since then, large-scale measures to address waterway pollution in the UK have had significant impact in terms of environmental rejuvenation. More recently, attention has turned to plastic in the oceans and the practice of exporting Western waste to other economies (Ritchie and Rosser), making the continued use of this setting in the miniseries a questionable choice. The particularly visible polluted state of the Uck indicates either anachronism or paradox.

This problematizes the themes of human agency and choice that run consistently through both the book and TV series. Early in the novel, Crowley justifies adding fully operational automatic weapons to a team-building paintball exercise. He espouses anti-deterministic philosophy when he argues that nobody actually has to "pull the trigger" (114). This foreshadows the climax of the narrative. However, the Horsemen seem to do more than personify the problems they represent; they exacerbate and introduce them. War is a North American war reporter who turns to arms dealing. The modern Famine is found not in a field of failed crops, but in a restaurant where socially constructed food fads and fashions are linked to deliberate starvation. Pollution, a man-made phenomenon, takes over the largely natural role of Pestilence.

The fact these are anthropogenic issues ties smoothly into the motif of man-made misery, but there is a thematic awkwardness between the notion of the Horsemen as reflective symbols shaped by human violence, and as independent forces that instigate violence. A person is infinitely more likely to pull the trigger if they are handed a gun or drive a polluting car if they are given the design for a petrol engine. The presence of Pollution by the river Uck implies that, just as the arrival of War precipitates a regional conflict and Famine is responsible for designing a brand of edibles with no nutritional value, Pollution has a direct effect on the environment.

If the three lesser Horsemen have agency beyond their role as external manifestations of the minds of men (Pratchett and Gaiman 359), then they threaten to displace the responsibility for nuclear annihilation and environmental degradation from mankind onto supernatural entities. This shadows the old narrative tendency to displace fear of nuclear risk away from the political reality and onto an ahistoric alien force (Hendershot). Both narratives insist the Horsemen are as ephemeral as nightmares (365), but while the novel treads an ambiguous line, the update offers more credence to a reading of the Horsemen as autonomous, agentive entities. The modern version of Pollution throws a cardboard box into the water, as if to drive the point home.

These adaptational choices create a thematic tangle in terms of responsibility. The novel suggests a tendency toward self-destruction is a permanent and inevitable part of the human condition. War muses that vanquishing Earth might bring an end to War, Famine, and perhaps even Pollution (344), which implies the existence of all three are contingent on the existence of sinful, violent, sentient life. However, the miniseries muddies the waters by showing the faces of the nuclear deterrent personnel, making it obvious none of the human operatives, whether on a Russian nuclear submarine or in an office in India, want the launch to go ahead, instead working frantically to shut the launch down (6: 7.55–8.10). These many faces allude obliquely to the changed political context of the narrative, but, more profoundly, the new dialogue indicates humanity's fate is explicitly taken out of humanity's hands. If this is the case, the narrative has lurched straight down the paranoiac path described by Hendershot. Nuclear War, like Pollution, is inevitable and beyond mortal control. And yet, the narrative also repeatedly emphasizes human agency and responsibility at the point of crisis.

It is clear that the Apocalypse, whether man-made or celestial, extends to the environment, and both narratives reach beyond purely anthrocentric considerations. Crowley first broaches the issue of planetary collateral damage. He notes the tragedy of gorillas dying during an apocalyptic starfall, and whales and dolphins becoming "seafood gumbo" (63). His image of boiling seas is a serviceable hyperbolic metaphor for climate change and the rising sea temperatures that are increasingly evident in recent years (Dahlman and Lindsey).

Here, too are subtle but notable changes between the novel and adaptation in terms of the ways environmental loss is framed, further muddling notions of agency and responsibility. In the book, Crowley rants that nobody gives a damn (63). Aside from the religious pun, this statement, aimed ambiguously at God, Heaven, Hell and mankind, hints at a sense of responsibility for the degradation of the skies and oceans. This emphasis changes in the show, where Crowley wails, "it's not their fault!" (1: 31.09)—shifting the focus onto passive victims rather than the agentive causes of the problem. Book-Crowley exhibits the "love and rage" (Knopps) displayed by anti-climate change activists, such as those in the Extinction Rebellion movement which emerged in 2018. In contrast, the televisual Crowley seems to be manifesting something akin to "ecological grief" (Cunsolo and Ellis), mourning the loss and damage wrought by a biome-shattering disaster. His grief, in the contemporary version of *Good Omens*, may not be misplaced. The dénouement of the show restores the status-quo—and that includes the pervasive presence of pollution.

Crowley and Aziraphale's position as preternatural, biblical entities offers an opportunity to interrogate the difficult and complex relationship between the environment and Christian doctrine, which imbued the early Western ecological movement with "tremendous social, cultural, and political power" (Stott, 53), but also promotes a theocentric and anthrocentric hierarchy identified as a justification for environmental exploitation (McCright and Dunlap). This hierarchy, which Crowley and Aziraphale inhabit, sits in opposition to the posthumanism of the ecocritical "fourth wave," which challenges "the construct of the Great Chain of Being, which places man at its head" (Marland). These notions of hierarchy and supremacy are inherited by late-stage capitalist ideologies, and here, too, the televisual text opens new opportunities to engage in pointed satire on current issues. For instance, the angels borrow a Silicon Valley aesthetic, and seem, with their open-plan Heaven, white suits, celestial Segways and slick, ruthless corporate-speak, to embody the most sterile, inhuman, and inhumane aspects of corporate culture. As Smetak writes, "capitalism is itself in its own way apocalyptic" (53). However, this goes unexplored—and, as noted earlier, the blunt critiques of materialism present in the novel are stripped out of the television show.

While Crowley and Aziraphale's positioning as double agents serves to satirize the binary opposition of antagonistic superpowers, it does not present as effective a challenge to the economic and ideological frameworks that drive environmental damage. The Cold War binarism model is ill-equipped to reflect a phenomenon driven by multiple agencies, the origins of which are often diffuse and murky.

In the end, the television version of *Good Omens* falls short as an ecological text precisely because of its fidelity to the pre-existing nuclear narrative. In the context of nuclear war, Adam's refusal to take action represents a triumphant form of pacifism. In a context of rising ecological risk, his decision is not a victory. Instead, it represents a potentially tragic return to the status quo.

Conclusion

While both texts grapple to some degree with the politics and philosophy of nuclear risk, the broader environmental concerns referenced in both the novel and miniseries are not accorded the same degree and depth of discussion and resolution. This is understandable in a narrative of the 1980s, before climate change emerged as a prime focus of cultural anxiety. It is less understandable now when climate change discourse has "witnessed a steep rise" (Moser). While a few added lines of dialogue reference climate change, they do not address it. This echoes the tendency for the phenomena to be "treated in fiction as just another environmental problem, alongside deforestation, urban development, toxic waste, and depletion of the ozone layer" (Trexler 9).

Shifting to an ecological narrative, updating the conflict to a modern arena of warfare, with its drones, cyber-attacks, and suicide-bombing and fears around biosecurity, or, indeed, reflecting what Feldmen calls the "new nuclear age" of rogue states, cross-border conflicts, and the undermined principals of nuclear deterrence, would involve moving away from the us versus them structure of the Eastern and Western blocs. Like the new geopolitics of nuclear risk, problems of ecology are less immediately obvious than those of Star Wars and MAD. As with modern warfare, it would be difficult to integrate environmentalism as a prime concern of the TV series without radically restructuring the *Good Omens* narrative. This is obvious when the novel and TV show are compared to environmental fictions. Perhaps *Stark* (Elton 1989) comes closest to *Good Omens* in terms of its contemporary publication, comic tone, and global scope, but despite sharing themes of paranoia and grand conspiracy, the resulting novel relies on a different biblical analogy, a David and Goliath struggle with ethnic minorities, environmentalists, and conspiracy nuts on one side and ultra-capitalists on the other. It is eminently applicable today. In contrast, despite being wrenched out of its political and historical context, the binary Cold War framework continues to underpin the *Good Omens* story, therefore limiting it.

Environmental degradation, as an incremental process that is not driven by intent, is difficult to pinpoint, articulate, and address, particularly by a story locked into a narrative shape that limits its flexibility. This replicates the difficult real-world problem of crisis communication. This lack of definitiveness in environmental narratives, particularly in terms of climate change, is part of a broader difficulty. It hinders the ability of activists and members of the scientific community to marshal enough public support to ensure political action, amid confusion and debate over "scientific certainty" which Trexler argues, has been used to mire the phenomenon in "dead-end debate" (4). Environmental issues go beyond dialectics and diametric conflicts, and solving them involves deep, multi-level structural change. Just as no single mechanism will trigger climate catastrophe, there is no passive method of avoidance. In contrast to nuclear de-escalation, fiction cannot present simple solutions, such as disengaging the "big red button."

Global interventions are needed to contain worsening environmental issues (Trexler), as well as a major "cultural transformation that cannot be described through a rubric of belief" (5). It is an understanding of this, perhaps, that makes Brian's vanquishing of Pollution particularly unsatisfying. It will take more than vaguely and symbolically believing in a clean world (5:12.06) to redress the damage done to land, sea, and air. While Adam reboots reality, the final lines of both the novel and miniseries, in which a nightingale sings beneath the sound and smog of London traffic, indicate nothing has really been "fixed," at least not in terms of anthropogenic damage. The implication is that, as Adam runs off to scrump apples and play, the Amazonian jungle is returned to its grave beneath the shopping malls of south America and the whaling fleets are back in action.

Good Omens is, ultimately, a story about choice and humanity, and it utilizes one of the great threats of our time as a pivot-point where the politics of brinkmanship are tested and exposed as flawed, arrogant, elitist, and defeatist. Hendershot, discussing the contemporary philosophical and psychological response to the detonation of the Hiroshima and Nagasaki bombs, writes: "The realization that a human agency could in turn be responsible for the total death of humanity defies the imagination." In narrativizing Armageddon, Gaiman and Pratchett attempt in the novel to confront the unimaginable through the filter of fantasy fiction, and to place the responsibility for planetary survival in the hands of mankind.

However, the time-lift adaptation confuses this message by clinging to the original structure of the story and transposing a Cold War narrative into a different era. This patchwork fidelity to the source material also affects the ecological elements of the text. While ecocide has, according to some, overtaken nuclear risk as the primary global threat, the *Good Omens* television series scarcely acknowledges this. It adds a few scraps of dialogue to remind us that climate change is a contemporary concern but removes or reworks several of the environmentally themed scenes and conversations in the book, while retaining outdated details that undermine any message of human accountability. Aravamudan voices concern that "climate change anxiety [could] voraciously incorporate nuclear anxiety." But the updated version of *Good Omens* does the very opposite: climate change, in the miniseries, is incorporated into the nuclear anxiety narrative almost as an afterthought.

By declining to set the television series in a moment when nuclear stalemate is crumbling but still baked into the political discourse of the day, and by applying a partial and piecemeal update that references but does not engage with contemporary global concerns, the adaptation of *Good Omens* has rendered the End Times less real. Rather than confronting us with a modern apocalypse, it lodges Armageddon somewhere indeterminate, between the political past and the material now. The satirical edge of the novel is blunted, and the Cold War analogy, which gives structure to the novel, disintegrates into dead weight. Nuclear anxiety is not effectively replaced by contemporary anxieties in any meaningful way. And yet, the adaptation does maintain narrative coherence, and it does so by shifting the core of the story away from Adam and the Horsemen and looking elsewhere.

Notes

1. Although published in 1990 by Victor Gollancz Ltd. narrowly before the collapse of the USSR, *Good Omens* evolved during the dying days of the Cold War. In correspondence with fans, Gaiman recalls how he and Pratchett worked on the book in the late 1980s (NeilGaiman.com). As Cordle suggests, "although the dramatic changes of 1989 seem so definitively to reduce the possibility of global nuclear war, there is a time lag during which nuclear concerns continue to work their way through the culture and appear in literary texts."
2. As elsewhere, the update renders some characters anachronistic. Though she makes reference to "everyday sexism," reviewers have noted that "Adam's tomboy friend Pepper is still quoting the same 1990s feminism talking points" (Kraiser).
3. Pepper's ecofeminist argument recalls the actions of the Greenham Common women who conducted a rolling protest at an RAF base housing nuclear weapons. In an action that spanned three decades, notions of motherhood were marshalled as a form of defiance (Shepherd). The missiles were removed in 1991, a year after *Good Omens* was published.

Works Cited

Aravamudan, Srinivas. "The Catachronism of Climate Change." *Diacritics*, vol. 41, no. 3, 2013, pp. 6–30.
Bracke, Astrid, and Marguérite Corporaal. "Ecocriticism and English Studies: An Introduction." *English Studies,* vol 91, no. 7, 2010, pp. 709–12.
Briggs, Raymond. *When the Wind Blows.* Penguin, 1986.
Carter, Chris, creator. *The X-Files.* Ten Thirteen Productions and Twentieth Century Fox, 1993.
CBC Radio. "With the Sandman Set to Hit Netflix, Creator Neil Gaiman Says It Will Stay True to the Comics," www.cbc.ca. November 22, 2019.
Clemens, Amy Lea. "Adapting Revelation: Good Omens as Comic Corrective." *Journal of the Fantastic in the Arts*, vol. 28, no. 1, January 2017.

Cordle, Daniel. "Protect/Protest: British Nuclear Fiction of the 1980s." *The British Journal for the History of Science*, vol. 45, no. 4, December 2012, pp. 653–669, doi: 10.1017/S0007087412001112.
Crompton, Richmal. *Just William*. Macmillan Children's Books, 1991.
Cunsolo, Ashlee and Neville R. Ellis. "Ecological Grief as a Mental Health Response to Climate Change-related Loss." *Nature Climate Change*, vol. 8, no. 4, 2018.
Dahlman, LuAnn, and Rebecca Lindsey. *Climate Change: Ocean Heat Content*. Climate.gov, 17 August 2020, https://www.climate.gov/news-features/understanding-climate/climate-change-ocean-heat-content.
Debs, Alexandre, and Nuno P. Monteiro. *Nuclear Politics: The Strategic Causes of Proliferation*. Cambridge University Press, 2017.
Derrida, Jacques. "No Apocalypse, Not Now (Full Speed Ahead, Seven Missiles, Seven Missives)," translated by Catherine Porter and Philip Lewis. *Diacritics*, vol. 14, no. 2, 1984, pp. 20–31.
Doherty, T. "Future Hell: Nuclear Fiction in Pursuit of History." *Human Architecture: Journal of the Sociology of Self-Knowledge*, vol. 7, no. 3, 2009, pp. 191.
Dowling, David. *Fictions of Nuclear Disaster*. University of Iowa Press, 1987.
Duffer, Mark, and Russ Duffer, creators. *Stranger Things*. 21 Laps Entertainment and Monkey Massacre, 2016.
Earth Vs. the Flying Saucers. Directed by Fred F. Sears, performances by Hugh Marlowe and Joan Taylor, Columbia Pictures, 1956.
Elton, Ben. *Stark*. Sphere Books, 1989.
Feldman, Noah. "Islam, Terror, and the Second Nuclear Age." *New York Times*. 29 October 2006, www.nytimes.com/2006/10/29/magazine/29islam.html.
Fey, Marco, Annika E. Poppe, and Carsten Rauch. "The Nuclear Taboo, Battlestar Galactica, and the Real World: Illustrations from a Science-Fiction Universe." *Security Dialogue*, vol. 47, no. 4, 2016, pp. 348–365.
Flahive, Liz, and Carly Mensch, creators. *GLOW*. Tilted Productions, Perhapsatron, and Fan Dancer, 2017.
Franklin, H.B. "Strange Scenarios: Science Fiction, the Theory of Alienation, and the Nuclear Gods." *Science Fiction Studies*, vol. 13, no. 39, 1986, pp. 117.
Gaiman, Neil, creator. *Good Omens*. Narrativia, BBC Studios, The Blank Corporation, and Amazon Studios, 2019.
Gaiman, Neil. "Several Days of Unposted Mailbag..." NeilGaiman.com, 4 May 2006, http://journal.neilgaiman.com/2006/05/several-days-of-unposted-mailbag.html.
Gaiman, Neil, and Terry Pratchett. *Good Omens*. Corgi, 2006.
Ganser, Daniele. *NATO's Secret Armies: Operation GLADIO and Terrorism in Western Europe*. Taylor and Francis, 2004.
Garrard, Greg. *Ecocriticism: The New Critical Idiom*. Routledge, 2012.
Gatta, John. *Making Nature Sacred: Literature, Religion, and Environment in America from the Puritans to the Present*. Oxford University Press, 2004.
Hendershot, Cyndy. "From Trauma to Paranoia: Nuclear Weapons, Science Fiction, and History." *Mosaic: An Interdisciplinary Critical Journal*, vol. 32, no. 4, 1999, pp. 73–90.
Hoban, Russell. *Riddley Walker*. New York: Summit, 1980.
Hofstadter, Richard. *The Paranoid Style in American Politics and Other Essays*. Harvard University Press, 1996.
It: Chapter One. Directed by Andy Muschietti, performances by Jaeden Lieberher and Bill Skarsgard, Warner Brothers Pictures, 2017.
James, Erin. *The Storyworld Accord: Econarratology and Postcolonial Narratives*. University of Nebraska Press, 2015.
Johns Putra, Adeline. "Climate Change in Literature and Literary Studies: From Cli-fi, Climate Change Theater and Ecopoetry to Ecocriticism and Climate Change Criticism." *Wiley Interdisciplinary Reviews: Climate Change*, vol. 7, no. 2, 2016, pp. 266–282.
Knops, Louise. "On the Love and Rage of Extinction Rebellion." *Green European Journal*, 18 March 2020, https://www.greeneuropeanjournal.eu/on-the-love-and-rage-of-extinction-rebellion/

Kraiser, Vrai. "The Good Omens Miniseries Is Definitely a Fanfic I Read in 2006." *Fanbyte*, 7 June 2019, www.fanbyte.com/features/the-good-omens-miniseries-is-definitely-a-fanfic-i-read-in-2006/.
Lueckel, Wolfgang. "From Zero Hour to Eleventh Hour?: German Fiction of the Nuclear Age Between 1945 and 1963." *Monatshefte*, vol. 107, no. 1, Spring 2015, pp. 84–107.
Mad Max—Beyond Thunderdome. Directed by George Miller and George Ogilvie, performances by Mel Gibson and Tina Turner, Warner Brothers, 1985.
Marland, Pippa. "Ecocriticism." *Literature Compass*, vol 10, no. 11, 2013, pp. 846–868, doi: 10.1111/lic3.12105.
McCright, Aaron, and Riley E Dunlap. "Challenging Climate Change: The Denial Countermovement," *Climate Change and Society: Sociological Perspectives*, edited by Riley E. Dunlap and Robert J. Brulle, Oxford University Press, 2015, pp. 300–332.
Moser, Suzanne. "Communicating Climate Change: History, Challenges, Process and Future Directions," *Wires Climate Change*, vol. 1, no. 1, 22 December 2009.
Nexon, Daniel H., and Iver B. Neumann. *Harry Potter and International Relations*. Rowman & Littlefield, 2006.
The Omen. Directed by Richard Donner, performances by Gregory Peck and Lee Remick, 20th Century Fox, 1976.
Pratchett, Terry. *A Slip of the Keyboard*. Corgi, 2015.
Ready Player One. Directed by Steven Spielberg, performances by Tye Sheridan, Olivia Cooke, and Ben Mendelsohn, Warner Brothers, 2018.
Ritchie, Hannah, and Max Roser. "Plastic Pollution," *Our World in Data*. September 2018, https://ourworldindata.org/plastic-pollution.
Rowland, Antony. *Tony Harrison and the Holocaust*. Liverpool University Press, 2001.
Shepherd, Laura J. *Gender Matters in Global Politics*. Routledge, 2010.
Smetak, Jacqueline R. "So Long, Mom: The Politics of Nuclear Holocaust Fiction." *Papers on Language & Literature*, vol. 26, no. 1, Winter 1990, pp. 41–59.
The Sound of Music. Directed by Robert Wise, performances by Julie Andrews and Christopher Plummer, Twentieth Century Fox, 1965.
Sutcliffe, Matthew. "Who Saved the Mersey?" Mersey Basin Campaign, September 2009, http://www.merseybasin.org.uk/archive/items/MBC176.html.
Taylor, Paul. "Where Fish Dare Not Swim." *Manchester Evening News*, 13 October 1984.
The Terminator. Directed by James Cameron, performances by Arnold Schwarzenegger and Linda Hamilton, Orion Pictures, 1985.
Trexler, Adam. *Anthropocene Fictions: The Novel in a Time of Climate Change*. University of Virginia Press, 2015.
20 Million Miles to Earth. Directed by Nathan Juran, performances by William Hopper and Joan Taylor, Columbia Pictures, 1957.
War Games. Directed by John Badham, performances by Matthew Broderick and Ally Sheedy, MGM/UA Entertainment Company, 1983.
Warrick, Patricia S. *The Cybernetic Imagination in Science Fiction*. MIT Press, 1980.
Zins, Daniel L. "Exploding the Canon: Nuclear Criticism in the English Department." *Papers in Language and Literature*, vol. 26, no. 1, 1990, pp. 13–40.

God Is a Woman
Good Omens, *Voice-Over, and the Female Gaze*

Julia Vanessa Pauss

> In the beginning was the Word, and the Word was with God, and the Word was God.
> —The Bible John 1:1

If there is something that the Bible and *Good Omens* (2019) agree on, it is the power of the spoken word. The Amazon Prime adaptation of the 1990s cult novel written by Terry Pratchett and Neil Gaiman starts with the voice of an invisible woman in space, prompting the big bang explosion on screen (1.01 "In the Beginning"). "God does not play dice with the universe," she explains, "I play an ineffable game of my own devising" (ibid.). This announcement marks a distinct deviation from the show's literary predecessor. Even though God is never physically described in the novel, he is referred to exclusively with capitalized male pronouns (Gaiman and Pratchett 10). But God's gender is not the only aspect of the character that changed in the process of adaptation. In the Amazon Prime series, God acts as the omniscient voice-over narrator leading through the events preceding the apocalypse. But does this change effectively introduce a female perspective or is God simply a functional means of transporting the distinct voice of the novel's narrator to screen? This essay aims to analyze the duality between voice-over as a functional necessity versus a carrier of the female gaze in *Good Omens*. How do the two different interpretations conflict and interact with each other and why does it matter that, in the universe of *Good Omens*, God is a woman?

Voice-Over and Gender

Voice-over describes the use of a narrative voice-track superimposed over the images on screen. U.S.-American art historian and film critic Kaja

Silverman points out that it always occupies "a different order from the main diegesis," which is often introduced by a "slight temporal and/or spatial dislocation" (48). It is to be differentiated from the voice-off, in which the source of sound is located out of frame but still within the same level of diegesis (ibid. 48, Doane 37). While the voice-off is directed at characters within the scene, the voice-over addresses the spectator and provides knowledge about character motivation, thoughts, and background information (Doane 43). The technique originated in the early cinema of the late 1890s and experienced its heyday in the 1940s, before it fell out of fashion due to its authoritative style in the following decades (Kozloff, *Storytellers* 33, Wolfe 149). Because of its tangible subjectivity, tendency to tell instead of show, as well as double-layering of information, voice-over has since been criticized as a technique unsuitable for the visual medium of film (Kozloff, *Voice of God* 41, *Storytellers* 13). However, not all agree with this assessment. Film studies scholar Sarah Kozloff argues that double-telling, the simultaneous presentation of the same information via visual and audio track, is technically impossible as "different information will always be provided by different sign systems" but admits that through voice-over, some information may overlap (*Storytellers* 20).

Although female voice-over is not uncommon, it is generally relegated to a different domain than its male counterpart. Based on the narrative theory proposed by French literary theorist Gérard Genette, Kozloff distinguishes between first-person and third-person voice-over narration (*Storytellers* 42, 72). First-person voice-over is derived from Genette's homodiegetic first-person narrator, who is also a character within the story. Third-person voice-over narration stems from Genette's heterodiegetic third-person narrator, who is not part of the story but lingers above it and has insight into everything within, including the characters' thoughts and feelings (ibid. 42, Genette 245). But to be applied to the visual medium of film, Genette's terms require some modification. As Kozloff points out, literary and voice-over narration are not identical, as voice-over constitutes one element of a film's "narrating agent" (*Storytellers* 44). This agent is what Kozloff calls the "image-maker," the entity who is responsible for the "primary diegesis," the "selecting, organizing, shading, and even passive recording processes that go into the creation of a narrative" in which the voice-over narration is one of many elements (ibid.). Accordingly, Kozloff argues, the voice-over narrator is "always embedded within the image-maker's discourse," which complicates the distinction between hetero- and homodiegetic levels (*Storytellers* 45, 76). For this reason, her suggested terms refer to the narrator's proximity to the story (*Storytellers* 41,72). The distinction between first-person and third-person voice-over is therefore not based on whether a character "is telling a story 'about himself,'" but rather "whether he or she exists in the same fictive world as the characters, whether he or she could possibly know them and they know him or her" (*Storytellers* 76). Thus, while not all third-person voice-over narrators are necessarily frame narrators, they must be far removed from the story and its characters, be it through time, space and/or a story's "status as *fiction*" (ibid.).

In cinematic history, female voice-over has been commonly associated with first-person character narration and employed as a narrative strategy to reflect personal experiences and emotions (Kozloff *Storytellers* 99f). This likely leads back to the woman's film of the 1940s, which dealt with women's domestic issues and had "the largest number of female first-person voice-over narrators of any Hollywood genre" (Hollinger 34). The technique was popularized by TV shows such as *Sex and the City* (1998–2004), in which the protagonist Carrie Bradshaw famously commented on her life via first-person voice-over, and is still frequently utilized in contemporary television (McHugh 195).

In contrast, the less common third-person voice-over narrator is traditionally associated with male speakers. Few female examples such as Mary Alice Young in *Desperate Housewives* (2004–2012) still count as an exception to the rule. Kozloff argues that because of their function as the "voice of the image-maker," third-person narrators mirror the male-dominated film industry and, due to their ability to "make sweeping pronouncements about human nature and society," have been "automatically assigned to authoritative male voices" (*Storytellers* 100). This is especially true for Voice of God narrators, a style of third-person voice-over commonly associated with documentary-style films. Voice of God narration is "construed as fundamentally unrepresentable in human form, connoting a position of absolute mastery and knowledge outside the spatial and temporal boundaries of the social world the film depicts" (Wolfe 149). As the name suggests, Voice of God narrators speak from a position of absolute truth and have insights into every aspect of the events on screen. They frequently use description as a method of relaying their knowledge to the audience, a controversial technique that is primarily employed in documentaries and has been frequently criticized by filmmakers (ibid).

Good Omens employs two different types of voice-over: Frances McDormand as God and third-person narrator and Josie Lawrence, who plays Agnes Nutter and recites the witch's ominous prophecies via voice track. But while Lawrence's voice-over mainly serves a practical function, McDormand's role quite literally personifies the omniscient Voice of God narration. With third-person voice-over so closely tied to matters of authority and knowledge, a female God as narrator embodies a uniquely complex and potentially empowering position within the *Good Omens* universe.

God Is a Woman

In an interview, writer and showrunner Neil Gaiman confirmed that casting a woman for the role of God was a conscious decision:

> I knew I wanted an American voice. I knew I wanted a female voice, and I was trying to figure out who I wanted because Whoopie [sic] Goldberg's already been the voice of God and the voice of death so I thought, "That's probably not right." So I was trying to figure it out and [sic] on the way back to America. I had just watched Three Billboards and my head was filled with Frances McDormand. About a day later she sent me an email about something completely different out of nowhere. I wrote back and said, "Would you like to be God?" She said it would confirm something her family already suspected [Gaiman, *Los Angeles Magazine*].

God is not the only character whose gender changed in the process of adapting *Good Omens* to screen. The demon Beelzebub is also referred to with masculine pronouns in the novel (Gaiman and Pratchett 334) but is portrayed by British actress Anna Maxwell Martin in the Amazon Prime series. Furthermore, Pollution, one of the Four Horsemen of the Apocalypse, is called "Mr. White" in the novel (Gaiman and Pratchett 58). In the series, Pollution is portrayed by the female actress Lourdes Faberes and while the mailman refers to the character as "Sir," God uses the gender-neutral pronoun "them" (1.04 "Saturday Morning Funtime"). This indicates an effort to include more empowered female and nonbinary characters in the adaptation. However, when it comes to the character of God, a gender swap entails a uniquely ideological and often controversial implication.

Good Omens is not the first to portray the divine feminine on screen. Some earlier instances include Cher in *Will and Grace* (1998–2006), Alanis Morrisette in *Dogma* (1999), Whoopi Goldberg in *It's A Very Muppet Christmas Movie* (2003), and Octavia Spencer in *The Shack* (2017). What unites these films and TV series is the considerable amount of backlash they received for their interpretation of a female Christian God and *Good Omens* is no exception to this rule. After the show's release, the American Society for the Defense of Tradition, Family and Property, a conservative Christian organization, issued a petition signed by over 20,000 people to remove the series from its streaming service based on several supposedly blasphemous offenses, one of which being that "God is voiced by a woman" (*Return to Order*). While the petition represents an extreme end of the religious spectrum, the concept of a male God is a pervasive idea throughout Christian religion, and representations of a feminine divine are hardly accepted. This is reinforced by common descriptions of God with terms like "Bridegroom, Husband, Father, [and] King" and the male pronoun

"He" that "seems to convey God's personhood without drawing attention to its limitations as a masculine metaphor" (Morley 309). Within religious spaces, it is often argued that the male address is all-encompassing, yet a reversal of pronouns is hardly permitted (ibid.). However, contrary to conservative readings of Christian mythology, depictions of the feminine divine can be traced back as far as the second century (Mollenkott 8). Furthermore, the Bible itself contains no clear references to God's masculinity but states that "God is a spirit" (John 4:24). Yet, these points are usually overlooked by opponents of female depictions of the Almighty. A male God seems to be taken as the universal standard, as if the male position constitutes an ungendered one. A female God as an omnipotent and infallible entity therefore contradicts the patriarchal order of Christian society and challenges traditional notions of the woman's role.

In *Good Omens*, gender is a blurred concept. In the novel, the angels treat gender as a fluid category (Gaiman and Pratchett 151), and in the series, Aziraphale and Crowley both shift gender, for example when Crowley applies as Warlock's nanny (1.01 "In the Beginning") and Aziraphale possesses Madame Tracy's body (1.05 "The Doomsday Option"). The show portrays bodies as fragile, exchangeable things—when Aziraphale arrives in Heaven after being accidentally discorporated, he is chastised for losing an expensive piece of equipment (ibid.). God's gender is not addressed within the narrative, but it is never suggested that she is perceived as female outside of the detached space she shares with the audience. On the contrary, when Aziraphale first meets the Metatron, he initially mistakes him for God (1.04 "Saturday Morning Funtime") and during his crucifixion, Jesus begs his "Father in Heaven" to have mercy with humanity (1.03 "Hard Times"). God never attempts to interfere with this notion and appears to have no interest in correcting her image on Earth. On the contrary, the misconception only adds to her position as a superior being and heightens the distance between her and the rest of the characters, who are entirely unaware of her motives. Her gender, then, becomes exclusive knowledge she shares with the audience as she invites them to watch the events unfurl.

Notably, aside from the brief flashback in episode three, Jesus is never mentioned in the series and his relation to God is never addressed, suggesting that he is human rather than a divine being. This also erases any motherly connotations that could be associated with a female God as maternal figure. Instead, she appears as distanced to the events on Earth as a narrator in a nature documentary and never intervenes, not even in the face of the impending apocalypse. Her gender exists for and matters only to the spectators and while it can be argued that *Good Omens'* female God has no sexed or gendered body within the diegesis, her voice alone challenges the preconceived notion of a universally accepted male perspective.

The Narrator as Image-Maker

Even though the omniscient Voice of God narrator is usually reserved for documentary-style films, it is a suitable choice for *Good Omens*. McDormand's rendition of God not only defies voice-over conventions but also goes against a trend established in earlier on-screen adaptations of Pratchett's and Gaiman's work. *Terry Pratchett's Hogfather* (2006) is narrated by Ian Richardson, *The Color of Magic* (2008) by Brian Cox, and *Stardust* (2007) by Ian McKellen. *Good Omens*' departure from sonorous male British voices towards an American woman marks a distinct break in tradition. In contrast to her precursors, McDormand's voice lacks the booming qualities of a male Voice of God narrator. Instead, she speaks with a medium pitch and a high, light timbre. Her words are well enunciated and while her neutral tone sounds informational, factual, and sometimes even educational, there is a slight tongue-in-cheek quality to her lines. Although her lighter, more melodic voice does not demand authority, her mastery of knowledge, time and space reveals her unconditional power. This is further enforced by her slight amusement and the humorous quality of her lines, reflecting her own description as a poker dealer "who won't tell you the rules and who smiles all the time" (1.01 "In the Beginning"). In effect, her authority does not derive from an ostentatious display of divine power, but from her all-encompassing knowledge of the world.

Similarly to Richardson's role in *Hogfather*, McDormand embodies the intersection between a homodiegetic book character and the novel's heterodiegetic narrator. While God as a character exists within the story, she must still be considered third-person voice-over narration due to her spatiotemporal distance to the characters. She inhabits a cosmic space between diegesis and audience, which is frequently emphasized through metafictional commentary. Often, God addresses the audience directly, for example when she cautions the viewers to not be deceived by the weather (1.01 "In the Beginning"). Moreover, she regularly introduces characters when they first appear on screen, for example when she invites the audience to meet Adam's parents when they first enter the scene (ibid.). In combination with her purposeful gender swap and the abundant use of voice-over in *Good Omens*, God as narrator appears to be a metafictional commentary on traditional Voice of God narration.

As narrator and character, *Good Omens*' God is defined by one essential trait: her ineffability. Throughout the series, Aziraphale and Crowley spend much of their time trying to decipher her plans to no avail and even prevent an apocalyptic war by appealing to the fact that neither Heaven nor Hell can be sure of God's true intentions. When Beelzebub cites God's Great Plan, according to which the world is bound to end in a war between angels and demons, Aziraphale wonders whether the Great Plan coincides with God's Ineffable Plan. Beelzebub struggles to offer an explanation and Crowley triumphantly declares that the Ineffable Plan is, by design, unknowable, which makes it impossible to determine whether God truly intended for the world to go down in flames. When Gabriel (Jon Hamm) objects and claims that the Almighty would not treat the fate of the universe as a game, Crowley disagrees and asks him, where he has been (1.06 "The Very Last Day of the Rest of Their Lives"). This exchange confirms God's own characterization of herself and even though she shares a space with the viewer, she never speaks about her plan and neither confirms nor denies if Aziraphale and Crowley are right. Her intentions are left to interpretation and her character remains unknowable to the characters, as well as the audience.

Even though as a homodiegetic character, God is mostly absent from the narrative, her role as narrator adds a metafictional element that emphasizes the distance between characters and narrator. Repeatedly, *Good Omens* appears to be a sort of game, staged by an omniscient entity testing her own creation. This idea is supported by the opening credits, in which Aziraphale and Crowley appear as paper dolls, walking through a scenery made up from various animation styles, mirroring the plot of the show like a miniature puppet theater. Even though the characters of *Good Omens* try to understand their creator's plans, they are ultimately unable to grasp even a fraction of her design, much like a puppet is unable to walk and act outside the confines of their stage. This idea of God as the puppet master not only breaches the fourth wall but also ultimately blends her character with the image-maker of *Good Omens*.

This aspect is distinct to the adaptation. Even though God never physically appears in a scene in the novel, he exists purely within the narrative. On screen, God interacts with the homodiegetic level only in a single sequence. During a flashback in the beginning of the third episode, she speaks directly to Aziraphale through voice-off, admonishing him for losing his flaming sword (1.03 "Hard Times"). However, her angry tone during this scene appears uncharacteristic in comparison to God's usual factual, yet slightly bemused intonation. Furthermore, later episodes reveal that although Aziraphale supposedly met God, he does not know what she looks or sounds like, indicating that God might have taken on a misleading form, or that Aziraphale maybe never interacted with the Almighty herself in person after all (1.04 "Saturday Morning Funtime").

This suggests that her brief voice-off appearance is a further facet of her unknowable plan and strengthens her position as mysterious entity.

The Female Voice as Maker of Meaning

In *Good Omens*, a woman speaks not only for herself, but for the entirety of creation, a privilege that is usually not assigned to female voices. Feminist film theorist Laura Mulvey points to the "silent image of the woman" that is subjected to the "linguistic command" of the patriarchal voice, which relegates her to the role of a "bearer of meaning, not maker of meaning" (58). By casting a woman as God, *Good Omens* challenges this notion of the silent woman. As voice-over narrator, God speaks regularly throughout the episodes, providing commentary on characters, places, and events. Her omniscient knowledge of the universe is not just a running gag but contextualizes the events on screen. This can, for example, be observed when she explains the misunderstanding between Sister Theresa Garrulous (Maggie Service) and Sister Mary Loquacious (Nina Sosanya), who misinterpret each other's winks and end up confusing the babies at the hospital (1.01 "In the Beginning"). Her tongue-in-cheek commentary is, then, an indispensable element within the series. Reflecting God's position as highest power within the story, the narrator becomes a crucial component in the process of meaning-making.

The impact is highlighted in comparison to *Dogma*, a film so heavily inspired by *Good Omens* that it lists Neil Gaiman as inspiration in its post-credits. Here, the female God does not speak and only uses her voice when she kills the fallen angel Bartleby with a silent scream. In *Dogma*, God is spoken for by the angel Metatron (Alan Rickman) and even though she is presented as the most powerful being in the universe, she appears almost child-like in her silence and dependence on the male voice.

In *Good Omens*, the power relations are reversed. British actor Derek Jacobi plays the role of the Metatron, but instead of undermining God's position, the series proves an awareness of the traditions it defies. Jacobi as Metatron marks a drastic change compared to his literary counterpart, who is described as a young man with fiery hair (Gaiman and Pratchett 333). In the series, he appears as a white-haired floating head, speaking with the conviction and the authority of a traditional Voice of God narrator, so much so that even Aziraphale initially mistakes him for the Almighty. However, he soon realizes that he is not in fact speaking with God and concludes that the Metatron wields no agency. He claims that the angel acts as the "presidential spokesman" to God and demands to speak to the Almighty directly. (1.04 "Saturday Morning Funtime"). In contrast to *Dogma*, *Good Omens*' Metatron is a pawn instead of a usurper and his claim to God's voice appears to be a test that Aziraphale passes with flying colors. While the Metatron functions as the leader of the heavenly army in the novel, the adaptation switches his role with the belligerent angel Gabriel, who has no more insight into God's will than his demonic counterpart Beelzebub. By weakening the position of the Metatron, *Good Omens* strengthens the sovereignty of God's voice, granting her an unrestricted position of power within the narrative.

Voice-Over, Literariness, and Humor in Adaptation

Gods power within *Good Omens* is simultaneously enforced and questioned by her proximity to the novel. For the majority of the miniseries, many of God's lines are adapted from the novel's heterodiegetic narrator, effectively blending a minor character with a major function. While God's words are spoken from a position of universal authority, the cult status of the novel serves as a constant reminder that they are not her lines after all. This begs the question of who is speaking: God as a character within the show, or God as mediator of Terry Pratchett's and Neil Gaiman's literary voices.

While historically, the issue of adaptation has often been associated with voice-over, many film scholars such as Kozloff disagree with the idea that novel narration and voice-over narration are essentially linked (*Storytellers* 18f). However, in the case of *Good Omens*, the connection is hard to deny. The distinct voices of Gaiman and Pratchett are a prominent feature of the novel and part of its peculiar charm. This increases the potential for recognition, even when the lines are spoken by a female voice. *Good Omens* references the novel's written word throughout the entirety of the series, starting with the first scene of the first episode, which begins with two minutes and twenty seconds of monologue. In this opening, God's lines largely correlate with the first two pages of the second chapter of the book (Gaiman and Pratchett 10f). Although some of the passages are shorted and slightly altered for screen, the pronounced similarity to the novel establishes a purposeful connection between the two texts. The most striking change from book to screen is the substitution of the masculine pronoun "He" to the first-person pronoun "I," which immediately situates the narrator within the diegesis and draws attention to the unarticulated, yet undisputable fact that *Good Omens*' God is a woman. She then fulfills not one but two essential functions: To introduce a female perspective that had been absent from the literary predecessor and to transport the characteristic literariness of the novel onto screen.

The merging of the narrator with no other than the role of God in the adaptation speaks volumes about the importance of the literary text in *Good Omens*. Forgoing all warnings about double-narration and showing versus telling, the show's propensity for voice-over narration indicates that Pratchett's and Gaiman's literary material will always hold a higher rank than the visuals. This can be observed during Death's exit in the sixth and final episode. Here, God's voice-over weakens the visual depiction of the scene by relying on the aesthetic of the written word borrowed from the novel. While the character Death exits the scene, God narrates: "Death opened wings of night. Wings that were shapes cut through the matter of creation to the darkness beneath and in which distant lights glimmered." (1.06 "The Very Last Day of the Rest of Their Lives").

The phrasing largely corresponds with the wording of the book (Gaiman and Pratchett 328), but while the novel aims to visualize the scene and create a striking image within the reader's minds, the cinematic version foregoes its major strength as a visual medium and instead circles back to the written word. As a result, the spoken word promises a spectacle that the visuals cannot deliver. On screen, Death spreads his wings but while they are described as magnificent constructs, they appear to be simple black feathered wings, reminiscent of a raven. While McDormand narrates the novel's description, Death turns into smoke and the screen fades to black. A skull appears, fades to a galaxy and eventually back to Adam and his friends (1.06 "The Very Last Day of the Rest of Their Lives"). The presence of *Good Omens*' literariness makes the images pale in comparison, enforcing a reading of the series adaptation as an homage to the written word.

As voice-over narrator, *Good Omens*' God not only preserves the distinct literariness of the material but also translates the characteristic humor of Pratchett's and Gaiman's writing to screen. Moreover, humor is one of the few characteristics that can be assigned to the otherwise ineffable narrator. When she claims that dinosaur fossils are a practical joke she planted for scientists to discover, she indicates that her own sense of humor is integrated into the Earth's design (1.01 "In the Beginning"). While God's propensity for amusement is not portrayed as malicious, it enforces her position as unknowable entity, as indicated by her description of herself as ever-smiling poker dealer (ibid.). Like any aspect of her character, her sense of humor is mysterious at best and in the face of the apocalypse the question arises as to what God considers funny.

God's humorous remarks not only work towards her own characterization but also further enforce the tie to the image-makers by capturing a distinct *Terry-Prachettness*. Prattchett, who was well-known for his satirical fantasy novels, habitually employed footnotes to provide amusing tidbits of information (Mendlesohn 269). This style of commentary appears to be well suited for the technique of voice-over, where the narrator is also able to share their remarks without interrupting the narrative. Even the recurrent use of double-narration mirrors Pratchett's humor, which heavily relies on repetition (Duvezin-Daubert 2). This is further supported by the fact that Gaiman revealed that he started working on the first episode directly after Pratchett's funeral and was inspired by one guiding principle: To do whatever would have made Terry Pratchett happy (Gaiman, *The Verge*). The show's tendency to preserve the nostalgia of *Good Omens*' literariness can, then, be interpreted as Gaiman's way of honoring his compatriot's literary voice over the strengths and weaknesses of the cinematic medium. In *Good Omens*, God transcends the boundaries of her literary counterpart and speaks not only as the creator within the story, but also acts as an extension of the image-maker's voice.

The Feminine Divine and the Male Gaze

Even though God in *Good Omens* serves as a means of translating the novels' distinct literary style to screen, she is more than just a mouthpiece for the image-maker. As a female Voice of God narrator, she challenges cinematic traditions, most strikingly because she never physically appears on screen. This is remarkable in the context of mainstream film culture, in which the female figure was created to be "seen but not heard" (Kozloff *Storytellers* 100). In her influential essay "Visual Pleasure and Narrative Cinema," Mulvey claims that in classic cinema, "the pleasure of looking has been split between active/male and passive/female" and thus "[t]he determining male gaze projects its phantasy on to the female figure which is styled accordingly" (Mulvey 62). Based on a psychoanalytic framework inspired by the work of Sigmund Freud, Mulvey suggests that women on screen "are simultaneously looked at and displayed, with their appearance coded for strong visual and erotic impact" (ibid.). The female body as a site of visual pleasure has become a central idea of feminist film theory and an essential foundation for understanding the visual coding of gender in art. Even before Mulvey's manifesto, British art critic John Berger claimed: "Men look at women. Women watch themselves being looked at" ("Ways of Seeing, Episode 2"). The idea of the female body as an observable object is crucial for the visual pleasure of the male gaze, so much so that Molly Haskell considers "the conception of a woman as idol, art object, icon, and visual entity" as "the first principle of the aesthetic of film as a visual medium" (7). In their coding as visual spectacles, female figures in mainstream cinema therefore usually possess a "to-be-looked-at-ness" and produce pleasure by being observed and displayed (Mulvey 62). According to Mulvey's essay, the male gaze works on three levels: The look of the camera, the look of the male characters within the film, and the look of the male viewer, which follows the gaze of the camera and the male characters (Mulvey 63f, Kaplan 30, de Laurentis 139). Feminist scholar and director E. Ann Kaplan points out that it "carries with it the power of action and of possession" and while women can "receive and return [the] gaze," they "cannot act upon it" (31). Although it "operates in a totalizing way through its premise of binary gender," the concept has become a "key phrase" in discussions about female objectification in the media (Paasonen et.al. 29).

The male gaze is therefore not just a singular phenomenon but translates to all cinematic representations of women—even when they personify the Almighty herself. This, again, can be observed in *Dogma*, where God is immediately objectified when she appears on screen at the end of the film and rewards the character Jay with a kiss on the cheek. Upon contact, Jay responds with erotic pleasure and voices his assessment of God's physical attractiveness:

> JAY: I got half a stock when she kissed me.
> BETHANY: Jay!
> JAY: I couldn't help it! The bitch was hot! [*Dogma*]

Even though his character serves as comic relief, Jay's objectification of God illustrates the leading principle of the male gaze: No matter how powerful, all-knowing, and divine a female body appears, it cannot escape the confines of sexualization.

This, however, is not the case in *Good Omens*. While, by virtue of not being male, McDormand's voice draws attention to her physical body, it is never presented as a site of visual pleasure. Throughout the series, aside from a brief sequence in which a set of hands that might or might not belong to McDormand shuffles a deck of cards (1.04 "In the Beginning"), God is never physically present on screen and thus forgoes the staging of her body as a site of visual pleasure. This also extends to her voice. McDormand speaks with a neutral register, sometimes inclining towards amusement, other times towards seriousness, but throughout the series, her voice never assumes a sultry or sexualized quality. By doing so, *Good Omens* transgresses the traditional organization of cinematic pleasure by evading the eroticization of her female body. While her alleged adversary Satan appears at the end of the series, God still eludes the camera. By presenting her physical form as a mystery to both viewers and characters, *Good Omens* prevents her objectification, and her position of power remains unchallenged.

God and the Female Gaze

The male gaze in cinema is, however, not simply a matter of being-looked-at, but also a matter of looking. While female characters are generally constructed to be seen, male characters function as objects for identification and command the look that guides viewers through the narrative (Mulvey 61). This means that the male gaze is also an instrument of agency. This idea is currently being challenged by various attempts to introduce a so-called female gaze to cinema. This, however, is a challenging task, as power relations are difficult to revert without replicating the problematic systems they rely on. As Mulvey herself points out, within a patriarchal system, the gaze cannot simply be reversed because "the male figure cannot bear the burden of sexual objectification" (Mulvey 63). Kaplan agrees and argues that the female gaze is lacking "the power of action and of possession" inert to the male look in cinema. Furthermore, Silverman observes that when the female gaze is constructed in visual media, it often entails a distortion of reality:

> [T]he female subject's gaze is depicted as partial, flawed, unreliable, and self-entrapping. She sees things that aren't there, bumps into walls, or loses control at the sight of the color red. And although her own look seldom hits its mark, woman is always on display before the male gaze. Indeed, she manifests so little resistance to that gaze that she often seems no more than an extension of it [31].

While in these cases, the female gaze can be utilized to express a character's viewpoint, it wields no power or agency within the narrative. The female gaze is therefore a difficult perspective to achieve, and many instances of strong female characters still move within the confines of the male gaze (Kaplan 41). This phenomenon also affects voice-over. Feminist film theorist Karen Hollinger points out that the concept of the female character, who "in most genres serve[s] only as an object of investigation, is now also the investigating subject" (35). Female voice-over narrators can therefore still be subjected to the male gaze and therefore be relegated to a position of powerlessness and objectification.

With the voice of a female God as narrator, *Good Omens* challenges these traditions. God's voice is omnipresent throughout the episodes and her gaze appears as the organizing principle structuring the plot. Her power is emphasized by her position as the invisible game-master, which is repeated throughout the show, most prominently when the babies Adam and Warlock are switched at the hospital (ibid.). God deals the metaphorical cards of the universe and therefore commands the way in which the audience experiences the narrative. "We need to begin earlier," she proclaims while the camera cuts to a scene in the past, highlighting her control of time and space (ibid.). Notably, many of these directorial lines have not been adapted from the book but are unique to the screen version. This strengthens God's position as more than just the mouthpiece of the image-maker and enhances her agency as an omnipotent being within the narrative. Where she looks, the audience looks, and the aspects she highlights are the aspects the audience pays attention to.

While her motives are unknowable, God is at no point an unreliable narrator. Here, the aspect of literariness plays a crucial factor. By merging God as a character with the novel's neutral heterodiegetic narrator, she obtains power over the narrative and thus becomes an unquestionable authority. In contrast to *Dogma*, where God is knocked unconscious and trapped in a comatose body for the majority of the film, *Good Omens*' God is never in danger or distress. Even Satan (Benedict Cumberbatch) himself appears to be nothing more than a further pawn in her game, which is emphasized by the fact that he appears both in the episodes as well as in the form of a puppet during the opening credits.

Even though characters continuously wonder about God's motives, neither her power nor her existence itself is ever questioned within the series. French screenwriter Pascal Bonitzer has claimed that through his lack of a physical body, the voice-over narrator escapes criticism (Kozloff *Voice of God* 48). While the general applicability of this statement might be questionable—there is more than enough criticism of voice-over narration and narrators alike—it applies to God's role in *Good Omens*. Characters might despair at the challenges they face, but God's ultimate authority is never questioned. As third-person narrator, God occupies a shared space with the image-maker and the audience that allows her command over the narrative, effectively introducing an omnipotent female gaze to *Good Omens*.

Conclusion

By introducing a woman as omniscient voice-over narrator, *Good Omens* puts a new twist on an outdated cinematic technique. Yet, God remains an ambiguous symbol. While the omnipresent, yet invisible female Voice of God narrator transgresses the traditional organization of visual pleasure in cinema, she also serves as a functional vessel to transport the literary style of Terry Pratchett and Neil Gaiman to screen.

While these two functions may intersect, they are not mutually exclusive. As narrator, God manages to convey the novel's characteristic tongue-in-cheek humor and creates a nostalgic appreciation for the authors' voices. But the proximity to the book's narrator also endows her with an unrestricted authority over the text. As female God, she not only challenges patriarchal religious practices but also becomes the main maker of meaning within the narrative. With the detached authority of a Voice of God narrator, Frances McDormand's voice guides the viewers through time and space, inviting them to follow the convoluted adventures of Aziraphale and Crowley. In *Good Omens*, God controls the gaze; she tells the viewers where to look, when to look and what to look for without ever making herself the subject of interest. Her authority remains unquestioned throughout the series, empowering a female perspective within the traditionally masculine space of third-person voice-over narration.

While the technique of the female Voice of God has the potential to further contribute to a female gaze in film and TV, there are many intersectional aspects like class and race to be considered. Nevertheless, *Good Omens* challenges the gendered standards of voice-over in which the male perspective has always been considered the neutral option. Voice equals power and in *Good Omens*, a woman is in charge of the universe.

Works Cited

Berger, John. "John Berger / Ways of Seeing, Episode 2 (1972)." *Youtube*, uploaded by tw19751, 9 October 2012, https://www.youtube.com/watch?v=m1GI8mNU5Sg.
The Bible. King James Version Online, accessed 20 May 2020. www.kingjamesbibleonline.org/.
The Color of Magic. Directed by Vadim Jean, performance by Brian Cox, Sky 1, 2008.
de Laurentis, Teresa. *Alice Doesn't: Feminism, Semiotics, Cinema*. London: Macmillan, 1984.
Desperate Housewives. Performance by Brenda Strong, ABC Studios, 2004–2012.
Doane, Mary Ann. "The Voice in the Cinema: The Articulation of Body and Space." *Yale French Studies*, vol. 60, 1980, pp. 33–50. https://doi.org/10.2307/2930003.
Dogma. Directed by Kevin Smith, performance by Alanis Morrisette, Lions Gate Films, 1999.
"The Doomsday Option." *Good Omens*, created by Neil Gaiman, performance by Frances McDormand, season 1, episode 5, Amazon Video and BBC Two, 2019.
Duvezin-Caubet, Caroline. "Elephants and Light Fantasy: Humour in Terry Prachett's Discworld Series." *Études Britanniques Contemporaines*, vol. 51, 2016, pp. 1–14. https://doi.org/10.4000/ebc.3462.
Gaiman, Neil. Interview by Liz Shannon Miller. *The Verge*, 30 May 2019, www.theverge.com/2019/5/30/18645935/neil-gaiman-interview-good-omens-amazon-adaptation-terry-pratchett-michael-sheen-david-tennant.
Gaiman, Neil. Interview by Ian Spiegelman. *Los Angeles Magazine*, 30 May 2019, www.lamag.com/culturefiles/good-omens-neil-gaiman. Accessed 10 May 2020.
Gaiman, Neil, and Terry Pratchett. *Good Omens*. 1990. William Morrow, 2006.
Genette, Gérard. *Narrative Discourse: An Essay in Method*. Cornell University Press, 1980.
Good Omens. Created by Neil Gaiman, performance by Frances McDormand, Amazon Video and BBC Two, 2019.
"Hard Times." *Good Omens*, created by Neil Gaiman, performance by Frances McDormand, season 1, episode 3, Amazon Video and BBC Two, 2019.

Haskell, Molly. *From Reverence to Rape: The Treatment of Women in the Movies.* Penguin Books, 1974.
Hollinger, Karen. "Listening to the Female Voice in the Woman's Film." *Film Criticism*, vol. 16, no. 3, 1992, pp. 34–52.
"In the Beginning." *Good Omens*, created by Neil Gaiman, performance by Frances McDormand, season 1, episode 1, Amazon Video and BBC Two, 2019.
It's a Very Muppet Christmas Movie. Directed by Kirk R. Thatcher, performance by Whoopie Goldberg, NBC, 2002.
Kaplan, E. Ann. *Women & Film: Both Sides of the Camera.* Routledge, 1983.
Kozloff, Sarah. "Humanizing the 'Voice of God': Narration in 'The Naked City.'" *Cinema Journal*, Vol. 23, No. 4, 1984, Pp. 41–53. https://doi.org/10.2307/1225263.
Kozloff, Sarah. *Invisible Storytellers. Voice-Over Narration in American Fiction Film.* University of California Press, 1988.
McHugh, Kathleen A. "'Sounds That Creep Inside You': Female Narration and Voiceover in the Films of Jane Champion." *Style*, vol. 35, no. 2, 2001, pp. 193–218.
Mendlesohn, Farah. "Narrative." *An Unofficial Companion to the Novels of Terry Pratchett*, edited by Andrew M. Butler. Greenwood World Publishing, 2007, pp. 264–267.
Mollenkott, Virginia Ramey. *The Divine Feminine: The Biblical Imagery of God as Female.* Eugene, Oregon: Wipf and Stock, 1984.
Morley, Janet. "In God's Image?" *CrossCurrents*, vol. 32, no. 3, 1982, pp. 308–315.
Mulvey, Laura. "Visual Pleasure and Narrative Cinema." *Feminism and Film Theory*, edited by Constance Penley. Routledge, 1988, pp. 833–44.
Paasonen, Susanna, et.al. *Objectification: On the Difference Between Sex and Sexism (Gender Insights).* London: Routledge, 2020.
"Saturday Morning Funtime." *Good Omens*, created by Neil Gaiman, performance by Frances McDormand, season 1, episode 4, Amazon Video and BBC Two, 2019.
Sex and the City. Performance by Sarah Jessica Parker, HBO, 1998–2004.
The Shack. Directed by Stuart Hazeldine, performance by Octavia Spencer, Summit Entertainment, 2017.
Silverman, Kaja. *The Acoustic Mirror. The Female Voice in Psychoanalysis and Cinema, Theories of Representation and Difference.* Indiana University Press, 1988.
Stardust. Directed by Matthew Vaughn, performance by Ian McKellen, Paramount Pictures, 2007.
"Tell Amazon: Cancel Blasphemous 'Good Omens' Series." Return to Order, accessed 5 May 2020. www.returntoorder.org/petition/tell-netflix-to-cancel-blasphemous-good-omens/.
Terry Pratchett's Hogfather. Performance by Ian Richardson, Sky1, 2006.
"The Very Last Day of the Rest of Their Lives." *Good Omens*, created by Neil Gaiman, performance by Frances McDormand, season 1, episode 6, Amazon Video and BBC Two, 2019.
Will and Grace. Performance by Cher, NBC, 1998–2020.
Wolfe, Charles. "Historicising the Voice of God: The Place of Vocal Narration in Classical Documentary." *Film History*, vol. 9, no. 2, 1997, pp. 149–167.

Ways of Mourning
Reading Grief as Friendship in Terry Pratchett and Neil Gaiman's Good Omens (1990)

Pavan Mano

Dedicated to my friend Jasper

The people you love become ghosts inside of you and like this you keep them alive.

—Montgomery

Grief is inextricably woven into the fabric of friendship. As the French philosopher Jacques Derrida reminds us, grief haunts the onset of friendship because "to have a friend [...] is to know in a more intense way, already injured, always insistent, and more and more unforgettable, that one of the two of you will inevitably see the other die" (Derrida, *The Work of Mourning* 107). To open oneself to the friendship of another is therefore to simultaneously open oneself to grief and mourning in a momentarily deferred future. It is precisely this acknowledgment of the lottery of loss that is to come that constitutes friendship for "there is no friendship without knowledge of this finitude" (Derrida, *Memoires for Paul de Man* 29). Death is a universal phenomenon—it happens to everyone. But amity underlies the path to grievability. It renders death specific by bringing it to reside within one and sounding the call to mourn a friend. As such, because grief is immanent in friendship, excepting the poetic possibility that two friends might die at precisely the same instant, so is the imperative to mourn.

We see Aziraphale come to terms with this in the cold opening of episode 3 of *Good Omens*. Scene after scene in this sequence of nearly thirty minutes chronicles Crowley and Aziraphale's friendship through history,[1] and finally concludes with them squarely confronting the specter of death. Seated in his car, Aziraphale tells Crowley that he has learnt of his plans to steal holy water from a church. For Crowley, this was an insurance policy of sorts in case he needed to take his own life to spare himself the reckoning of his master. After briefly attempting to dissuade him, Aziraphale spells out in no uncertain terms how holy water would effectively obliterate his friend ("Holy water won't just kill your body. It will destroy you completely" [Mackinnon, "Hard Times" 27:17–27:21]). Having said that, he then hands Crowley a flask of holy water—the very thing that would kill and destroy his friend completely.

Instead of reading this as an act of resignation, we should read it as a confirmation of their friendship—Aziraphale understands completely that friendship brings with it the inevitability of death and grief. It is precisely because he considers Crowley his friend and cares for him deeply ("But I can't have you risking your life. Not even for something dangerous" [Mackinnon, "Hard Times" 27:27–27:31]) that Aziraphale grants Crowley the gift of death. The look that they share at the point of exchange is also the moment the weight of Derrida's words bears down fully—for this is when they realize that, even as supernatural beings, they are not spared from the absolute rule that "one of the two of you will inevitably see the other die" (Derrida, *The Work of Mourning* 107).

This cold opening that celebrates friendship and simultaneously grapples with its attendant notion of death is one of the most significant additions—certainly the lengthiest—that Neil Gaiman makes to the miniseries. It reflects the context leading up to Gaiman writing the miniseries where he had to come to terms with the impending death of his friend and *Good Omens*' co-author, Terry Pratchett. Ever since Pratchett's diagnosis with Alzheimer's, the shadow of his death had become harder to ignore and in his foreword to *A Slip of the Keyboard*, Gaiman writes about how "[a]s Terry walks into the darkness much too soon, [...] I rage at the imminent loss of my friend" (*A Slip of the Keyboard* xvii).

Pratchett died on March 12, 2015. His death catalyzed the process of bringing *Good Omens* to screen. In an interview with *Los Angeles Magazine*, Gaiman said:

> Terry had asked me to write [*Good Omens*] for him the year before he died. He wrote me an email saying, "I want to be able to see this, and you're the only person out there who has the same understanding of and passion for the old girl that I do. So, you have to do it, and I want to watch it." And then he died. We thought he'd have a lot of time [Spiegelman].

Immediately after the funeral, Gaiman began writing the script for what would eventually become a six-episode television miniseries of *Good Omens*. He said:

> I came home from his funeral, and I started writing episode one. [... It] also felt like a very good way to go head-on into the grief for my friend, and a way to

get really determined. I was writing this for Terry. I was writing a *Good Omens* that Terry would want to see, and that became huge for me [Spiegelman].

Bringing Good Omens *from Page to Screen*

Nominally, *Good Omens* is a story of two friends working together, trying very hard to track down the Antichrist—who has quite unfortunately been misplaced—and, in the end, saving humanity. But it is also much more than that. It is the story of two friends—Terry Pratchett and Neil Gaiman—telling each other a tale. As they put it, when *Good Omens* was published in 1990, it was the result of "two blokes with an idea, who were telling each other a story" (Gaiman and Pratchett 402). Throughout the time they collectively wrote it, they called each other up, read what they had written to each other, and repeated this process everyday all whilst simply "trying to make each other laugh" (Gaiman and Pratchett 400–02).

Whereas the book was a work of friendship, written as a collaborative effort between two friends, adapting *Good Omens* for television was done in the aftermath of Pratchett's passing which gives the miniseries a different timbre. It might help here to think of adaptation as a form of translation from one medium to another, a dialogue "between two historical moments" (Pevear 27). Writing the miniseries was for Gaiman a "way to go head-on into the grief" (Spiegelman) and thus, even as he was bringing words to life on screen, the embers of death and mourning flicker in the background. Unlike the book, then, *Good Omens'* television adaptation is a writing of grief that, amongst other things, also does the work of mourning a friend. Pratchett's specter haunts the miniseries as a function of his death prior to its writing and, as we tail this ghost, the background of grief against which the miniseries is written comes to the fore, inviting us to meditate upon friendship, death, and grief.

Some might say that death has always been a part of *Good Omens* and they would be right. It is, after all, a story about the end of the world—literally the death of everyone. But the arc of its own genealogy also allows us to step beyond the teleology of the story world and read it as a story within our world, a story of our world, and perhaps as a story for our world. Even as the book was an extended dialogue about death, the story behind *Good Omens'* journey from page to screen means that death is no longer merely a theme of the story—it is transformed into an active interlocutor involved with the writing of the miniseries, compelling us to consider what we see on screen as a work of mourning. At the same time, it remains a work of friendship. Put differently, it is a work of mourning precisely because it is a work of friendship; and a work of friendship precisely because it is a work of mourning.

Attending to the miniseries as both a work of mourning and a work of friendship allows us to read *Good Omens* as a requiem for Terry Pratchett. In this way, it demonstrates how friendship is mediated by death and opens the question of mourning that haunts all friendship. In the 2010 *Richard Dimbleby Lecture*, Pratchett took the opportunity to consider "the nature of our relationship with death" (Pratchett, "The Richard Dimbleby Lecture: Shaking Hands with Death" 267). I would like to do something similar through the prism of friendship by asking what Gaiman's adaptation of *Good Omens* in the aftermath of Pratchett's death might tell us about mourning a friend. Specifically, how might one mourn a friend?

Instead of focusing on either the book or the miniseries, I am more interested in their differing contexts—in particular, the death of Pratchett that catalyzed the television adaptation of the book. I take the miniseries' genealogy as an invitation to interrogate the relation between friendship and death and ask what *Good Omens* could tell us about the challenges of mourning and remembering a friend. Reading the miniseries as a work of mourning and friendship, I suggest, offers a responsible way of mourning a friend by (re)telling the stories they told. This is not to say that (re)telling stories ought to be elevated above other ways of mourning or that it is a superior memorializing mechanism in any sense. But I suggest it is responsible because it is a way of mourning someone that ensures the kind of remembering it instantiates happens on their terms instead of ours.

Specters of Friendship

When Derrida famously asserted "il n'y a pas de hors-texte" [there is no outside-text] (Derrida, *Of Grammatology* 158), the point he was making was that language is, by definition, an imperfect system of representation. A text's meaning is always-already reliant on its individual context—and since context is required to assemble a text's meaning, it cannot be considered "outside" a text as such. Without an "outside" of language, all forms of signification necessarily fall short of complete presence; and this representational absence itself could be read as a form of presence that makes itself known through that very absence—absence/presence.

This is not a problem exclusive to written texts. Roland Barthes makes a similar point in his *Camera Lucida* about the limits of representation through the medium of the photograph. He points out that "what the photograph produces to infinity has occurred only once; the photograph mechanically repeats what could never be repeated existentially" (Barthes

4). The photograph captures a moment that has passed and, in freezing it, simultaneously functions as an instrument that allows that moment to endure. The photograph is thus a placeholder representing something that is absent/present—a moment both there and not there at the same time. Ghosts are the paradigmatic signifiers of this state of absence/presence. For, what are ghosts but markers of something absent that continues to haunt us through its presence? Their very presence signifies their absence—the simple fact that they are not there—whilst simultaneously negating that very presence.

The most obvious manifestation of this absence/presence occurred at *Good Omens'* premiere at the London Odeon theatre. A seat was left empty for Pratchett with his hat and scarf placed upon it. In a straightforward sense, this seat was unoccupied—nobody was sitting in it. At the same time, however, it was "occupied"—it was plainly unavailable for anyone else to occupy. The hat and scarf functioned as (imperfect) representations of Pratchett, maintaining him in a state of absence/presence. The imperfection of representation—the absolute impossibility of complete signification—is obvious here. It was precisely Pratchett's hat and scarf that meant his presence could be felt even as these placeholders that stood in for him simultaneously accentuated his absence. They signaled his presence and signified that he was there with everybody at the premiere whilst, at the same time, betraying the fact that the place they were holding was nonetheless empty. Placeholders are necessary only because what they are standing in for is not there. The state of occupation, however, is still marked and realized through a presence and this instance demonstrated how Pratchett's absence made itself felt as presence. For, it was not as if Pratchett was actually there at the London Odeon sitting in his chair. Rather, he was there not *in spite of* his absence but *through* his absence. In other words, it was the presence of absence that marked Pratchett's seat as occupied. The emptiness of the seat functioned as a marker that allowed Pratchett's absence to be imagined as presence.

It was precisely this absence/presence that meant everybody at the premiere could behave and act as if he was there with them, as if his ghost were present. In this sense, one could say that Pratchett's seat was not, in fact, empty; it was occupied by his ghost. We catch glimpses of this ghost in the miniseries as well. In Aziraphale's bookstore, for example, Pratchett's hat and scarf are placed on the coat rack. *Good Omens'* cinematographer Gavin Finney acknowledges this on-screen curatorial choice, elaborating that "[i]t was cool not to foreground it, but just to have it in the background" (Vineyard). For Gaiman, too, this was a way to make sure that "Terry would always be there" (Carr). Pratchett's absence/presence thus haunts the miniseries, perceptible to those who know how to look.

His specter exists in the writing of the script, in between the lines of dialogue, in the spaces between words. Even though he had passed and was no longer present, neither was he completely absent. After all, just because we do not see something does not mean it is not there.

The Responsibility of Friendship: Keeping a Friend Alive

There is an instructive exchange in Pratchett's *Going Postal* where Princess one day asks Grandad about John Dearheart. Dearheart was a clacks worker who had fallen to his death whilst working on the towers and whose name had continually been sent up and down the clacks lines. Princess notices this one day and wants to know the reason his name continues to be circulated. "We keep that name moving in the Overhead," Grandad tells Princess, before adding, "Haven't you ever heard the saying 'Man's not dead while his name is still spoken'?" (Pratchett, *Going Postal* 105).

The Slovenian philosopher Slavoj Žižek spells out the point that Pratchett is gesturing towards by arguing that there are "two deaths" (Žižek 147). The first death is a biological one whilst the second is a symbolic death (Žižek 160). Biological death is strictly governed by the physical laws of nature. With perhaps one singular exception a little over two thousand years ago, one's final breath generally signals one's departure from the physical realm with no return; this is very much a one-way trip. When John Dearheart fell from the clacks lines, he was physically dead and there was no changing that. But the symbolic dimension of death is far more porous and permeable because it does not have to bend the knee for natural law. For, the symbolic dimension of death is both sustained and governed by memory.

Dearheart's symbolic death was thus kept at bay through the act of clacks workers continually sending the dispatch with his name up and down the line (Pratchett, *Going Postal* 150), memorializing him and keeping him suspended between two deaths. In this way, memory becomes both the limit and condition of death's symbolic dimension—which is both its beauty and its peril. What Grandad failed to mention was that for Dearheart's name to still be spoken and his symbolic death kept in abeyance, somebody had to remember to do the work of speaking it. In other words, absence must be marked for it to figure as presence. But it is precisely this requirement that configures the danger of the symbolic dimension of death. Because it relies on somebody continuing to mark absence, in very much the same way it only needs one person to remember, it only needs one person to forget for one's symbolic death to be pronounced.

The call of friendship therefore brings with it a temporarily deferred promise to mourn through which one preserves the ghosts of one's friends. And it is important to remember, even though their ghosts prefigure their symbolic deaths, they do not belong to them. Their ghosts do not belong to them because they are not theirs to bring into being. Instead, we instantiate our friends' ghosts from the moment we befriend them. The instant of friendship is also the instant one begins to make space within oneself for the presence of another, and like this we defer the symbolic deaths of our friends. As Robert Montgomery puts it, it is in allowing friends to "become ghosts inside of you" that we "keep them alive" (Montgomery). This is the responsibility that friendship brings—to turn one's friends into ghosts and carry them within us. But this turning *into* is also potentially a turning *upon* because the ghosts that they become are ghosts of our making; and it is entirely possible that we are turning them into ghosts they do not recognize at precisely the moment they are no longer able to defend their name.

In this way, friendship confers upon us the responsibility of remembering our friends. If one's symbolic death being deferred is contingent on being remembered, then the responsibility of doing the work of this remembering falls upon the shoulders of one's friends. In other words, responding to the call of friendship, calling another a friend, is also to accept the call to remember the other, and keep them alive, such that they can continue to defy death. Friendship in this sense always carries the weight of responsibility to keep another alive by remembering them—the mark of an impossible mourning that is already to come. The task of friendship thus becomes the task of keeping the ghosts of our friends within us such that we keep them alive.

Remembering a Friend

When Terry Pratchett died, a shared sense of grief and loss spread collectively across plenty of people—many of whom had never met him in their entire lives. I was one of them. The acuity of grief merely served to highlight that there is always an element of unknowability embedded in any loss. How do we articulate the loss we feel at losing someone we did and did not know at the same time? How do we "know" another? In fact, can we ever know if we "know" another? These are not particularly new questions. After all, the question of knowing the "other" is one of the foundational questions of psychoanalysis.

Sigmund Freud reminds us that the slipperiness of mourning owes much to the enduring difficulty of plotting the exact coordinates of loss because "one cannot see clearly what it is that has been lost" (245). For

Freud, the difficulty of precisely locating loss is that even though one might be able to name whom we have lost, it is difficult to be certain of exactly what we have lost in the person who is no longer with us—thus, one can speak of loss "in the sense that one knows *whom* [one] has lost but not *what* [one] has lost" (Freud 245). This is why Judith Butler argues that

> when one loses, one is also faced with something enigmatic: something is hiding in the loss, something is lost within the recesses of loss. If mourning involves knowing what one has lost, [...] then mourning would be maintained by its enigmatic dimension, by the experience of not knowing incited by losing what we cannot fully fathom [Butler 21-22].

However, it is not just loss that carries an element of unknowability within it. Inasmuch as we cannot be sure what we have lost, it is equally difficult to pin down the way someone was with us in the first place. Even if we know all too well that they are absent, no longer physically present with us, how do we articulate the way they were present with us before? After all, nobody is ever-present and physically with us every second of the day. This is patently not what we mean when we say someone is with us. What, then, is this *with*? When we say someone is still with us, or no longer with us, it is a *with* that suggests a part of someone else, from outside and beyond ourselves, is now a part of us.

At the same time, it is not a *with* in the sense of completely and utterly subsuming the other such that they have now become us for that would only efface them. It is a *with* that suggests they are a part of us and apart from us at exactly the same time, a discrete elemental way of being *with* such that they make us up whilst still maintaining their individuality. To put it in Derridean terms, friendship is a supplementary relation because one's friends are a part of one whilst remaining apart from one at the same time. The "logic of supplementarity" is that the supplement is at once, in its absence, external to—and yet in its very necessity, always-already part of—the whole (Derrida, *Of Grammatology* 144–45). The way that our friends are with us is therefore precisely the way that we allow them to be with us. If friendship is a relationality, it is also a relationality whose condition and limit is the individual. When we say someone is still with us, it is a *with* of our own making. And when we say they are no longer with us, it is not the same as saying they are absent—rather, it is an absence that continually highlights its presence. It is a *with* that even in its negation continues to assert itself by shifting one into a position of mourning.

The difficulty of mourning lies in the entwinement of object and subject. The object of mourning, the very reason that one is taken over by grief and feels compelled to mourn in the first place, is simultaneously a part of the subject who is mourning. This inseparability is evident in

Good Omens—and, in particular, the writing of the miniseries. Whilst the book was written by Pratchett and Gaiman, the miniseries was ostensibly only written by Gaiman. Yet, the very friendship that rendered Pratchett grieve-able to Gaiman also renders Pratchett a part of Gaiman and his writing. Thus, even though Pratchett may not have formally written the miniseries, his specter cannot quite be detached from it. When we mourn someone whom we carry with us, there is no possibility of detachability. One cannot extricate oneself from the one we are mourning—object and subject are entwined with each other because those whom we mourn are always-already a part of us. Any distinction between the self and the other crumbles because "the attachment to 'you' is part of what composes who 'I' am" (Butler 22). Or, as Butler beautifully puts it, "Who 'am' I, without you?" (22).

Mourning therefore cannot be considered a process where one neatly detaches another from ourselves in the way a surgeon might clinically remove an unnecessary appendage. It is not an elimination or evacuation of the other. Neither is it, like self-help gurus would have us believe, simply a process of healing—as if all that is necessary is a period of rehabilitation to make us whole again. The discourse of healing applied to mourning is also the seductive snake oil of nostalgia that promises we can be returned and restored to a previously imagined order of being—as if once mourning is complete, we will be complete, with the gaping hole of loss having been magically filled by the putty of acceptance. But mourning cannot be like this because the death of a friend is, fundamentally, a rupture—it involves the loss of someone who was a part of us, someone whom we carried within ourselves as a part of our being. The very relationality that we have with a friend is itself constitutive of who we are. By severing that relationality, the death of a friend threatens to sever one of the threads that composes the fabric of our being—irrevocably, changing who we are.

It is not that healing is impossible or that one will not learn to live differently; what is impossible is being returned to the way one used to be. Mourning reorders, rearranges, and remakes us both as we are and as we will be. It is a process of navigating a radical transformation of ourselves and grieving a certain loss whilst simultaneously learning how to live with a new and different version of ourselves; and even if this is a version that we are not necessarily ready to live with, it is one we are compelled to live with. What has been lost, for which there is possibly "no ready vocabulary, is a relationality that is composed neither exclusively of [ourselves] nor [the other]" (Butler 22). And consequently, there is always bound to be a slippage in mourning that derives and arrives from this entanglement of being mutually constituted with and by others.

The (Im)possibility of Mourning

In his eulogy for Barthes, Derrida reflects that:

he will receive nothing of what I say here of him, for him, to him, beyond the name but still within it, as I pronounce his name that is no longer his. [...] But if his name is no longer his, was it ever? I mean simply, uniquely? [Derrida, *The Work of Mourning* 45]

The simple answer to the question is no; Barthes' name was never his alone. Even when alive, in the best of times, our names are never ours alone because they are always invoked by others in our absence. As a consequence, the one being named is at the mercy of memory. To be named is to be memorialized, even if only momentarily; and, in death, to be named is to be at mercy of the memory of the mourner. This is the risk embedded in the act of mourning and memorializing another. For, when we mourn someone, we are destined to mourn only a part of them—the piece of them that we know and have known, the version that was made known to us, the fragment we think we remember. Our friends who are a part of us, who make up a part of who we are, are also never wholly with us; instead, it is only fragments of them that are embedded in our being. That is to say, they are with us only as we know them and remember them.[2]

It is worth pointing out at this juncture that remembering is an enterprise fraught with considerable difficulty. Primarily, this is because one can never remember perfectly. More precisely, even if a perfect memory were possible, one could never be sure of it because forgetting does not have an object—to know what one has forgotten one would have to remember it. "Are you remembering correctly?" is the devil's question for there is always-already a dimension of the unknown to every act of remembering and memory-making. The act of remembering is an act of abstraction that is also immediately a subtraction from a specific, experienced, present. In remembering, the "abstract sense [of one's memories] remains ... but the acousticovisual concreteness of the situation of the situation in all its continuity is lost" (Kundera 126). It is impossible to pin down, get a grip on, or hold onto, the present because the present is slippery and continually in movement. It is experienced but it cannot be spoken of because it can only be spoken of after the fact. The present perpetually passes into the past and so it can only be recounted as a kind of translation where our lived reality is turned into a memory—instantly rendering it a slight stranger even to itself.

Memory therefore should not be thought of as holding any particular fidelity to truth or reality. It is susceptible to betrayal without us knowing it; it is always in the process of potentially becoming an impostor to itself; and it is always necessarily imperfect. The point here is not just that remembering is destined to remain a perpetually incomplete project besieged by the possibility of forgetting. Rather, it is to let go of the illusion that remembering exists in an antonymic relation with forgetting because, as Milan Kundera puts it, "[r]emembering is not the negative of forgetting. Remembering is a form of forgetting" (Kundera 126).

The shadow of forgetting therefore casts itself over all acts of mourning. For, in mourning someone, we are mourning nothing other than who we think they are, as we have imperfectly imagined and constituted them, as we remember them to be. In mourning one's friends, one inadvertently turns them into ghosts who will also always be slight strangers to themselves. This is something we do from the instant of friendship—we begin assembling the ghosts of our friends that we carry with us from the moment of getting to "know" them. The difference with mourning, however, is that it occurs at the point they are no longer able to defend their name in a way they could have whilst physically alive. They who are remembered will inevitably be remembered on our terms, the terms we define, the terms we render them in.

If one accepts the basic Freudian point that there is a certain slippage to all mourning, then Butler and Kundera show us that this specter derives from the curse of forgetting imbricated in any act of remembering. It comes both from the knowledge that in remembering someone, something has already slipped our mind as well as the fact that the slippage was entirely out of our control. For, slips happen when we least expect them to—in that precise moment when one loses one's hold, grasp and grip on something. Slips always come from beyond us—if one could foresee a slip, one could forestall it; and they are always beyond us—one can never plan to slip or slip deliberately.

Mourning thus becomes a triangular process of remembrance where we are made aware that we might have forgotten something, not knowing what it was, and also knowing there was nothing we could have done about it—all in the same instant. Grief, in this sense, is fundamentally discombobulating as a response to the rupture that death brings. Because the "disorientation of grief … posits the 'I' in the mode of unknowingness" (Butler 30). Placing grief's capacity for disorder alongside the ambiguity of memory, one is left with the question of exactly how to mourn. If it is destined to always be slightly beyond our reach, how do we mourn? For, mourning pronounces its enigma upon itself. Its enigmatic dimension engulfs it entirely. It is a black hole unto itself and perhaps when we mourn, we mourn nothing other than the very impossibility of mourning itself.

If the responsibility of friendship is to keep the ghosts of our friends within us and thus keep them alive, the task of friendship is remembering and resurrection—with all of the responsibility that this entails. For, remembering is an imperfect enterprise that is always already slightly tainted by forgetting. When Montgomery reminds us that the people we love become ghosts within us, it should not escape us that this *becoming* is not a state but a process. It is a process that we actively participate in where, even as we keep our friends alive, we also take the risk that this likeness, the way in which we keep them alive, is one that they might well have actively refused if they could have. This is the risk of friendship—what one opens oneself up to when remembering another. It is also the risk when one befriends another. For, this is the trust we bestow upon our friends: the deep responsibility of resurrecting us any way they like because of the impossibility of mourning within itself.

Good Omens carries the weight of this impossibility. The writing of its script was also the writing of grief; and as such, in addition to all the work it was doing as a television series, it was also doing the work of mourning. If the difficulty of mourning a friend is always haunted by the danger of fossilizing a version of them estranged from themselves, then I suggest that reading *Good Omens* as a work of mourning opens the possibility of keeping someone alive by (re)telling the stories they told as a responsible way of mourning. By no means is this because stories have some particular fidelity to the truth. In fact, here, perhaps the very opposite is true—after all, one must not forget that to tell a story is often also to tell a lie, and to spin a tale is to fib. What lies in favor of (re)telling our friends' stories is not that it remembers them in some authentic way; rather, it simply means that all of the remembering and resurrection built into mourning will happen on their terms, in their words, and with some luck, perhaps even in their worlds.

Post-script

Good Omens was picked up by Amazon Studios as well as BBC Studios, airing on *Amazon Prime* in May 2019 before coming to *BBC Two* in January 2020. At its conclusion, after the screen credits have rolled, one of the penultimate title cards has just two words in the center resting on a wave of poignance. "For Terry" (Mackinnon, "The Very Last Day of the Rest of Their Lives" 54:06). Gaiman's dedication carries an air of closure and absolution for it signals the fulfilment of a promise he had made to his friend—a promise that called on him to take *Good Omens* from its original incarnation and bring it to life on screen. In this gesture of bringing to life, there lay a laying to rest.

It is possible that against this backdrop of friendship, grief, and mourning, after watching all six episodes of *Good Omens*, reading its ending title card, and having heard the context against which the miniseries was written, some will continue to insist it is simply the story of two friends saving humanity. Perhaps they would not be wrong because, in some way, a story of humanity is exactly what *Good Omens* is.

Notes

1. This is admittedly a Eurocentric depiction of history and Aziraphale reflexively alludes to this in the Mesopotamian scene, saying, "I don't believe the Almighty's upset with the Chinese. Or the Native Americans. Or the Australians" (Mackinnon, 'Hard Times' 01:31-01:41).

2. This line of thought owes much of its genesis to a conversation with my friend Jasper Quek in Singapore, July 2018.

Works Cited

Barthes, Roland. *Camera Lucida: Reflections on Photography*. Translated by Richard Howard, Hill and Wang, 1981.
Butler, Judith. *Precarious Life: The Powers of Mourning and Violence*. Verso, 2006.
Carr, Flora. "Neil Gaiman Confirms Good Omens Cameo." RadioTimes, 31 May 2019, https://www.radiotimes.com/news/tv/fantasy/2019-05-31/good-omens-cameo-neil-gaiman-tv-series/.
Derrida, Jacques. *Memoires for Paul de Man*. Translated by Cecile Lindsay et al., Columbia University Press, 1989.
_____. *Of Grammatology*. Translated by Gayatri Chakravorty Spivak, Johns Hopkins University Press, 1998.
_____. *The Work of Mourning*. Edited by Pascal-Anne Brault and Michael Naas, University of Chicago Press, 2001.
Freud, Sigmund. "Mourning and Melancholia." *The Standard Edition of the Complete Psychological Works of Sigmund Freud*, translated by James Strachey, Hogarth Press, 1957, pp. 243–58.
Gaiman, Neil, and Terry Pratchett. *Good Omens: The Nice and Accurate Prophecies of Agnes Nutter, Witch*. Gollancz, 1990.
Kundera, Milan. "Testaments Betrayed: An Essay in Nine Parts." Translated by Linda Asher, Faber & Faber, 1996.
Mackinnon, Douglas. "Hard Times." *Good Omens*, season 1, episode 3, Amazon Prime Video, 2019.
_____. "The Very Last Day of the Rest of Their Lives." *Good Omens*, season 1, episode 6, Amazon Prime Video, 2019.
Montgomery, Robert. *The People You Love Become Ghosts Inside of You*. 2010.
Pevear, Richard. *Translating Music*. The Center for Writers & Translators, American University of Paris and Sylph Editions, 2007.
Pratchett, Terry. *A Slip of the Keyboard: Collected Nonfiction*. Doubleday, 2014.
_____. *Going Postal*. HarperTorch, 2005.
_____. "The Richard Dimbleby Lecture: Shaking Hands with Death." *A Slip of the Keyboard: Collected Nonfiction*, Doubleday, 2014, pp. 266–84.
Spiegelman, Ian. "Neil Gaiman Made Good Omens a Show Terry Pratchett Would Want to See." *Los Angeles Magazine*, 30 May 2019, https://www.lamag.com/culturefiles/good-omens-neil-gaiman/.
Vineyard, Jennifer. "Some of the Coolest Good Omens Easter Eggs, According to Neil Gaiman, David Tennant and Crew." SYFY WIRE, 2 June 2019, https://www.syfy.com/syfywire/some-of-the-coolest-good-omens-easter-eggs-according-to-neil-gaiman-david-tennant-and-crew.
Žižek, Slavoj. *The Ticklish Subject: The Absent Centre of Political Ontology*. Verso, 2000.

Good Omens and Fan Culture

"Okay, Crowley, Junior"

Subversions and Transformations of Good Omens in Supernatural and Its Fandom

Cait Coker

The 2019 Amazon television adaption of *Good Omens* created a new surge within an older fandom. While stories and references to the 1990 collaborative novel by Neil Gaiman and Terry Pratchett could previously be found in mass fanfiction aggregators like Fanfiction.net (with the earliest stories appearing in 2001, while the site itself was founded in 1998), and Archive of Our Own (AO3) (early stories first appearing in 2008, after its 2007 creation), under categories for "Books" and "Books and Literature," the revitalization categorized as "Television" was as profound as it was sudden. For a period of months, new stories would be posted daily by the dozen on AO3; Fanfiction.net was significantly sparser due to its age, yet notably new material was still being added while many other fandoms lay dormant. The new fan texts consciously modeled themselves on the adaptation with its description of characters drawn from their embodiments by actors David Tennant and Michael Sheen, while their transformative contexts varied extensively, and most often, romantically. However, arguably one of the major transformations of the text of *Good Omens* was drawn from the novel, and was itself a TV series: *Supernatural* (2005–2020).

Supernatural as a television series is a postmodern text that derives both its meaning and its interpretations from other works. Creator Eric Kripke has famously said that much of his main characters, Sam and Dean Winchester, were drawn from Jack Kerouac's Sal Paradise and Dean Moriarty from his 1957 novel *On the Road* (Zubernis and Larsen 5), but other influences permeate the text—most especially Neil Gaiman's work. At 2007's San Diego Comic Con, Kripke noted that he'd hoped to meet Gaiman there "because he's a huge influence on *Supernatural*, between

American Gods and *Sandman*" (Boris 2007). References to *Good Omens* abound in the series: a demon named Crowley, a reluctant young Antichrist (Jesse Turner in 5.06 "I Believe the Children Are Our Future"), plentiful usage of classic rock (albeit no Queen), Chuck the Prophet's ill-fated publishing career,[1] and angels and demons teaming up with humans to avert an Apocalypse that few of them want. (A notable sequence in which a convention center is filled with a convocation of gods in 5.19 "Hammer of the Gods" is also an homage of Gaiman's solo novel *American Gods*, itself adapted for television in 2017–2021 to mixed reviews.)

Supernatural's textual revisions of *Good Omens* took place over the course of a decade, a period which itself saw a significant cultural shift in depicting queerness and queer relationships. During this period, the notion of subverting the power of the author-creator went mainstream as broader mass culture came to understand and to some extent even embrace fan practices. Far from bringing intellectual anarchy, these practices of reading (and writing) queerly underscore the splendid range of textual meanings that are possible in popular texts. This chapter argues that *Supernatural* (hereafter SPN) is a subversion of *Good Omens* as a text rather than a derivation: the elements that it chooses to copy are utilized in specific and sometimes troubling ways. SPN is a problematic text for many reasons, including its longevity and its multiple authors on and offscreen. As such it lacks the narrative cohesion and consistent authorial intentions which both *Good Omens* and its television adaptation maintain. However, the ways SPN revises, references, and plays on *Good Omens* makes it a fascinating case study for twenty-first-century textual revisionary readings.

Good Demons and Dick Angels

A peculiar charm of *Good Omens* as both novel and mini-series television is how it recasts the familiar elements of Jewish and Christian lore at a slant through the appearances of such figures as Gabriel and Beelzebub. The Amazon adaptation goes even further with its added sequence showing Aziraphale and Crowley's meetings throughout history, often in the context of (quasi-historical) events from the Bible. These include the lead-up to the Great Flood and the crucifixion of Christ, with the addition of a Monty-Python-esque scene in 537 AD. Wessex in which our angel is masquerading as one of King Arthur's knights on the quest for the Grail while our demon is "the Black Knight" (1.03 "Hard Times").[2] Above all, the focus remains on the oppositional duo of Aziraphale and Crowley, who are in fact not that oppositional. The text undercuts what we know about the "goodness" of angels and the "evil" of demons by giving us characters that are morally (but not ethically) slippery in a universe predicated on the notion that such beings must function as dichotomies.

SPN, in contrast, situates the divide between angels and demons with humans in the middle, and the Apocalypse with billions dead as only collateral damage in a narrative in which the end has already been written (or so it is assumed). Heroes Dean and Sam Winchester roam continental America on their family business of "saving people and hunting things" in a world where, seemingly, everything is chaos. Over the course of the first few seasons, however, they find that they have been forced to enact roles in a storyline that God himself has already written. Season Five's Apocalypse arc featured the Winchesters teaming up with their own angel (Castiel) and demon (Crowley) who would become fixtures for most of the series. While Castiel was primarily motivated by his friendship and love for Dean Winchester, Crowley saw the chaos caused by the End's aversion as a ladder, moving upwards from the King of the Crossroads to the King of Hell. (He also insisted that his reason for assisting the Winchesters was self-preservation.) As such the storyline became closer to what Gaiman and Pratchett's Crowley imagines, with "Heaven and Hell against humanity" (463). The final arc of the show in Season Fifteen played with this notion of opposition between Heaven, Hell, and Humanity even further by showing God in direct conflict with his own creations.

Further, SPN's Season Fifteen began production in the summer of 2019, soon after the Amazon adaptation of *Good Omens* first streamed online. References to the series were direct on the textual and meta-textual levels. For instance, in the season opener (15.01 "Back and to the Future") the team allies with a demon named Belphegor. Belphegor uses the dead body of the Nephilim Jack, who had been killed by God with his eyes burned away in the preceding season; Belphegor immediately uses a pair of sunglasses to hide his disfigurement similarly to the way Amazon's Crowley consistently uses glasses to hide his snake-like eyes. Dean immediately calls out the reference, addressing him as "Crowley Jr." and thus implying that *Good Omens* is a fictional media property within the popular culture world of SPN, along with *Game of Thrones*, *Star Trek*, *Star Wars*, and other media which are also frequently referenced.[3] (Within the context of SPN's own Crowley, it's unlikely that Dean would be referring to jokingly referring to the previous King of Hell, who was his frenemy and whose death Dean actively grieved. Later, in the episode 15.13 "Destiny's Child" angel Anael and demon Ruby are shown, via flashback, making plans to escape the Apocalypse. This flashback is also a retcon of previous continuity, which had established that Anael came to Earth and possessed her human vessel in the wake of the angels' fall from Heaven in 2013, rather than during the Apocalypse of 2008–2009 [as previously mentioned in 13.13 "Devil's Bargain"].) This brief storyline therefore functions as another direct homage to *Good Omens* with its depiction of angel/demon friendship and cooperation, albeit at the expense of previous storytelling decisions earlier in the show.

Angel/demon partnerships elsewhere in SPN are much more fraught, and indeed, only seen in the context of enforcing order. Much of Season Six is given over to a second war in Heaven after the aversion of the Apocalypse, with Castiel competing with the Archangel Raphael for leadership of the angels. Raphael's plan is to reset the Apocalypse, which Castiel plans to thwart by partnering with Crowley. The episode 6.20 "The Man Who Would Be King" details Crowley's "temptation" of Castiel, which hinges on an arrangement to keep Dean safe as well as ignorant of these machinations. While Aziraphale is often conflicted about his "arrangement" with Crowley (though he eventually capitulates to a joyful "Temptation accomplished!" in the end), Castiel is shown to be guilt-ridden by his choice. In another example, set in Season Fifteen, we see that God is manipulating both Heaven and Hell to punish the Winchesters for refusing to obey him. God opens Hell and resurrects Lilith, the first demon created by Lucifer, and orders her to find the Archangel Michael. She in turn reminds Michael of the last time they "worked together" to jumpstart the Apocalypse in order to force God to return, ten years previous (15.08 "Our Father, Who Aren't in Heaven"). God is shown to be a selfish and destructive force here, rather than a beneficent one.

In short, the relationships between angels and demons—and Heaven and Hell—are primarily but not totally antagonistic in both texts. Both view humans as God's creations, but creations that are to be used and exploited as metaphysical natural resources. Both Kripke and Gaiman/Pratchett view humanity's free will as an afterthought of possibility rather than as a meaningful variable in their calculations: the Apocalypse will always happen, and its aversion in both texts is presented as a surprise that could only be foreseen by an otherwise-absent God. While this metaphysical worldview is perhaps not groundbreaking to serious theologians or readers of genre, within the context of mainstream American television it is noteworthy. Further, the gulf between cult television (which SPN inhabits) and prestige television (which *Good Omens* inhabits) is wide enough to force a deeper reckoning with the portrayals of Christian mythology in mass popular culture. Both texts also require examination as queer texts that successfully subvert many of our expectations regarding theological representations.

As It Was Written? Queer(ing) Texts as an Ineffable Plan

Queer texts do not necessarily need to be written by queer authors nor chronicle queer characters per se. Instead, queerness is read in the "gaps" in texts, in which that which is not directly explained can only be assumed, and that assumption provides narrative closures which cannot otherwise be found directly in the text. For example, as I have written elsewhere, Marvel's "Civil War" comic book arc is queer in that narrative tension is maintained through the emotional arc of Captain America and Iron Man's dissolution of friendship, while the narrative is closed by Steve's death and Tony's mourning; the ostensible problem of superhero legislation is never directly solved, while all of the emotional catharsis is created by celebrating doomed friendship.[4]

Similarly, one of the main plots of *Supernatural* revolves around the friendship of Dean Winchester and the angel Castiel, whose relationship is identified as a romance by other characters though not always by themselves. The narrative gaps referenced on the show which relate events off-screen consistently circle around to shared emotional experiences between the two: the year of prayers Dean sent to Castiel in Purgatory (8.02 "What's Up, Tiger Mommy?"); the mixtape Dean gave to Castiel, which is only seen when Castiel attempts to return it after an argument (12.19 "The Future"); numerous times the pair have spent watching films together and, apparently, times where Castiel has woken Dean up out of sound sleep and then made him coffee (13.06 "Tombstone"). Such moments allude to an extensive off-screen relationship that parallels the (equally extensive) one seen on-screen, and which highlights smaller, more domestic interactions that contrast heavily with the drama usually seen.

Good Omens as a television production is likewise queer through its absences; for example, Aziraphale's exasperated statement to Crowley in 1.06 "The Very Last Day of the Rest of Their Lives," "Come up with something, or.... Or I'm never going to talk to you again!" However, it is also directly stated to be queer through its authorial and actorial intentions. Neil Gaiman admitted that the adaptation needed additional material for the pairing, which led to a revision of their relationship from book to screen:

> I felt, well, why don't I essentially take the beats of a love story and see how that works? ... I think that gave us something very special, because people of every and any sexual orientation and any and every gender looked at Crowley and Aziraphale and saw themselves in it, or saw a love story that they responded to.... Things like this, you can't manufacture, they have to happen from a fandom [Jeffery].

These specific choices contrast with authorial decisions that leave the matter totally up to the viewer, who can choose to see (or not see). While arguably this could remain the case with *Good Omens*, which lacks traditionally overt romantic signifiers between Aziraphale and Crowley such as kisses or direct professions of love, it nonetheless contains numerous queer signifiers instead. Crowley's costuming is consistently genderfluid, and more than once he is shown wearing feminine clothing (the scarf over his hair at the Crucifixion in 1.03 "Hard Times," or his dress as Nanny in 1.01 "In the Beginning"). Aziraphale is referred to by Shadwell, in both the adaptation and in the original novel, as a "Southern pansy," a derogatory turn of phrase for an urban (specifically London) gay man.

Queer signifiers in the original book are largely limited to brief text like the "Southern pansy" comment, with the context of 1990s homophobia. It is important to note, however, how the novel utilizes text and its revisions, and how this can be utilized to further queer readings. For example, Jessica Walker (2012) has linked the portrayal of Agnes Nutter to the history of women's writing from the period of the English Civil War and the acts of recovery inherent in locating and reading such writings. Indeed, Anathema Device is very much indicative of a certain kind of literary reader or student, examining and re-examining her ancestress's *True Prophecies* to locate meaning and to take her own place in a story that is foretold. I argue that Aziraphale is the flip side of this portrayal, as his role as a bookseller speaks to the historical place of booksellers in the circulation and dissemination of texts.

However, Aziraphale bumps up against this expectation by virtue of being a bookseller who does not actually like to sell books, and indeed, tries to avoid it as much as possible. Gaiman and Pratchett write that "he used every means short of actual physical violence to make a purchase. Unpleasant damp smells, glowering looks, erratic opening hours—he was incredibly good at it" (36). A footnote in the novel also places Aziraphale in the role of textual editor in the case of the "Buggre All This Bible" with its extensive compositor's errors and additional verses. The footnote addresses these textual transgressions before concluding that "since the whole print run was burned anyway, no one bothered to take up this matter with the nice Mr. A. Ziraphale, who ran the bookshop two doors along and was always so helpful with the translations" (37).

Rereading and revision in *Good Omens* lay the groundwork for acts of interpretation that are key to saving the day—and to making meaning for the audience. The characters push past the assumption that the Apocalypse and the End are foretold to change the story, which they do; they make new meanings. These tools are likewise there for critics and for fans engaged in making transformative works: The ability to see something new within a text in order to reread and revise it. Henry Jenkins called such work "resistant readings" in his seminal work *Textual Poachers* (1992), and much more work has been done since to look at how fan works have meaningfully revised media texts.

Reading SPN itself as a kind of fan work of *Good Omens*, which resists authorial intentions regarding text, and especially as centering itself around a transformative queer romance, enhances the show with additional layers of meaning. As mentioned above, the multitudinous direct references to *Good Omens* can be found easily, but the more subtle relationships between Dean, Castiel, and Crowley also lend themselves to this reading. It is also telling that popular media have picked this up, as with *SFX Magazine*'s June 2019 issue specifically devoted to the *Good Omens* series. A sidebar entitled "Team Heaven" in the piece asks, "If Aziraphale wasn't available who [sic] else from Up There could team-up with Crowley?" and goes on to answer with several fictional characters from other works, including Castiel. The text goes on:

> Dean Winchester's biggest fan has some form when it comes to tackling the Apocalypse, though after years of saving Dean, resurrecting Dean, dying for Dean and staring at Dean with puppy dog eyes, it may be tricky partnering up this angel with anyone else [Edwards 43].

Though playfully and humorously meant, the piece reiterates the queer reading of Castiel and Dean through popular media rather than through a specifically fannish lens, therefore providing additional weight to that reading—which is often otherwise mitigated through fandom's ship wars.[5] In short, public media attention to a queer pairing whose canonicity was not outright at the time[6] helps to build the case for its legitimacy among the viewership.

Angelic Romance and Devilish Companions

As mentioned previously, SPN began to insert references to *Good Omens* in 2009. SPN fandom did the same[7] but more directly, name-dropping or inserting Aziraphale and Crowley as characters in fan fiction crossovers and fusions. Unlike such figures as Michael and Gabriel, angels named in the Bible and related texts, Aziraphale is instead the fictional invention of Gaiman and Pratchett. His appearances in SPN fic range in roles from minor cameos to lead character, and in period from 2009 until the present (with a significant bump dating after May 31, 2019). Crowley's appearances range across similar spans, but with pains taken to either differentiate the *Good Omens* version of the character from the SPN version (such as stories where

68 *Good Omens* and Fan Culture

King of Hell Crowley meets Anthony J. Crowley), or alternatively to meaningfully fuse them into the same character (in which he is King of Hell and frenemies with Dean Winchester and also a friend of Aziraphale).

There is also an impulse among some to view the relationships between, respectively, Aziraphale and Crowley and between Castiel and Crowley as parallel in nature since, after all, they are both angel/demon relationships. This does, however, overlook or even mischaracterize some key elements of both pairs. For example, a major distinction between the Crowleys regards their fall from grace: the *Good Omens* Crowley was originally a fallen angel who, in his own words, "didn't fall so much as saunter vaguely downwards" ("Hard Times" 1.03), while the SPN version of the character was initially a human from the seventeenth century named Fergus MacLeod who sold his soul for what is politely described as "an extra three inches below the belt" ("Weekend at Bobby's" 6.04). For the better part of his run on SPN, Crowley was a villain and an antagonist who only periodically assisted the Winchesters—*if* doing so was in his own best interests.

Further, Crowley and Castiel are arguably romantic rivals for Dean Winchester rather than thwarted lovers themselves. As the "Righteous Man" who was sent to Hell and then raised from perdition and was later turned into both a demon Knight of Hell and an archangel's vessel, Dean has deep connections both to Heaven and Hell and to Castiel and Crowley. Likewise, both Castiel and Crowley have ties to Dean that they have periodically held above those to their own side, to the consternation of the other angels and demons. As a lower-ranked angel, Castiel has been punished by Heaven multiple times for getting too close to Dean, as well as slowly losing his powers due to his literal fall from grace. Crowley faced several attempted coups by demons who believe that he has gone soft, with his metaphorical "fall" being instead a renewal of human emotions. Intriguingly, a deleted scene from 10.14 "The Executioner's Song" plays with these tensions directly. Crowley notes that Castiel has been "running errands all over the U.S., burning through that rather finite supply of grace all in a desperate effort to save your boyfriend." An irked Castiel replies, "What about you, Crowley? Dropping everything, bringing the First Blade.... Maybe he's your boyfriend."[8] By the finale of the twelve season, Dean is faced with the death of both men, and in 13.01 "Lost and Found," he makes an impassioned prayer:

> Okay, Chuck ... or God, or whatever. I need your help. ... We've lost everything. And now you're gonna bring him back. Okay? You're gonna bring back Cas, you're gonna bring back Mom, you're gonna bring 'em all back. All of 'em. Even Crowley.

That Dean puts Castiel first in this private moment, even above his mother, is especially meaningful, and perhaps why the silence is so loud in this scene.[9] Eventually, Castiel returns due to his own devices, as does Mary

Winchester. Crowley's definitive death, as a genuine self-sacrifice for Dean Winchester, is left as it is.

In addition to the previously discussed friendship of Anael and Ruby, the other recurring angel/demon partnership is that of Castiel and Meg—who canonically *are* thwarted lovers. Meg Masters is a demon who was introduced in the first season and had multiple run-ins with the Winchesters until her death at the hands of Crowley in Season Eight. Appearing initially as an antagonist, Meg eventually becomes an ally of sorts, as well as starting a flirtation with Castiel (and engaging in a passionate clinch in 6.10 "Caged Heat"). Before her self-sacrifice, she calls him her "unicorn" to parallel Sam's own doomed romance with a woman named Amelia: "You fell in love with a unicorn. It was beautiful, then sad, then sadder. I laughed, I cried, I puked in my mouth a little. And honestly, I kind of get it" (8.17 "Goodbye Stranger").

This profession of love, albeit without Castiel present, is a mirror to the one that Dean and Castiel have in the same episode, in which Dean breaks through Castiel's Heaven-induced mind-control by stating that "We're family. We need you. I need you." The contrast of the Castiel/Meg and Castiel/Dean relationships puts the inherent queerness of Castiel and Dean in stark relief, both as the female is violently discarded in the text and as the queer relationship is the one that overcomes eons of mind-control. The "queerness as absence" motif is also reiterated through the revelation that the original script for the episode had Dean saying, "I love you" rather than "I need you," with actor Jensen Ackles requesting that the line be changed since he felt that "was not in character for Dean," with script-writer Robbie Thompson stating on Twitter that he supported Ackles' call on the decision (@rthompson1138).

The shift in line did not necessarily change the relationship between the characters—statements of love need not be romantic, after all—but it absolutely reinforced the queer-coding of Dean as a man who has an incredibly deep relationship with another man. This is further reinforced during the sequence in 13.01 "Lost and Found" in which he prepares the body of the dead Castiel for burning. This is the only such sequence we see on the show where wrapped bodies are burned on funeral pyres on a semi-regular basis. We see Dean lay out Castiel on a table, and physically rend white curtains into sheets of wrapping, imagery that is most typically associated, visually and historically, with widows and widowers.

Unfortunately, the ultimate conclusion of this arc would again involve Castiel's death via self-sacrifice in 15.18 "Despair." After proclaiming his love for Dean, he is removed to the cosmic void. Though he is briefly referenced in the finale as being in the new and improved Heaven (a place of love and without walls), he is not seen again. Hammering the problematic trope home, however, was the disappearance of lesbian couple Charlie and Stevie earlier in the same episode. While all of these absences were, according to the actors, due to the challenges of shooting in the wake of pandemic-related lockdowns, they also seemed to imply a lack of concern for queer treatments onscreen. In contrast, Aziraphale and Crowley not only survive, but celebrate their victory with luncheon at the Ritz, champagne flutes in hand: their "Temptation accomplished" not only underscores the romantic reading of the scene but reasserts the choices they have made in asserting their own destinies.

Ways of Reading? Textual Free Will and Certain Conclusions

The recurring theme of free will is one of the keys to both *Good Omens* and SPN, and indeed is the intellectual endgame of both texts. The ability to choose one's own destiny—and family, and friends, and life—is at the heart of both stories, and in many ways is one that is also, inherently, resoundingly queer. The verbal echoes of Castiel's "We're making it up as we go" in 4.22 "Lucifer Rising" and Aziraphale's "Oh well I'll figure it out as I go" in 1.05 "The Doomsday Option" resound with the anxiety and the hope deep-rooted in the very concept of free will's ability to choose: One can choose well, and one can choose poorly, and one always hopes for the former while fearing the latter. Likewise, in choosing to read queerly, one surveys the text looking for evidence of the author's supposed Great Plan but wondering if it's the same as the reader's Ineffable Plan. After all, they are not guaranteed to be the same plan, and no one (not even the author, at times) knows for sure.

Supernatural's textual revisions of *Good Omens* took place over the course of a decade, a period which itself saw a significant cultural shift in depicting queerness and queer relationships. During this period, the notion of subverting the power of the author-creator went mainstream as broader mass culture came to understand and to some extent even embrace fan practices. Far from bringing intellectual anarchy, these practices of reading (and writing) queerly underscore the splendid range of textual meanings that are possible in popular texts.

Notes

1. God, actually. Chuck's meta-narrative is literalized as he composes text and events onscreen and watches his "favorite show" about the Winchesters as a truly capricious and cruel audience.

2. Let us take a moment to reflect on the cultural loss inherent in Crowley choosing not to threaten to bite Aziraphale's kneecaps off. The "fomenting" exchange was pretty great, though.

3. SPN's relationships to other media is much fuzzier. For instance, in the *Legends of Tomorrow* season 5 episode "Zari, Not Zari," the time-traveling heroes arrive in 2020 Vancouver on the set of *Supernatural*. Character Sara Lance expresses dismay that another character hasn't seen the show, and they see signs referencing filming-in-progress, examine the iconic 1967 Impala with its props, and must fight zombified set crew members controlled by a malevolent time deity. This entire episode implies that *Legends* may well take place in our own world, *or* in the alternate universe shown in "The French Mistake" (6.15) where Sam and Dean find themselves taking the place of their actors Jared Padalecki and Jensen Ackles while shooting an episode of *Supernatural* (a universe differentiated from our own due to the fictional deaths of actor Misha Collins and previous show-runner Eric Kripke which take place). However, *Legends* may well be a show in SPN's world as well, given that the angel Zachariah mockingly calls Castiel "Constantine" in the episode "Lebanon" (14.13), referring to the characters' near-identical costumes. (Although, it is worth noting that the character has also appeared in an eponymous 2005 film, albeit sans the famous costume, as well as a short-lived television show, several animated features, and numerous comics. It is also worth noting that Neil Gaiman has also famously written that character numerous times for DC Comics.) To further complicate matters, Lucifer, as played by Tom Ellis in the titular FOX series which later moved to Netflix (and which is based on a DC character created by—you guessed it—Neil Gaiman), cameoed on the CW's *Crisis on Infinite Earths* crossover event (1.03/6.09) to speak with Constantine and transport him and other characters to Purgatory (which is shown to be visually and locationally identical to the Purgatory shown on SPN). And finally, on *Lucifer* ("Orgy Pants to Work," 4.06) the angel Amenadiel asks his sister Remiel if she is visiting because she is "sick of Castiel's Singing" in Heaven. Audiences would prove to be utterly sympathetic to this comment a few months later when we do indeed hear Castiel's "singing" in the SPN episode "The Rupture" (15.03). *Supernatural*'s presence is thus transcendent across networks, digital platforms, and universes.

4. See Coker 2013.

5. In fannish parlance, a "ship" is a relationship between two fictional characters, in this case Castiel and Dean Winchester. A "ship war" is the disagreement (to put it lightly) between two or more factions as to the most canonical, most romantic, or even the One True Pairing (OTP) among fictional characters. While Castiel/Dean, or Destiel, is very popular, other ship factions include Sam/Castiel (Sastiel), Dean/Crowley (Drowley), and even Sam/Dean (Wincest). Particularly hostile shippers are known as "antis," who may not be *for* any given ship but are definitely *against* certain ships—including Destiel. Indeed, virulent antis foment hatedom rather than fandom, with the two largest such factions in SPN being the Destihellers (or just Hellers, fans of Destiel who are a bit too fanatic for their ship; this name has been reclaimed somewhat, however) and the Bronlies (those who focus on the relationship between Dean and Sam, often but not always Wincest shippers). See "Destihellers."

6. Or what we might call "Schrodinger's Queerbaiting." For more on queerbaiting, see Brennan 2019.

7. It is notable that the fictional angels of both Gaiman and Pratchett and *Supernatural* differentiate themselves by not adhering to the traditional "-el" ending convention, which in Hebrew denotes "of God." "Aziraphale" does not convey meaning of itself, unlike Castiel ("Shield of God"), or Azazel ("Arrogance to God"), who in theological literature is a fallen angel and who on *Supernatural* is a Knight of Hell.

8. The quoted dialogue begins at timestamp 0:26 at the following video link: https://youtu.be/Xg4c_LWjUck.

9. That and Chuck's a dick, obviously.

Works Cited

@rthompson1138. "@GreensieBeans He did. and yeah, I think he made the right call #supernatural." *Twitter*, 5 November 2013, 7:54 pm, https://twitter.com/rthompson1138/status/397904791604441088.

72   *Good Omens* and Fan Culture

Amazingbecca. "Cas and Crowley 10x14 Deleted Scene." *YouTube*, 26 July 2017, https://youtu.be/Xg4c_LWjUck.
American Gods. Dev. By Bryan Fuller and Michael Green. Starz. Three seasons, 2017–2021.
Archive of Our Own (AO3). archiveofourown.org.
"Back and to the Future." *Supernatural*, season 15, episode 1, CW, 10 October 2019. *Netflix*, netflix.com/watch/81193703.
Boris, Cynthia. "Eric Kripke: Satan's Head Writer." *TV of the Absurd*. 25 July 2007. web.archive.org/web/20080214083340/http://tvoftheabsurd.com/2007/07/25/eric-kripke-satans-head-writer/. Accessed 4 May 2020.
Brennan, Joseph, ed. *Queerbaiting and Fandom: Teasing Fans Through Homoerotic Possibilities*. Iowa City: University of Iowa Press, 2019.
"Caged Heat." *Supernatural*, season 6, episode 10, CW, 3 December 2010. *Netflix*, netflix.com/watch/70223143.
Coker, Catherine. "Earth 616, Earth 1610, Earth 3490—Wait, What Universe Is This Again?: The Creation and Evolution of the Avengers and Captain America/Iron Man Fandom." *Transformative Works and Cultures* 13 (June 2013). journal.transformativeworks.org/index.php/twc/article/view/439. Accessed 27 May 2020.
"Crisis on Infinite Earths: Part Three." *The Flash*, season 6, episode 9, CW, 10 December 2019. *Netflix*, netflix.com/watch/81193681.
"Despair." *Supernatural*, season 15, episode 12, CW, 5 November 2020. *Netflix*, netflix.com/watch/81193720.
"Destihellers." *Supernatural Wiki*. www.supernaturalwiki.com/Destihellers. Accessed 11 June 2020.
"Destiny's Child." *Supernatural*, season 15, episode 13, CW, 23 March 2020. *Netflix*, netflix.com/watch/81193715.
"Devil's Bargain." *Supernatural*, season 13, episode 13, CW, 8 February 2018. *Netflix*, netflix.com/watch/80216357.
"The Doomsday Option." *Good Omens*, episode 5, Amazon Prime, 31 May 2019. *Amazon Prime*, amazon.com/gp/video/detail/B07FMHTRFD/.
Edwards, Richard. "Good Omens." *SFX Magazine*, June 2019, pp. 32–43.
"The Executioner's Song." *Supernatural*, season 10, episode 14, CW, 17 February 2015. *Netflix*, www.netflix.com/watch/80061146.
"Family Remains." *Supernatural*, season 4, episode 11, CW, 12 November 2009. *Netflix*, netflix.com/watch/70223100.
Fanfiction.net. fanfiction.net.
"The French Mistake." *Supernatural*, season 6, episode 15, CW, 25 February 2011. *Netflix*, netflix.com/watch/70223148.
"The Future." *Supernatural*, season 12, episode 19, CW, 27 April 2017. *Netflix*, netflix.com/watch/80144959.
Gaiman, Neil. *American Gods*. New York: HarperCollins, 2001.
Gaiman, Neil. *The Quite Nice and Fairly Accurate Good Omens Script Book*. New York, William Morrow, 2019.
"Galaxy Brain." *Supernatural*, season 15, episode 12, CW, 16 March 2020. *Netflix*, netflix.com/watch/81193714.
"The Girl Next Door." *Supernatural*, season 7, episode 3, CW, 7 October 2011. *Netflix*, netflix.com/watch/70245742.
"Goodbye Stranger." *Supernatural*, season 8, episode 17, CW, 20 March 2013. *Netflix*, netflix.com/watch/70283560.
"Hammer of the Gods." *Supernatural*, season 5, episode 19, CW, 22 April 2010. *Netflix*, netflix.com/watch/70223130.
"Hard Times." *Good Omens*, episode 3, Amazon Prime, 31 May 2019. *Amazon Prime*, amazon.com/gp/video/detail/B07FMHTRFD/.
"I Believe the Children Are Our Future." *Supernatural*, season 5, episode 6, CW, 15 October 2009. *Netflix*, netflix.com/watch/70223117.
"In the Beginning." *Good Omens*, episode 1, Amazon Prime, 31 May 2019. *Amazon Prime*, amazon.com/gp/video/detail/B07FMHTRFD/.

Jeffery, Morgan. "Neil Gaiman: 'Good Omens Fan Response to Crowley and Aziraphale's Love Story Caught Me by Surprise.'" *RadioTimes*. 4 June 2019. radiotimes.com/news/tv/2020-02-04/good-omens-crowley-aziraphale-romance/. Date accessed 28 May 2020.

Jenkins, Henry. *Textual Poachers: Television Fans & Participatory Culture*. New York, NY: Routledge, 1992.

"Lebanon." *Supernatural*, season 14, episode 13, CW, 7 February 2019. *Netflix*, netflix.com/watch/81029353.

"Lost and Found." *Supernatural*, season 13, episode 1, CW, 12 October 2017. *Netflix*, netflix.com/watch/80216345.

"Lucifer Rising. *Supernatural*, Season 4, Episode 22, CW, 14 May 2009. *Netflix*, Netflix.com/watch/70223111.

"The Man Who Would Be King." *Supernatural*, season 6, episode 20, CW, 6 May 2011. *Netflix*, netflix.com/watch/70223153.

"Orgy Pants to Work." *Lucifer*, season 4, episode 6, Netflix, 8 May 2019. *Netflix*, netflix.com/watch/81012154?.

"Our Father, Who Aren't in Heaven." *Supernatural*, season 15, episode 8, CW, 12 December 2019. *Netflix*, netflix.com/watch/81193710.

"The Real Ghostbusters." *Supernatural*, season 5, episode 9, CW, 12 November 2009. *Netflix*, netflix.com/watch/70223120.

"Reichenbach." *Supernatural*, season 10, episode 2, CW, 14 October 2014. *Netflix*, netflix.com/watch/80061134.

"The Rupture." *Supernatural*, season 15, episode 3, CW, 24 October 2019. *Netflix*, netflix.com/watch/81193705.

"Tombstone." *Supernatural*, season 13, episode 6, CW, 16 November 2017. *Netflix*, netflix.com/watch/80216350.

"The Very Last Day of the Rest of Their Lives." *Good Omens*, episode 6, Amazon Prime, 31 May 2019. *Amazon Prime*, amazon.com/Inside-Look-Good-Omens/dp/B07FMHTRFF/.

Walker, Jessica. "'Anathema Liked to Read About Herself': Preserving the Female Line in *Good Omens*." *Feminism in the Worlds of Neil Gaiman: Essays on the Comics, Poetry and Prose*, edited by Tara Prescott and Aaron Drucker. Jefferson, NC: McFarland, 2012, pp. 246–260.

"Weekend at Bobby's." *Supernatural*, season 6, episode 4, CW, 15 October 2010. *Netflix*, netflix.com/watch/70223137.

"What's Up, Tiger Mommy?" *Supernatural*, season 8, episode 2, CW, 10 October 2012. *Netflix*, netflix.com/watch/70283545.

"Zari, Not Zari." *Legends of Tomorrow*, season 5, episode 8, CW, 21 April 2020. *Netflix*, netflix.com/watch/81235596.

Zubernis, Lynn, and Katherine Larsen, eds. *Fan Phenomena: Supernatural*. Chicago, Intellect Press, 2014.

Fan Desire and Normative Masculinities in *Good Omens* Gift Exchanges

MARY INGRAM-WATERS

December 1, 2020, marked the beginning of the 16th season of the *Good Omens* Holiday Gift Exchange (https://go-exchange.dreamwidth.org/). Hosted on the Dreamwidth social media platform, the 2020 Exchange featured 31 gifts, at the rate of about one per day for the entire month. Like most fandom gift exchanges, the *Good Omens* Exchange allows fans to anonymously create gifts for and receive gifts from other fans. Gifts are created in response to prompts. Even a casual perusal through the gifts from the 2019 and 2020 Exchanges shows the influence of the 2019 release of *Good Omens* on Amazon. The fan art gifts featuring Aziraphale and Crowley present the most striking evidence of the success of the 2019 version in solidifying fan interpretations of these two characters. One of the primary goals of this chapter is to explore the ways in which the 2019 *Good Omens* changed how fans conceptualize Aziraphale and Crowley.

Terry Pratchett and Neil Gaiman co-authored the standalone novel, *Good Omens: The Nice and Accurate Prophecies of Agnes Nutter, Witch*, in 1990. The 16-year history of the *Good Omens* Exchange illustrates the depth of activity of the long-running book-based fandom. With Amazon Studios' release of the television series, *Good Omens*, in 2019, new fans joined the existing book fans. The six-part series, adapted by Neil Gaiman and starring Michael Sheen as the angel Aziraphale and David Tennant as the demon Crowley, follows the two supernatural friends' unconventional "odd couple" relationship and their efforts to subvert the biblical apocalypse. The long-awaited adaptation achieved both critical acclaim and, perhaps more importantly for this chapter, fan acclaim.

The 2019 *Good Omens* inspired a huge wave of new fans who were eager to consume fanworks and to interact with other fans. For the 1990 book fans, the 2019 adaptation brought in new ideas, new canon, especially visual canon, and thus, new transformative works that were anchored completely in the 2019 series instead of the 1990 book. That meant that most of the newer fanworks definitively depicted Aziraphale and Crowley as similar to how Michael Sheen and David Tennant, respectively, portrayed them. At the *Good Omens* Exchange, most gifts of fanart clearly conformed to the visual canon for Aziraphale and Crowley established in the 2019 film series.

Conceptions of Aziraphale and Crowley

While Sheen's Aziraphale and Tennant's Crowley maintain an odd couple status as an angel and a demon, the way they look as a couple does differ from how book fans had previously conceived of them. In the 2019 series, Aziraphale and Crowley seem similarly aged and while their body types are different, they are not extremely so. Their primary visual differences come down to details such as their hair, clothing, eyes, and comportment. Aziraphale's hair is blond and curly, his clothing always outdated, and his comportment is somewhat feminized. Crowley's hair is dark auburn and usually wild and flowing. His clothing is always stylish and modern. Underneath his sunglasses are bright snake-like eyes. And his comportment is more masculine. These physical characterizations are arguably more aligned than what might be expected from the 1990 book canon descriptions. By aligned, I simply mean that the two could easily pass as a couple because neither is so different looking as to disrupt normative expectations for couples.

For the 1990 book fans, Aziraphale was usually conceptualized as older, frumpy, overweight, and stereotypically gay while Crowley was younger, stylish, thin, and sensuous, but without a defined sexuality. These characterizations are anchored in the brief descriptors from the 1990 book. A second goal for this chapter is to explore how book fandom representations have largely softened some of those descriptors, especially for Aziraphale so that he is not visibly old or chubby, and thus is in closer alignment with Crowley and also cultural expectations of normative masculinity. In other words, long before the 2019 filmic *Good Omens* softened the 1990 book's differences between Aziraphale and Crowley, fans were visualizing the two characters together in more palatable, attractive, and conventional ways.

Beyond noting that recent *Good Omens* fanart reflects fans' collective preference for the new visual canon set by Tennant and Sheen, we can draw on the work of critical fans studies scholars (Stein 2006; Åström 2010; Rowland and Barton 2011; Hunting 2012; Ingram-Waters 2010, 2015), to ask what these preferences might mean. Aziraphale and Crowley are both white, similarly aged, and to some extent, conventionally attractive and appropriately gendered, with Crowley as more traditionally masculine and Aziraphale as less so. Thus, fanart inspired by the 2019 series also reflects fandom's preferences for conventional norms for race, bodies, and gender presentation.

Recent *Good Omens* fanart of Aziraphale and Crowley is often categorized as slash, or the genre for romantic same sex relationships between males. Though slash, to some degree, is always progressive in its transformative depictions of same sex relationships, critical fanfiction studies helps us understand how slash simultaneously remains conventional in how it reflects a range of normative desires for its presumably female audience (Stein 2006; Åström 2010; Hunting 2012; Ingram-Waters 2010, 2015).

For example, in both the source texts and all of the fanworks studied in the chapter, Aziraphale and Crowley form a conventional dyadic relationship. Had they been depicted in a triadic romantic relationship with another character, that would be non-normative (Hunting 2012). Aziraphale and Crowley have recognizable dates at restaurants and spend time together in conventional ways, such as walking through the park, drinking wine, and discussing art and books. In neither the source texts nor fanworks do Aziraphale and Crowley move beyond the parameters of a normal romantic relationship, and, for this chapter, these parameters include how the two characters are visually portrayed.

Aziraphale and Crowley, despite being an odd couple, are usually depicted fairly similarly by fans, regardless of whether fans are inspired by the 2019 or 1990 text. I explicitly mean that their bodies seem to be similarly visibly aged. Their body types have minor differences. They are both masculine, with Crowley more so and Aziraphale less so. Their relationship is recognizable as a dyadic romantic relationship. My argument in this chapter is that fans' desires, in collectively conceptualizing Aziraphale and Crowley in these ways, are normative and reflect cultural values of masculinity more so than canon representations, especially 1990 book canon.

With this research, I examine fans' normative desires as they emerge in Aziraphale and Crowley slash fanart from both the 1990 book fandom and 2019 film series fandom. Using fanart from the 2016 to 2020 *Good Omens* Holiday Exchanges, I show how fans made the 1990 characters normatively attractive and then seized on the opportunity to do it more with the 2019 characters. These five years were selected to capture samples of the relatively coherent fanon characterizations of Aziraphale and Crowley from pre- and post–2019 *Good Omens*.

Fan Studies Scholarship

In this chapter, I analyze how *Good Omens* fans' fanart gifts contribute to a fanon understanding of normative masculinity; however, it is important to situate this research goal in relevant fan studies scholars' works. Thalia Ester de Candido Girardi's thesis, which examines gender and sexuality in *Good Omens* fanworks starts with a recognition of whether the fanartist intends their art to either celebrate or critique canon texts. This initial question is similar to the fan-developed categorical device of assessing whether a particular fanwork is affirmational, meaning it reaffirms source material, or transformational, meaning it challenges, critiques, or expands source material (Zygutis 2021). As I am looking closely at slash as a site for fans' meaning-making, I turn to scholars who have noted the simultaneously progressive and normative tenets of this same-sex genre of fanworks (Stein 2006; Åström 2010; Hunting 2012; Ingram-Waters 2010, 2015). Gift exchanges, like the one studied in this chapter, are important sites for fandom communities precisely because the exchange of gifts affirms social cohesion, especially around shared fandom values. Lastly, I look at previous research for insights on how fandom communities come to understand what constitutes not just fanon but "good" and "accurate" fanon and how these processes of reaching agreement also reaffirm larger cultural values.

Despite enjoying an active fandom since 1990, *Good Omens* fans have not been as extensively studied as other book, film, and television fandoms. One exception is Girardi's work on gender and sexuality as depicted in *Good Omens* fanfiction. Girardi notes that gender and sexuality are performative and as such, can be identified through authors' choices about characters' actions, feelings, and dialogue. By doing a content analysis of the most well-liked fanfiction at Archive of Our Own, most of which was written just after the 2019 television series, Girardi notes two main findings: one, social and behavioral markers of gender and sexuality are unusually fluid; and two, Aziraphale and Crowley are almost always portrayed as male, even when in gender-swapped situations.

Girardi argues that fans utilize the characters' supernatural origins to facilitate the breakdown of normative gender and sexuality behaviors, such that both Aziraphale and Crowley engage in both masculine- and feminine-coded behaviors, especially during romantic and erotic scenes. However, Girardi notes that Aziraphale and Crowley are primarily depicted as male, with fans writing male pronouns even while the characters are in gender-swapped, gender-ambiguous, or genderless bodies. Girardi concludes by pointing out the discrepancy between how the presumably female fans who choose to create fanworks use *Good Omens* fanfiction to subvert some stereotypes associated with gender and sexuality while simultaneously reaffirming the supremacy of the preferred male gender for Aziraphale and Crowley.

Girardi's work is a helpful point of departure for this chapter because Girardi shows us that *Good Omens* fans, much like other fandom communities, use fanworks to both resist and accommodate normative values associated with gender and sexuality (Stein 2006; Åström 2010; Hunting 2012; Ingram-Waters 2010, 2015). Thus, slash, which is the genre of fanworks studied in this chapter, is not as progressive as it might seem. Slash relationships are often normative, meaning they are monogamous dyads. Erotic elements are also normative, with penetrative sexual relations, ending in mutually attained orgasms as the norm. There are recognizable gender roles, with one part of the dyad more feminine and the other part more masculine. While this certainly does not describe all fanworks, it does describe most.

In Jessica Seymour's article on scholars appropriately interpreting fanart, she argues that the fanartist's intent behind the art offers useful information for interpreting specific pieces that can supplement a fan's initial categorization of a piece as either affirmational or transformational. She offers three categories of intent: homage, collaboration, and intervention (100). For Seymour, homage is used to interpret fanart that intends to celebrate and reflect canon texts while collaboration refers to fanart that extends details of canon texts without altering the canon. Intervention, however, classifies fanart that intends to challenge or change canon texts, with Seymour offering non-canonical slash or racebending as examples of this category.

For each of the categories, Seymour recognizes the primacy of the fan communities to the fanartist. Fanartists know that other fans share the common language of the canon text enough to be able to recognize different intentions for fanart. For fanartists intending their art to intervene with canon texts, Seymour emphasizes the importance of collective knowledge on the part of the fandom. Further, the scholar hoping to interpret the fanart would be best able to do so by knowing the canon text and the fandom dynamics in relation to it, what others would recognize as fanon (Pugh 2005: 11; Busse and Hellekson 2006).

Scholars who study the gift economy of fandom argue that as fans create and share transformative works, they do so as gifts to the fan community (Hellekson 2009; Turk 2014). These gifts of fanworks, when given and received, engender a reciprocal gifting economy that brings about social cohesion (Hellekson 2009; Turk 2014). Even during a fandom gift exchange, in which one fan creates a specialized gift for another, that fan's gift is always meant to reach a larger audience (Turk 2014). Karen Hellekson writes, "Writer and reader create a shared dialogue that results in a feedback loop of gift exchange, whereby the gift of artwork or text is repetitively exchanged for the gift of reaction, which it itself exchanged, with the goal of creating and maintaining social solidarity" (Hellekson 115–116). Though Hellekson is focusing on the community that is continuously maintained and reaffirmed through the mutual recognition of fan labor, the "shared dialogue" can be understood to relate to fans' specific sets of commonly held meanings, what others have called the democratic processes that give rise to fanon (Pugh 11).

Fanon is the collective knowledge of fans that challenges or extends canon (Gray 2010). Notably, canon, much like fanon, relies on fans' collaborative, iterative knowledge creation. Canon would seem to imply the facts as they exist in the source text. Yet, those facts are not always clear, and fans must work together to arrive at a meaning for more obscure facts or meanings of the source text. Fanon is the extension of that process of collective knowledge production. Fanon relies on collective meaning-making processes that yield a set of shared understandings, usually about characters, from a source text.

In studies of male pregnancy (mpreg) fanfiction, I have noted that the iterative fanfiction creative processes between author, beta, reader, and reviewer, yield a collectively held understanding of what constitutes "good" and "accurate" mpreg (Ingram-Waters 2010, 2015). But these interactions also show more than just the ideal form for a particular fanfic trope as good and accurate mpreg translates into largely normative portrayals of masculine bodies that are going through a recognizably normative feminine experience of pregnancy.

However, even though the bodies are normatively masculine and the pregnancy is realistic, the very act of a normatively masculine body going through a realistic pregnancy is itself evidence of a queering of the boundaries of masculinity and pregnancy. Thus, mpreg is a genre that, similar to fanon, is a product of fans' meaning making strategies that lies at the intersection of resisting and accommodating normative understandings of gender, bodies, and, in the case of mpreg, pregnancy.

Sites of fans' collective meaning-making, such as genres, fanon, and even canon, reveal rich understandings of cultural values. By deciding on what constitutes good or accurate portrayals of characters in fanworks, fans do two things: one, they reify canon by agreeing on the range of acceptable iterations of in-character portrayals; two, they showcase their collectively held, and likely normative, desires. For example, when fans come together and laud a piece of fan art of Aziraphale and Crowley, they will likely give praise on multiple fronts: how in-character the depictions are, whether or not the depictions are aesthetically pleasing, and if the depictions conform to normative expectations.

Given the literature on fans' expectations for canon-recognizable characters, preferences for normatively desirable masculine males, and respect for the circular gift economy of exchanges, I expect to find that fanart images of Aziraphale and Crowley present them as a relatively good-looking odd couple, with softened differences between the two. While I expect that Aziraphale will be portrayed as less attractive and less masculine than Crowley, I do not expect that their differences will be great. Further, I expect that the post–2019 versions of Aziraphale and Crowley will have even fewer visual markers of difference than the pre–2019 versions.

Methodology

To analyze fans' collectively held and reinforced normative desires for attractive and masculine men, I selected Aziraphale and Crowley fanart from the *Good Omens* Exchange, a long-running fandom holiday gift exchange that wrapped up its 16th season in 2020. I looked at all the entries coded as "art," "slash," and "Aziraphale and Crowley" or "Aziraphale/Crowley" from the Exchange's 2016–2020 seasons. As previously mentioned, I selected these five years to assess two different time periods: three years before the 2019 *Good Omens* series and the two years after its release. I selected the Exchange because all gifts were explicitly created by fans for fans in response to desired prompts.

I sorted all pieces of fanart in two passes. On the first pass, I asked if either Aziraphale or Crowley was portrayed with normative masculine attractiveness, meaning explicitly, is the character meant to be attractive as a normal and conventional man? In addition to viewing the gifts, I took notes on the titles, artists' notes, gift prompts, and comments, for each gift. Though I did not formally analyze these details, I did use them to confirm whether a particular gift was meant to portray a romantic or potentially romantic situation. Because Crowley was always depicted as normatively masculine and attractive, except for one time in which he was comically depicted as an attractive and masculine snake, I used the following codes to analyze Aziraphale's depiction in each piece of fanart: body size, the presence of spectacles, style of clothing, body size differences between characters, height differences, age differences, and hair styles. These codes emerged inductively, meaning that I looked at all of the art and noted all of the markers of difference for Aziraphale. Essentially, at this second pass of coding, I wanted to know how fans presented Aziraphale in relation to Crowley. How did they maintain the odd couple nature of their relationship while also keeping Aziraphale attractive and masculine? I also noted whether the work was pre- or post–2019 *Good Omens*.

Data Analysis and Discussion

Between 2016–2020, there were 31 pieces of fanart that featured Aziraphale and Crowley in either a definite romantic setting or a possible romantic setting. In general, the two were depicted as different or opposite, thus maintaining their odd couple status, though Crowley was also depicted as more attractive and more masculine than Aziraphale. In Table 1, I have noted that fanartists depict Crowley as normatively attractive, which I describe further below, in every piece of art, regardless of year. Aziraphale is depicted as normatively attractive about half the time, though this rate increases during the 2019 and 2020 Exchanges.

Table 1: Crowley and Aziraphale's Attractiveness by Year

Year	# Of Art Pieces	Attractive Crowley?	Attractive Aziraphale?
2016	7	7	4
2017	6	6	3
2018	5	5	3
2019	4	4	3
2020	3	3	3

During 2016–2017, Aziraphale is marked as different in what I have noted as soft non-normatively masculine ways. Where Crowley is often portrayed as handsome, young, stylishly dressed, with nicely coiffed hair, and a slender body, Aziraphale is portrayed differently. In the 1990 book, Aziraphale is depicted as frumpy, older, with old-fashioned clothing, and a plump body. While these canon characteristics are charming and help to create an interesting juxtaposition with Crowley, none of these would typically be considered as attractive and conventionally masculine. But in slash fan art, those non-normative aspects are softened so that Aziraphale and Crowley are in closer alignment. Notably, Aziraphale usually has frumpier hair and glasses. By frumpier, I mean that Aziraphale's hair is mussed, too long, too curly, or just generally unstyled, especially compared to Crowley's. He is also often wearing glasses. About half the time, he is portrayed as chubbier than Crowley, though not extremely so. He is not usually shown as older or shorter. Aziraphale and Crowley are almost always depicted as similarly aged and in 2016–2017, they are both usually shown as young adults.

The 2018 Exchange marks a slight shift for how artists portray Aziraphale which might be attributed to the early promotional stills, posters and trailers which feature Michael Sheen as Aziraphale from the forthcoming 2019 *Good Omens*. In 2018, only one work of art has Aziraphale with glasses, although the rates for frumpy hair, body size, and clothing are about the same as those in 2016–2017. In 2018, I noted the first of only two examples of an artist using age to distinguish Aziraphale from Crowley.

During 2019–2020, Aziraphale is still marked as different with the softened non-normative markers of difference though the shifts seen in 2018 have continued. There are no pieces of art in which Aziraphale is wearing glasses. He is still more likely than not to have frumpier hair and clothing and a slightly larger body size. Further, artists remain less inclined to present him as older or shorter than Crowley. There is an important caveat, though, with regard to age. Though Aziraphale is rarely portrayed as older in any fanart studied in this chapter, in the 2019–2020 seasons, Aziraphale and Crowley are both portrayed as older than they are in pre-2019 seasons. If we return to Table 1, we can see that despite some of these markers of difference, Aziraphale is still presented as attractive at a higher rate than during the 2016–2018 Exchanges.

Table 2: Aziraphale's Markers of Difference in 2016–2020 Fan Art Entries

	Hair: is Aziraphale's Hair Less Stylish?	Body Size: Is Aziraphale's Body Larger?	Clothing: Is Aziraphale's Clothing Less Stylish?	Age: Is Aziraphale Older?	Height: Is Aziraphale Shorter?	Glasses: Does Aziraphale Wear Glasses?
2016	7 out of 7	2 out of 7	5 out of 7	0 out of 7	0 out of 7	5 out of 7
2017	7 out of 7	4 out of 7	3 out of 7	0 out of 7	1 out of 7	7 out of 7
2018	3 out of 4	2 out of 4	3 out of 4	1 out of 4	2 out of 7	1 out of 4
2019	4 out of 6	4 out of 6	1 out of 6	1 out of 6	1 out of 6	0 out of 6
2020	2 out of 3	3 out of 3	2 out of 3	0 out of 3	0 out of 3	0 out of 3

In sum, analysis of the data shows three primary trends. First, regardless of the year of the *Good Omens* Exchange, Aziraphale is likely to be portrayed as more normatively attractive and masculine than he is in the 1990 book. Second, though Aziraphale is still depicted with non-normative markers of difference that would not usually be associated with normative masculine attractiveness, these markers are softened so that he and Crowley are visually compatible as a couple. Aziraphale and Crowley are almost always portrayed as similarly aged, though in the pre-2019 seasons, they are both depicted as young adults and in the 2019–2020 seasons, they are both shown as older adults. Finally, the 2019–2020 fan art also coheres around Sheen's and Tennant's respective portrayals of Aziraphale and Crowley.

Conclusion

Conducting a Google image search of *Good Omens* fan art yields a trove of stunning and creative work by hundreds of fanartists. Even an open search like that shows the fandom's favorite subject: Aziraphale and Crowley. Further, a current search clearly shows the absolute dominance of the 2019 *Good Omens* series on how Aziraphale and Crowley are conceptualized by fans. Michael Sheen and David Tennant have fundamentally shaped the way that Aziraphale and Crowley, respectively, are depicted. In doing so, the 2019 *Good Omens* has become the new canon, refining the 1990 book canon with its descriptors of a frumpy, older, and chubbier Aziraphale, and a stylish and sleek Crowley. Sheen's portrayal has softened these descriptors so that Aziraphale still has questionable fashion sense, a modest waistline and might be in his fifties while Tennant's Crowley is always stylish, quite thin, and, notably, also in his fifties.

In many ways, pre–2019 and post–2019 *Good Omens* Exchange fanartists have always portrayed Aziraphale and Crowley as a normatively attractive and aligned couple. In the 2016–2018 seasons, Aziraphale may have had different attributes signaling him as less normatively masculine and attractive, such as glasses, for example, but these attributes were all softened so that he was still convincingly one half of a good-looking couple. Also, similar to post–2019 versions, Aziraphale is usually shown as similarly aged with Crowley, though unlike post–2019, they are often portrayed as young adults.

There are plenty of limitations to this study. Looking only at the fanart from a gift exchange may have led to oversampling of art that is specifically designed to meet another fan's highly detailed expectations. A broader survey of fanart might have yielded images that explored the physical differences between Aziraphale and Crowley more so than the ones studied here. The 2019 *Good Omens* series starred extremely well-known and well-regarded actors who were largely embraced by fans, and the author, Neil Gaiman. Had the actors been less effective, less known, or not liked by Gaiman, who also has an active relationship with fans through social media, fans may have been less likely to embrace Sheen and Tennant as the embodiments of Aziraphale and Crowley. Finally, other methods of gathering data, including interviewing fan artists or analyzing fan reviews of art, might have led to other explanations regarding fans' desires for how Aziraphale and Crowley should look.

Though fan scholars have long demonstrated that fans want fanart and fanfiction, first and foremost, to be recognizable with the source texts, they have also shown that fans, precisely because they share the language of canon, enjoy fanworks that explore their favorite characters in transformatively new ways. What I have tried to show here is that fans also want to see what they like. In the case of Aziraphale and Crowley, they want their odd couple, but they don't prefer them to be as odd as Neil Gaiman and Terry Pratchett have written them. Rather, they prefer them to be normatively aligned as they are in the 2019 *Good Omens*.

Works Cited

Åström, Berit. "'Let's Get Those Winchesters Pregnant': Male Pregnancy in 'Supernatural' Fan Fiction." *Transformative Works and Cultures*, vol. 4, no. 1, 2010, https://journal.transformativeworks.org/index.php/twc/article/view/135.

Girardi, Thalia Ester de Candido. *Fandom tribe: The Depiction of Gender Inside* Good Omens *Fanfiction*. Thesis. Universidade De Caxias Do Sul. *Repositorio Institucional*. 2019. https://repositorio.ucs.br/xmlui/handle/11338/6206.

Gray, Melissa. "From Canon to Fanon and Back Again: The Epic Journey of *Supernatural* and Its Fans." *Transformative Works and Cultures*, *Transformative Works and Cultures*, vol. 4, no. 1, 2010, https://doi.org/10.3983/twc.2010.0146.

Hellekson, Karen. "A Fannish Field of Value: Online Fan Gift Culture." *Cinema Journal*, vol. 48, no. 4, 2009, pp. 113–118.

Hellekson, Karen, and Kristina Busse, editors. *Fan Fiction and Fan Communities in the Age of the Internet: New Essays*. McFarland, 2006.

Hunting, Kyra. "'Queer as Folk' and the Trouble with Slash." *Transformative Works and Cultures*, vol. 11, 2012, https://journal.transformativeworks.org/index.php/twc/article/view/415.

Ingram-Waters, Mary. "When Normal and Deviant Identities Collide: Methodological Considerations of the Pregnant Acafan." *Transformative Works and Cultures*, vol. 5, no. 1, 2010, https://journal.transformativeworks.org/index.php/twc/article/view/207.

Ingram-Waters, Mary. "Writing the Pregnant Man." *Transformative Works and Cultures*, vol. 20 no. 3, 2015, https://journal.transformativeworks.org/index.php/twc/article/view/651.

Pugh, Sheenagh. *The Democratic Genre: Fan Fiction in a Literary Context*. Seren, 2005.

Rowland, Thomas D., and Amanda C. Barton. "Outside Oneself in *World of Warcraft*: Gamers' Perception of the Racial Self-Other." In "Race and Ethnicity in Fandom," edited by Robin Anne Reid and Sarah Gatson, special issue, *Transformative Works and Cultures*, no. 8, 2011. https://doi.org/10.3983/twc.2011.0258.

Seymour, Jessica. "Homage, Collaboration, or Intervention: How Framing Fanart Affects Its Interpretation. *Participations*, col. 15, no. 2, 2018, pp. 98–114.

Stein, Louisa E. "This 'Dratted Thing': Fannish Storytelling Through New Media." *Fan Fiction and Fan Communities in the Age of the Internet: New Essays*, edited by Karen Hellekson and Kristina Busse. Jefferson, NC: McFarland, 2006, pp. 245–260.

Turk, Tisha. "Fan Work: Labor, Worth, and Participation in Fandom's Gift Economy." *Transformative Works and Cultures*, vol. 15, 2014, https://journal.transformativeworks.org/index.php/twc/article/view/518.

Zygutis, Linda. "Affirmational Canons and Transformative Literature: Notes OnTeaching with Fandom." In "Fan Studies Pedagogies," edited by Paul Booth and Regina Yung Lee, special issue, *Transformative Works and Cultures*, no. 35, 2021. https://doi.org/10.3983/twc.2021.1917.

The Theology
of *Good Omens*

"In the beginning, it was a nice day"
Aziraphale and the Subversive Miltonian Angelology of Good Omens

Melissa D. Aaron

The opening line of *Good Omens*—"in the beginning ... it was a nice day"—sets it up as a quasi-sequel to John Milton's *Paradise Lost*. It begins exactly where *Paradise Lost* ends, with the "hast'ning Angel" Michael taking Adam and Eve to the Eastern Gate, where a "flaming Brand" bars their re-entrance (12.632–44). Neil Gaiman and Terry Pratchett's "hast'ning angel" Aziraphale, however, nudges other canonical angels out of the way, thrusts the sword into the couple's hands, suggesting that it might help them, and then proceeds to admit his moment of rebellion to a demon, and, in the streaming Amazon series, to shelter said demon from the First Thunderstorm (Gaiman and Pratchett 4, Gaiman 8–9).[1] Thus begins *Good Omens'* subversion of Milton's epic, with its focus on first things, free will, and obedience. In particular, the character of Aziraphale, usurping the place of Raphael, inserts himself into the narrative with that first hasty dash and remains there. As he does, despite his best attempts to be obedient and to adhere to Heaven's Great (or Ineffable) Plan, he brings about the slow wreckage of *Paradise Lost's* stated agenda "to justify the ways of God to men."

Terry Pratchett and Neil Gaiman's angelology deliberately draws from Pseudo-Dionysius, Thomas Aquinas, cabalistic tradition, and almost certainly Milton. This essay situates *Good Omens* into a historical, theological, and literary framework.[2] It begins with a brief look at traditional angelology, using Pseudo-Dionysius and Thomas Aquinas as touchstones, and the ways in which *Paradise Lost* breaks with these traditions. It goes on to discuss Raphael—the healer, the helper, and Milton's "sociable spirit"—and how Aziraphale reproduces his characteristics and abilities in a reduced and ridiculous form. Finally, it looks at Milton's subversion in his presentation of angels and Gaiman and Pratchett's subversion of that subversion through the character of Aziraphale: free will, food, books and materiality, imagination and intelligence, obedience and the utter explosion of the idea of a Great Plan.

Paradise Lost is one of the most influential books in Anglophone literature: solemn, pious, very English, and also, quite literally, epic. Its status and ubiquity make it a perfect target for the blasphemous, irreverent humor of *Good Omens*. This is complicated because *Paradise Lost* is already subversive, both as an epic and in its theology. The language in which it is written, the subject matter, and its objective represent a radical break with the classical past. Milton's theology, as set forth in his *De Doctrina Christiana* (*Christian Doctrine*) was far from orthodox. He was not a Trinitarian, and rejected Calvinistic predestination, insisting instead on free will. To Milton, without free will, obedience and love mean nothing. His angelology is also radically different from almost all prior theological interpretations. Joad Raymond, in *Milton's Angels: The Early Modern Imagination,* states that angels are central to *Paradise Lost*:

> Angels are fundamental to the execution of Milton's design in *Paradise Lost*. They are necessary because without them the story does not work…. The story of *Paradise Lost* is told by and of angels [9].

Angels are also fundamental to *Good Omens*, and without them, the story does not work, but its story is not by angels. It is, in part, a work about angels, fallen and unfallen. According to Neil Gaiman, *Good Omens* began as 5,000 words of a short story called "William the Antichrist," beginning with the character of the demon, then called Crowleigh. Terry Pratchett phoned to say that he knew what happened next, wrote the next 5000 words, and then the joint process of writing *Good Omens* began.[3] While Gaiman has given various versions of this origin story, it is not unreasonable to assume that just as Gaiman created "Crowleigh," Pratchett added Aziraphale. This relationship between an angel and an angel who did not fall, but who "Saunter[ed] Vaguely Downwards" is essential to the book (7). The idea that an angel and a demon could be friends is impossible in most previous angelology, theological and fictional. In order to understand why this relationship is impossible in Milton and the theological traditions he rejected, it is necessary to look more deeply at angelology.

Something like angels are found as far back as Sumerian and Mesopotamian culture, but in the three major Abrahamic religions, it begins with the Book of Genesis. It is impossible to cover angelology in its entirety, including over two millennia of the Common Era, but in order to situate Milton's angelology and therefore *Good Omens*' in context, here are some relevant elements of Christian angelology. The angelic hierarchy was first laid down by Pseudo-Dionysius in *De Coelesti Hierarchia* ("The Celestial Hierarchy"), written sometime in the fourth or fifth century.[4] There are nine ranks of angels, divided into three sets or "ternions." The first are the Seraphim (love), Cherubim (intelligence) and Thrones (justice); the second ternion are the Dominions, Virtues, and Powers; while the third ternion are those most concerned with the world and human beings: Principalities, Archangels, and Angels. Thomas Heywood, in *The Hierarchie of the Blessed Angels* (1635), dedicated to Charles II's Catholic wife Henrietta Maria, sums it up:

> Now we know,
> The third descends t'have care of things below,
> Assisting good men, and withstanding those
> That shall the rule of Divine Lawes oppose.
> Aziraphale belongs to the highest rank of the third ternion, described thus:
> The Principates, of Princes take the charge,
> Their power on earth to curbe, or to enlarge,
> And these work miracles.
> [194; qtd in Raymond 52–53]

Note that Principalities, the class to which Aziraphale belongs, are one of the lower classes, and specifically intended to interact with humans, and to "work miracles."

St. Thomas Aquinas' opinions on angels in *Summa Theologicae*, (Q50–64), are still the orthodox Roman Catholic theological view, and probably the strongest influence on *Good Omens*.[5] Aquinas maintained that angels are important, as a bridge, or intermediary, between God and humans. They are perfect. They do not have corporeality, so they do not eat and certainly do not make love, although he does state that angels feel love. They are intelligent, but their intelligence is different from that of human beings, since they do not have human senses. Because of this, they do not learn from experience, and do not need memory: they simply know. Perhaps most importantly, "beatified," or "good" angels "cannot sin" (Q62 A 8; p. 582). Their initial choice, before their fall, was to obey or not to obey. After that, as Aquinas puts it, they have "inflexible free choice after once choosing" (Q63 A7; p 595). They have no choice, no change, and no imagination. On the surface, at least, both the angels and demons of *Good Omens* are Thomistic: their initial choice has determined who they are and what they do. As Aziraphale suggests at the very beginning of *Good Omens*, Crawly can't do anything good, because that's part of his very essence—to which Crawly replies sarcastically that in that case, Aziraphale can't do anything evil (Gaiman and Pratchett 3–4). Six thousand years later, Crowley is still reflecting on this lack of free will (20). Aziraphale's lament that he can't "disod—not do what I'm told. 'M an angel," at that point, may be true (Gaiman 62).

Milton had significantly unorthodox opinions about angels, which can be seen in Chapter Nine of *De Doctrina Christiana*, "On the Special Government of Angels" (990–92). Milton's angels have senses. They eat, they make love, and they feel pain. Angels are intelligent, but they do not know everything. Good angels, however, do not disguise themselves, and they do not have extreme emotions which visibly distort their appearance: Uriel recognizes a disguised Satan by this in Book 4 of *Paradise Lost*. Good angels experience love: demons only feel "fierce desire," which is why Satan is so jealous of Adam and Eve. Milton even considers that angelic ongoing obedience might be a choice:

> It seems, however, more agreeable to reason, to suppose that the good angels are upheld by their own strength no less than man was before his fall ... that it is not from any interest of their own, but from their love to mankind, that they desire to look into the mystery of our salvation [990].

To sum up, Aquinas maintained that angels and demons don't have free will and therefore do not and cannot befriend one another, assuming that they desired to do so. Milton, who suggests that angels and demons may have free will, makes their interactions explicitly antagonistic, from Zephon's cutting remark that Satan is not as attractive as he once was in Book 4 (835–40) to Satan's battle with Michael in Book 6. Aziraphale's and Crowley's friendship would never happen in *Paradise Lost*. It is forbidden and unlikely in both the Heaven and Hell of *Good Omens,* for reasons more Thomistic than Miltonian, but it happens all the same.

The novel is somewhat clearer than the series that the friendship began in antagonism. Crowley thinks of Aziraphale as The Enemy in capital letters, but over the course of six thousand years, during which they have largely been abandoned by their superiors, they have become friends, or at least frenemies. The book plays out as a sort of mismatched buddy story. Gaiman describes the relationship in his script book of the television series, and elsewhere, as a love story (Gaiman, Neil, @neilhimself, 9/21/2020).

It takes a very long time for Aziraphale to acknowledge that Crowley is his friend. He explicitly denies that they are acquaintances in the Renaissance at the Globe Theatre and vehemently denies their friendship to Crowley during the Last Week with the force of a slap in the face (Gaiman 179, 231). Uriel is not so easily fooled, and refers to Crowley as though he were Aziraphale's romantic partner (297).

In other words, *Paradise Lost* ruptures tradition by giving its angels and demons free will, while *Good Omens* doubly subverts this idea: it initially removes free will, and allows an angel and a demon to be friends: Aquinas' "could not" becomes "would not" in *Paradise Lost*, and "cannot, but do anyway" in *Good Omens*.

Paradise Lost states its objective in the first twenty-six lines: to tell of "Man's first Disobedience/ ... Assert Eternal Providence, /And justify the ways of God to men" (1.25–25). Its purpose is to reconcile the seemingly irreconcilable and, explicitly, to reveal the Divine Plan. *Good Omens* derails that purpose by beginning with a nervous angel, worrying whether or not he's done the right thing, and an unimpressed serpent, expressing his doubt about God's rationale (Gaiman and Pratchett 3–4). Aziraphale falls back onto what will become his keyword, "ineffability." The plan is "ineffable," or unknowable, and therefore, the best course of action is to assume that ultimately God intends everything to turn out for the best, and in the meantime, to be obedient.

Paradise Lost is about aetiology, or "first things": Genesis, first disobedience, first sin, first rebellion, and first pain. *Good Omens* is about eschatology: *Revelation*, the original copy of which resides in Aziraphale's bookshop, and the Four Last Things—Death, Judgment, Heaven and Hell. It ends in a barely averted apocalypse, with the angel ruefully comforting the demon with the thought that everything could have been much worse if they'd been better at their jobs (Gaiman and Pratchett 339).

What IS the Plan? Raphael's entire purpose is to communicate the Divine Plan to Adam and Eve in Books 5–8 of *Paradise Lost*, although God already knows that this mission will prove futile. His humbler replacement in *Good Omens* can't even begin to do that. How is it possible to justify the ways of God to men when even the Angel of the Eastern Gate doesn't know what they are? Is "it's ineffable" enough?

God's plan is very effable in *Paradise Lost*. Book 3 begins with His all-seeing eye taking in Earth, the Heavens, the depths of Hell, and Satan clinging to the outside of the world (lines 55 ff). God then explains everything that's going to happen to the entire heavenly host:

> Man will heark'n to his glozing lies.../
> So will fall
> Hee and his faithless Progeny: whose fault?
> Whose but his own? ingrate, he had of mee
> All he could have; I made him just and right
> Sufficient to have stood, though free to fall [94–99].

This is the crux of *Paradise Lost's* agenda, the problem it attempts to solve: if God is omniscient and omnipotent, why didn't he prevent Adam and Eve from picking the apple? Milton's God's answer is that he has left mankind the ability to choose, and therefore to choose wrongly. This much would be obvious to Aziraphale: it all comes back to Right and Wrong, reward and punishment, but mostly punishment (Pratchett and Gaiman 4). This isn't a satisfactory answer to Crawly, or to many humans. Even the Tree of the Knowledge of Good and Evil is badly placed (Gaiman 7).

In Book 3 of *Paradise Lost,* God goes on to explain that while He knows the Fall will happen, it is Adam and Eve who will choose to do Wrong. Not to worry, though, God continues: "Man therefore shall find Grace" (131). While there's some conversation about how they're going to get around the issue of original sin, and there's an awkward pause in which no one volunteers to die on mankind's behalf, everything is wrapped up by the Son offering, "account mee Man; I for his sake ... Let Death wreck all his rage" (238, 241). The Father bestows Kingship on the Son, "by Merit more than Birthright Son of God," (309) and describes the entire history of the universe through the Apocalypse and beyond, when "God shall be all in all" (341). After that, there's nothing for the angels to do but burst into "thir Sacred Song" to perfectly tuned harps, "such concord is in Heav'n" (370, 72), or what Crowley dismissively suggests is tedious in *Good Omens* (Gaiman and Pratchett 41). The Divine Plan is not a secret in *Paradise Lost.*

In contrast to the over-sharing God of *Paradise Lost,* God does not explain or talk to anyone in *Good Omens.* He (or She, in the series), plays a game with no known rules, in the dark, in which the smallest mistake is catastrophic for the other player: a sort of celestial Calvinball (Gaiman 4).[6] Both Crowley and Aziraphale know the broad outlines of what the end will be like, which adhere to the prophecies in the Book of Revelation. It is a question of when, how, and as Adam Young suggests at the end, why.

Every epic is supposed to have an epic norm, and in *Paradise Lost,* it is obedience to a very clear Divine Plan. In *Good Omens,* it is impossible to know what the Ineffable Plan is, because it is Ineffable. Disobedience might be obedience, or as Crawly suggests in the beginning, his choice—to push humans towards knowledge—might have been the good one, while Aziraphale's choice—to arm the humans—might have been the bad one. (Gaiman and Pratchett 5). This is a problem, because, theoretically, what defines an angel from a demon is obedience—in Aquinas, because after that first choice to obey they have no more free will, and in *Paradise Lost,* because obedience is freely chosen.[7] Obedience in *Good Omens,* in practice, is what Aziraphale and Crowley's respective Head Offices have determined their jobs to be in the Official Grand Plan: but note the shifting descriptors of Divine, Grand, and Ineffable Plans. It is this confusion that allows Crowley to get around Aziraphale in the first place and convince him to help head off Apocalypse. The Antichrist is a diabolic plan, and so to interfere with it, thus delaying Armageddon, must be an angelic one, or as Crowley puts it more succinctly, "you see a wile, you thwart" (Gaiman and Pratchett 51).

Ultimately, Aziraphale concedes the point, but given that allowing the Antichrist to grow up and Armageddon to take place would ruin his bookshop and his supply of Châteauneuf-du-Pape, his motives are mixed at best, and on some level, he knows it. He becomes a "godfather" to the Antichrist partly in order to save himself, and partly to save humanity and the world, of which he's become rather fond. Aziraphale, therefore, is editing himself into the Book of Revelation, just as he previously edited himself out of Genesis, 3:25–27, in which he lied to God and claimed to have lost his flaming sword (Gaiman and Pratchett 44).[8]

Good Omens also has Aziraphale taking over the roles of several more important angels in *Paradise Lost*, particularly that of Raphael. Since I maintain that the much less powerful Aziraphale has taken on his qualities and his "job," it is important to know who he is. A great deal of Aziraphale's character is Raphael's, reduced for humorous effect.[9]

In Jewish, Christian, and Islamic tradition, there are important angels such as the seven spirits of God in Revelation 1:4. One of these groups consist of the four major Archangels: Gabriel, Michael, Uriel, and Raphael. Michael and Gabriel appear in the Protestant Bible—Gabriel in Daniel, the Gospel of Luke, and the book of Enoch, and Michael in Daniel, the Book of Revelation, and the Epistle of Jude. Michael is also, according to Crowley, a "wanker" (Gaiman 511). Uriel is from the deuterocanonical book 2 Esdras, and Raphael from the deuterocanonical Book of Tobit. Those who studied and invoked angels in magic assigned them to the four cardinal directions, the four seasons, and inscribed their names onto scrying balls.[10] Gabriel, Michael, and Raphael are still honored as a group on September 29, the Feast of St. Michael and All Angels. Considering his importance, Raphael is quite conspicuously missing from *Good Omens*.

Raphael, whose name means "God has healed," and who in some sources is the Angel of the East, is first seen in the Book of *Tobit*, where he introduces himself to Tobit as Aziriah, or "God has helped."[11] While Pratchett and Gaiman claimed not to have done this on purpose, only maintaining that they had followed the rules in creating an appropriate angelic name, "Aziraphale" can be read as a portmanteau of "Aziriah" and "Raphael."[12] Raphael volunteers to guide Tobit's son Tobias on a journey to Media. His real mission is more extensive: to heal the lives of several people, and he has acquired this mission by sorting through the prayers of people on earth and bringing Tobit's case directly to God (*Tobit* 12:12). It is too much to suggest that he interferes, but he does intervene, asking the Almighty's permission, of course, which is something Aziraphale does not and cannot do.

Tobit has lived according to the law and buried his fellow Jews, suffering, as a result, exile, the confiscation of his property, and blindness no physician has been able to cure. The money that might help Tobit's family is in Media, but it is too dangerous to travel there. Meanwhile, there is a young kinswoman in Media, Sarah, who would make an ideal wife for his son Tobias. Unfortunately, she is being tormented by a demon who has killed seven previous bridegrooms on the wedding night. Raphael has been sent to heal and help both of them, remove the white film from Tobit's eyes, arrange the marriage of Sarah and Tobias, and get rid of the demon (*Tobit* 3: 16–17).[13]

Raphael doesn't mention any of this, or that he is an angel when Tobit hires him as a guide for his son. But, in the course of the journey, Raphael instructs Tobias what to do with the magic fish he catches, negotiates the marriage and the exorcism, and personally goes to collect the money. On their return, Raphael heals Tobit. In Christian art, Raphael is usually depicted wearing a traveling cloak and staff, holding Tobias by the hand. He usually is much bigger than Tobias and has gigantic wings, which makes it less than credible that no one realizes that he is an angel until he reveals himself in Chapter 12:

> 16 I am Raphael, one of the seven holy angels, which present the prayers of the saints, and which go in and out before the glory of the Holy One.
> 17 …. Fear not, for it shall go well with you; praise God therefore.
> 18 For not of any favour of mine, but by the will of our God I came; wherefore praise him for ever.
> 19 All these days I did appear unto you; but I did neither eat nor drink, but ye did see a vision.

Note that Raphael, like all angels, doesn't eat: he merely pretends to eat to fit in. This is not true of Milton's Raphael, but he's retained the willingness to mingle with and help humans.

In *Paradise Lost*, Raphael is the "sociable spirit," whom God sends to spend a day with Adam "as friend with friend" (*PL* 5.221, 229). He is to explain exactly who and what Satan is, so that later, Adam can't claim he wasn't warned (4.243–45).

Raphael likes humans. This is in sharp contrast to Satan, who feels only contempt and hatred for them. He explicitly says that he enjoys conversing with Adam, and that angels do not consider humans to be beneath them (8.217–28). He also states that angels and people are different, but not superior, in types of intelligence: "Discursive, or Intuitive; discourse/ Is oftest yours, the latter most is ours, /Differing but in degree, in kind the same" (5.488–90). Conversations between humans and angels, or humans and God, are straightforward and egalitarian. One of the most heartbreaking moments in *Paradise Lost* is when Adam bids Raphael to "oft return" (8.651), since the reader and Raphael know that this is never to be. Aziraphale, even in a post-lapsarian world, has also had human friends and socialized with them, taking lessons from John Maskelyne on how to perform magic, however badly, dancing the gavotte, and proofreading various printings of the Bible, removing some important, incriminating passages from Genesis in the process.

Raphael is a Seraph, of the highest rank of angels, and Milton depicts him with the traditional six wings. However, Feisal Mohamed, in his book *In the Anteroom of Divinity: The Reformation of the Angels, from Colet to Milton*, has suggested that Raphael is of a "lower rank" than Michael, and that this may be connected not only to Michael's higher mission, but also his less friendly attitude: "not sociably mild/As Raphael" (*Paradise Lost* 11.234–5; Mohamed 115, 166). Mohamed also points to an extensive lineage of Raphael in both Rabbinical and Christian traditions as "celestial physician" or "celestial apothecary," including the healing of Abraham and Jacob, a "medieval cult of Raphael" the physician, and multiple instances of the angel being called upon to assist with the plague, a disease as incurable as Tobit's blindness (119).[14]

Aziraphale is a Principality, much further down the hierarchy than Raphael or the other primary archangels. This is also the class of angels that has the most to do with human welfare. More specifically, according to Heywood: "these work miracles" (4, 294). Aziraphale retains Raphael's attributes of healing and performing miracles. Like Raphael, Aziraphale heals bodies. He also heals bicycles but goes too far with the healing, adding gears, lights, and a pump that it didn't have (Gaiman and Pratchett 84, Gaiman 153–4).

The miracles can be frivolous, or at least his superiors think so (Gaiman 185), and their ethics can be questionable. Aziraphale arranges for an executioner to go to the guillotine in his place, which benefits only himself and is not going to put a stop to executions. Possibly this is more merciful than the actions of an angel like Sandalphon, who particularly enjoyed punishing the entirety of Sodom and Gomorrah (Gaiman 95). It is nice that he prevents a bloodbath at an eleven year old's birthday party, but he also creates the circumstances in which it almost happens. On the other hand, in one of the deleted scenes found in the script book, while he is explaining to a customer that he does not, in fact, have *The Nice and Accurate Prophecies of Agnes Nutter, Witch*, he off-handedly redirects a runaway baby carriage that is about to go into the street (Gaiman 10). His fellow angels Upstairs probably would not think to do such a thing. They don't understand humans and look down on them, as Gabriel and Sandalphon's loud announcement that they are purchasing pornography suggests. They think they have successfully hoodwinked the humans. Aziraphale knows better, especially as the volume of "pornography" they've attempted to purchase is Mrs. Beeton's Book of Household Management (Gaiman 94).

In *Paradise Lost*, Raphael is shown to like human food. When Adam first sees him coming, he tells Eve to prepare their best food, and only when he asks Raphael to sit down does Adam consider that perhaps Raphael can't eat it. He can, and he enjoys it.

> So down they sat,
> And to their viands fell, nor seemingly
> The Angel, as in mist, the common gloss
> Of Theologians, but with keen dispatch
> Of real hunger … [5.433–36].

Almost every depiction of angels states, as in *Tobit*, that their eating is an illusion, or that the food simply dissolves, but Milton's Raphael is able to digest the food: "Wonder not then, what God to you saw good/ If I refuse not, but convert, as you, /To proper substance" (5.491–93). It is hard to over-emphasize how iconoclastic this is. Raphael even suggests that humans may someday be able to subsist on angelic food and become more like angels over time (5.493–503). However, Raphael also spends a considerable amount of time lecturing Adam on temperance, and so does Michael later on, in Books 11 and 12. There are limits to the enjoyment of food. It is not supposed to become self-indulgent.

Like Milton's Raphael, Aziraphale also eats, but he conspicuously does not need it. Angels in *Good Omens* can eat, but don't. In fact, doing so is seen as repellant, as Gabriel makes clear in the series. When he first approaches Aziraphale, the latter is happily eating sushi. Aziraphale immediately recognizes that his superior disapproves, and tries to convince him that he's just eating sushi in order to fit in, somewhat undermined by the fact that the proprietor knows him and has prepared a dish of all his favorites (Gaiman 27).

"Fitting in" is a rather thin excuse. Raphael in the Book of Tobit states that he pretends to eat not to arouse suspicion (12:19). Milton's Raphael is eating a meal with human friends. Aziraphale, here, is eating alone. The proof that he doesn't need the food is that he's plump, a word used to describe him multiple times. In the book, he takes offence at what might be a joke about a dieting aid—Crowley's confusion of "Compline" and "Complan" (Gaiman and Pratchett 87). At another point, he eats all of his own deviled eggs before helping himself to Crowley's angel cake (63). In the television series, the buttonholes of his well-loved velvet waistcoat are worn and rubbed from strain and he has a habit of pulling it over his belly. He goes into a war zone because he wants some tasty brioche and crêpes, and he's fussy about his food. Furthermore, Milton's angels would have coronaries, if they could, over Aziraphale's enjoyment of Châteauneuf-du-Pape, because Milton's definition of temperance includes abstention from alcohol.

Aziraphale's indulgence in food is closely related to his indulgence in books. As Raphael says in Book Seven, "Knowledge is as food, and needs no less/Her Temperance over Appetite" (7.126-27). Raphael remembers; Aziraphale collects. His bookshop is a place to put his books, which he goes to considerable effort not to sell, including nasty smells and erratic business hours (Gaiman and Pratchett 43).

Milton's angels, unlike Aquinas', have memory. Raphael's function as Divine Historian requires it. Through Raphael, Adam hears the entire story of the demons' revolt, the war in heaven, Satan's fall—or rather, jump—into Hell, and the creation. There is no question about the truth of Raphael's narration; he only has to consider whether or not it is lawful to transmit a particular piece of information (5.569-70).

Like Raphael, Aziraphale is an historian, but the books he specializes in are the Infamous Bibles, which contain significant printer's errors, and works of prophecy, some of which are signed by the authors, including Nostradamus and St. John of Patmos. All these books, the narration informs us, are wrong. There is no conceivable need for them, except for the pleasure of collecting them. He does want the one completely correct book of prophecy, Agnes Nutter's *Nice and Accurate Prophecies,* but it falls into his hands by chance, just when it might be needed. Aziraphale has the Thomistic intuitive knowledge of comprehending an entire idea all at once and thousands of years of experience (Gaiman and Pratchett 151-52). While he has angelic intelligence, he uses human historic methodology: collecting information, checking sources, and primary research, which Thomistic angels don't do. Agnes' prophecies require interpretation, even though they are correct to the point of directly addressing Aziraphale and noting that his cocoa is cold.

Aziraphale retains or borrows Raphael's fondness for humans, ability as a healer and miracle worker, ability to eat and enjoy food, and to collect and parlay knowledge. In Book 8 of *Paradise Lost,* Adam asks "love not the heavenly spirits?" or "do angels have sex?" at which Raphael blushes "celestial rosy red, love's proper hue." The answer is yes—perhaps—but more specifically that it involves total unity with the beloved.

> we enjoy
> In eminence, and obstacle find none
> Of membrane, joint, or limb, exclusive bars:
> Easier than Air with Air, if Spirits embrace,
> Total they mix, Union of Pure with Pure
> Desiring; nor restrain'd conveyance need
> As Flesh to mix with Flesh, or Soul with Soul [8: 623-29].

Raymond points out that Milton's unorthodoxy here is not of that of the interpenetration of angelic bodies, but that it involves sexual pleasure. He also suggests that Satan's lament that demons don't experience "love,/But fierce desire" (4:509) indicates that sex is unknown to them (282).

By contrasts, in *The Seeds of Things: Theorizing Sexuality and Materiality in Renaissance* Representations, Jonathan Goldberg states that:

> The body that impedes is replaced by the possibility of total oneness, total interpenetration.... Raphael's description of angelic sex is one where likeness is sameness, a coupling that is undeniably homo (194).

Mohamed pushes back against the arguments for Milton's heterodoxy in angelic sex and insists that "what the angel describes isn't really 'sex' in any recognizable form" (131). This may perhaps be an extreme response to over analysis of this passage, but Mohamed's interpretation of "Let it suffice thee that thou know'st/Us happy, and without Love no Happiness" (*PL* 8:620–21) makes sense. Sex is not absent in Hell, but Love is, and here Satan's lament follows naturally from the passage beginning "Hail, wedded Love, mysterious Law, true source/Of human offspring" (PL 4.760 ff).

If Aziraphale indulges in food, is there the potential for sex? What does *Good Omens'* "angels are sexless unless they really want to make an effort" mean? (Gaiman and Pratchett 151) Does it refer to gender, sexual activity, or both? Gaiman and Pratchett's novel does not elaborate further. The 2019 series brings this question into sharper relief. Pollution and Beelzebub are referred to as "they": Sandalphon is, jarringly, an "it," making the character curiously sub-human.[15] Neil Gaiman states that Aziraphale and Crowley are in love, and elaborated in two posts on Twitter on June 2 and June 8, 2019.[16] This is a complex issue on its own and not within the scope of this essay, but it is worthwhile pointing out that Milton's angels have bodies and make love, even if it isn't explicable in human terms. In *Good Omens*, various non-human characters have chosen worldly, human things in which to indulge, but not necessarily the same things. Aziraphale likes food, books, and music; Crowley is never shown eating, but he drinks coffee and alcohol. He also likes sleep, which Aziraphale does not understand: "You don't need sleep. I don't need sleep. Evil never sleeps, and Virtue is ever-vigilant" (Gaiman and Pratchett 101).

Gabriel is attached to his bespoke Bond Street suits; Aziraphale, in the series, has not changed his hairstyle in 6,000 years but shares Gabriel's fondness for haberdashery: this may be because Aziraphale pays for his clothing, rather than creating them *ex nihilo* (Gaiman and Pratchett 92). The simplest answer revolves back to "really making an effort." Milton's angels do, the *Good Omens* angels theoretically could; and neither precisely reflect human experience.

So much for every aspect of angelic existence except for the most important one and the one which separates angels from demons: obedience. This is where *Good Omens* dramatically parts company with *Paradise Lost*.

Obedience, in *Paradise Lost*, is knowing where to stop. Raphael warns Adam:

> Solicit not thy thoughts with matters hid,
> Leave them to God above, him serve and fear....
> Be strong, live happy, but first of all
> Him whom to love is to obey [8.169–70; 633–34].

Even Satan agrees that obeying God is easy (4.45–47). Disobeying is also easy, but not necessarily worthwhile. In *Paradise Lost*, Satan declares:

> Fall'n Cherube, to be weak is miserable
> Doing or Suffering: but of this be sure,
> To do ought good never will be our task,
> But ever to do ill our sole delight,
> As being the contrary to his high will
> Whom we resist. If then his Providence
> Out of our evil seek to bring forth good,
> Our labour must be to pervert that end,
> And out of good still to find means of evil [1.157–165].

God makes something good, Satan makes something evil come from that good, God makes something good come from that evil, ad infinitum, or as Crowley puts it earlier, "you see a wile, you thwart."

Satan knows this is futile. So does Crowley.

> CROWLEY: So we're just working very hard in damp places and canceling each other out? [Gaiman 177]

In *Paradise Lost*, it is clear that there is a right and wrong side, a winning and a losing side. Satan, whatever he says to his followers, knows he's going to fail.

The outcome, the Plan, and what obedience is is not so obvious in *Good Omens*. Early in the book, Aziraphale states directly that "we," meaning the angels, will win (Gaiman and Pratchett 40). In the first episode of the series, "In the Beginning," he also takes it for granted that his side is the good side, that the results will be wonderful, and that the Ineffable Plan must make sense (Gaiman 48). His discomfort is more obvious in the series' third episode, "Hard Times." Watching the Flood clearly distresses him, blurring the seemingly clear line between officially good and officially evil. Crowley is there, pointing out that the impending flood will kill children. To him, it seems demonic. To Aziraphale, everything's been decided on a higher bureaucratic level, but it still bothers him (Gaiman 171).

Early in the unwinding of the Last Week, Aziraphale confidently states that the plan with the Antichrist was bound to fail, as evil always ultimately does. Crowley shoots this down with the cynical observation that it was "an ordinary cock-up" (Gaiman 137).

There are curious parallels between Milton's Raphael and Aziraphale in the arguably pointlessness of their missions. In *Paradise Lost*, Raphael is sent to explain absolutely everything to two charming new friends, in the certain knowledge that the entire thing is an exercise in futility. God has told him and everyone else that Adam and Eve are going to eat the fruit, whatever he does. When reporting back to Heaven, Aziraphale relays that he is having great success with the Antichrist, only to be told that what he is doing is very good, but futile. To make things worse, Gabriel quotes *The Sound of Music* at him, a musical Aziraphale hates, and which later serves as the kindling to his beloved bookshop (Gaiman 70).

In the Book of Tobit, Raphael volunteers to help someone, is sent by God, and brings his task to a successful conclusion. Milton's Raphael has the advantage of knowing the Plan and being sent directly by God to do a specific mission. In fact, one advantage of obedience to God in *Paradise Lost* is that it is never blind obedience. Even if his mission is ultimately to be futile, he knows that it is God who is telling him to do it. Aziraphale, on the other hand, has six thousand years on Earth cancelling out actions by his opposite number, directed by angels higher up the chain. He tries not to question this, but the truth is that he began with an act of disobedience—giving away his sword—because it felt like the right thing to do.[17] Evidently, that conversation about where the sword went was the last talk he's had with the Almighty. Everything else has gone through intermediaries like Gabriel.

In a last-ditch attempt to clarify what obedience to an unclear plan amounts to, Aziraphale even tries to contact God in the same way that scholarly humans tried to contact angels. Sophie Page, in "Speaking with Spirits in Medieval Magic Texts," describes the texts dealing with Hermetic and Solomonic magic and the rituals designed to invoke angels and demons, including circles and seals (129–30).[18] It makes sense that since humans use these in order to communicate with angels, who are one step up in the spiritual hierarchy, Aziraphale uses the same apparatus to attempt to talk to God, some of which is practical, and some of which is aesthetic (Gaiman and Pratchett 221).[19]

Aziraphale is sure that if he can communicate directly with God, God will make things all right. Crowley is stunned at his seemingly intelligent friend's naiveté and apparent idiocy (Gaiman 286). The Metatron, whom Aziraphale reaches instead, historically was a perfectly acceptable intermediary for humans practicing ceremonial magic in order to attain knowledge. For an angel desperately attempting to contact God, he is a disappointment, especially when he too, like Gabriel, insists that the point is to have a war and to win it.

Aziraphale may have rushed in to take Raphael's place, exactly as angels aren't supposed to do, but he doesn't seem to have Raphael's strength, position in the hierarchy, moral fiber, or even the knowledge to be able to help humanity, something both the Raphaels of Tobit and of *Paradise Lost* have always tried to do. Milton's Raphael knows the Great Plan and communicates it to humanity, even when it won't do any good. Aziraphale doesn't know anything, and surprisingly, turns this into a positive. He may be weaker than Raphael, but he has retained Aziriah/Raphael's desire to help humans. He doesn't know what the Great Plan is, so he weaponizes his ignorance. On the very brink of Armageddon, he interrupts the leaders of both opposing sides, Gabriel (or the Metatron, in the book) and Beelzebub, and politely points out that no one else knows either. He plays on the slippage between "Great Plan," "Divine Plan," and "Ineffable Plan," acting like the one nuisance at a meeting who holds up the agenda (336–37).

Because none of Aziraphale's superiors can parse the distinction between Great Plan and Ineffable Plan, and because they don't and can't know for sure, Beelzebub and Gabriel can't push the Antichrist into doing what they want. Uncertainty has helped to save humanity, for the present. As Aziraphale and Crowley leave, Aziraphale takes up the fiery sword he lost and brandishes it for one last time, protecting one particular important little human.

Aziraphale can't fulfill *Paradise Lost's* promise to "assert Eternal Providence/ And justify the ways of God to men" because he doesn't know what they are. The moral agenda is gone. There may be a Great Plan or an Ineffable Plan or some sort of plan, but since it is unknowable, Aziraphale's approach works better for the world he (and probably we) live in. He can, however, take the advice of Milton's Raphael: "be lowly wise" (*PL* 8.173).

Aziraphale fails to be Milton's Raphael, not just because of his un-angel-like attributes or his relative lack of strength, but because Milton's Raphael exists in a world of moral certainties and Aziraphale does not. His seeming self-indulgence and sentimentalism are connected to his deep love for the world and the humans in it. His inability to know the ineffable Plan, let alone to communicate it, are important elements in what ultimately saves the world. That is where he ends, in the series, at least, joining in a toast with his opposite number: "to the world."

Notes

1. I will be doing my best to distinguish between *Good Omens*, the book (Gaiman and Pratchett), the *Quite Nice and Fairly Accurate Good Omens* script book, published in 2020 (Gaiman), and the six-part Amazon mini-series, identified as such in the text.
2. There are fan theories to the effect that Crowley used to be Raphael or that Aziraphale

was demoted for disobedience. In theological and literary context, neither of these ideas work, and therefore they are not within the scope of this essay.
  3. "Good Omens: How Neil Gaiman and Terry Pratchett Wrote a Book."
  4. *Pseudo-Dionysius*,"The Celestial Hierarchy." *Pseudo-Dionysius, the Complete Works*. Translation by Colm Luibheid ;Foreword, Notes, and Translation Collaboration by Paul Rorem ; Preface by Rene Roques ; Introductions by Jaroslav Pelikan et. al. Paulist Press, 1987. 143–91. Entry on Principalities, 171.
  5. See Raymond 30. The edition of Aquinas I am using is Anton C. Pegis' *Basic Writings of St. Thomas Aquinas*.
  6. This game-playing God is much like the gods in Terry Pratchett's *Small Gods*, eternally playing games with human lives in Dunmanifestin. The gods in *Small Gods*, however, demonstrably do not care about human life at all, until another god—Om—literally twists their arms and hits them over the head with their own cornucopias (Pratchett, 324–27).
  7. Satan's "Better to reign in Hell than serve in Heaven" (*PL* 1.263) has become a popular quote, and one often taken out of context. The less important angel Abdiel's "Reign thou in Hell thy Kingdom, let mee serve/In Heav'n God ever blest, and his Divine/Behests obey, worthiest to be obey'd (6.183–5) is much less well known, but it exemplifies how important obedience is in *Paradise Lost*.
  8. The footnote adds that he helpfully destroyed this passage in one of the "incorrect" Bibles, n. 44–45.
  9. Sandalphon appears only in Cabalistic tradition.
  10. Owen Davies describes these practices in "Angels in Elite and Popular Magic," 305.
  11. Which of the four major Archangels rules which cardinal direction varies; Heywood states that Michael rules the Eastern Gate.
  12. Katherine Sueda, in "Milton in Science Fiction and Fantasy," notes that Aziraphale's name is "Raphael" with the Hebrew word for "help" in front of it. Gaiman and Pratchett claimed merely to be following angelic naming conventions, but I think that it is important to note that his name contains both Raphael's name and that of his human alias.
  13. The demon's name is Asmodeus. In the television series, Aziraphale suggests that Crowley may have chosen it as his new name while they both watch the very unpleasant crucifixion of Jesus.
  14. Mohamed's chapter on "Raphael, the Celestial Physician" examines this in great detail (115–40).
  15. Sueda suggests that the casting of female actors might be significant but Gaiman claimed that the casting was explicitly gender-neutral (147–8).
  16. Neil Gaiman's Twitter feed, June 2 and June 8, 2019. He also corrected "make" to "male."
  17. Sueda asserts that "Even more in line with Milton's portrayal of angels is Aziraphale's compassionate treatment of Adam and Eve after the Fall," noting also that "An obvious difference between these cases is that Michael helps the humans at God's behest while Aziraphale acts on his own initiative" (149).
  18. Davies also discusses the use of seals and planetary influence (308–09).
  19. Walter Stephens describes this process as "interspecies communication."

Works Cited

Aquinas, Thomas. *Summa Theologicae*, Part 1. *Basic Writings of Saint Thomas Aquinas*. Anton Pegis, editor. Random House, 1945. Volume 1.

Davies, Owen. "Angels in Elite and Popular Magic, 1650–1790." Marshall, Peter, and Alexandra Walsham, editors. *Angels in the Early Modern World*. Cambridge, 2006. 297-319.

Gaiman, Neil. *The Quite Nice and Fairly Accurate Good Omens Script Book*. London: Headline Publishing Group, 2020.

Gaiman, Neil [@neilhimself] Twitter. 8 June 2019, https://twitter.com/neilhimself/status/1137370226931228672.
Gaiman, Neil [@neilhimself] Twitter. 24 June 2020, https://twitter.com/neilhimself/status/1308052211222687749.
Gaiman, Neil, and Terry Pratchett. *Good Omens: The Nice and Accurate Prophecies of Agnes Nutter, Witch*. Workman Publishing, 1990. 2nd edition HarperCollins, 2006.
Goldberg, Jonathan. *The Seeds of Things: Theorizing Sexuality and Materiality in Renaissance Representations*. Fordham University Press 2009.
"Good Omens: How Neil Gaiman and Terry Pratchett Wrote a Book." BBC.com/news/magazine-30512620. Retrieved 3.21.2021.
Gordon, Bruce. "The Renaissance Angel." Marshall, Peter, and Alexandra Walsham, editors. *Angels in the Early Modern World*. Cambridge University Press, 2006. 41–63.
Harkness, Deborah E. *John Dee's Conversations with Angels: Cabala, Alchemy, and the End of Nature*. Cambridge UP, 1999.
Heywood, Thomas. *The Hierarchie of the Blessed Angels*. 1635.
Marshall, Peter, and Alexandra Walsham, editors. *Angels in the Early Modern World*. Cambridge University Press, 2006.
Milton, John. *The Christian Doctrine. John Milton: Complete Works and Major Prose*. Prentice Hall, 1957. Reprint, Hackett, 2003. 900–1020.
Milton, John. *Paradise Lost*. Edited by Merritt Hughes. *John Milton: Complete Works and Major Prose*. Prentice Hall, 1957. Reprint, Hackett, 2003. 207–469.
Mohamed, Feisal G. *In the Anteroom of Divinity: The Reformation of the Angels, from Colet to Milton*. University of Toronto Press, 2008.
Page, Sophie. "Speaking with Spirits in Medieval Magic Texts." Joad Raymond, editor. *Conversations with Angels: Essays Towards a History of Spiritual Communication, 1100–1700*. Palgrave Macmillan, 2011, pp. 125–49.
Pratchett, Terry. *Small Gods*. HarperCollins, 1992. E-book edition: HarperCollins, 2007.
Pseudo-Dionysius, et al. *Pseudo-Dionysius: The Complete Works* .Translation by Colm Luibheid; Foreword, Notes, and Translation Collaboration by Paul Rorem; Preface by Rene Roques; Introductions by Jaroslav Pelikan et. al. Paulist Press, 1987.
Raymond, Joad. *Milton's Angels: The Early Modern Imagination*. Oxford University Press, 2010.
Raymond, Joad, editor. *Conversations with Angels: Essays Towards a History of Spiritual Communication, 1100–1700*. Palgrave Macmillan, 2011.
Stephens, Walter. "Strategies of Interspecies Communication, 1100–2000." Raymond Joad, editor. *Conversations with Angels: Essays Towards a History of Spiritual Communication, 1100–1700*. Palgrave Macmillan, 2011. 25–48.
Sueda, Katherine Calloway. "Milton in Science Fiction and Fantasy." *Milton Studies*. Volume 63, Number 1, 2021, 136–53.
West, Robert H. *Milton and the Angels*. Athens: University of Georgia Press, 1955.

Eschatological Ambiguity in *Good Omens*

How Concerns for Survival Blur the Lines Between Good and Evil

Morgan Shipley

Its meaning, particularly within popular discourse, appears ubiquitous. Pressed into the psyche of those raised within western, monotheistic cultures, this is especially true in my undergraduate introduction to religions course. Every semester, when we arrive at the Tree of Knowledge, students respond to the query regarding the role/meaning of the serpent in almost identical ways. In a class where students often engage with new religious ideas and practices for the first time, this is a moment where their confidence emerges, a reference to their own faith (or broader culture) that they can share with others. Responding with variations of "evil," "the devil," "sin," or "the fall," these students demonstrate not religious bias, but rather a tendency to read biblical moments through narratives popularized by both the private and public spheres. Within popular culture, references and tropes abound, cementing the legacy of the serpent as the embodiment of evil, the source that pulls humanity away from God/goodness through acts of evil and into a state of permanent sin. Such association furthers an interrelated dynamic, one that connects acts of free will to conditions of evil—and therefore obedience to that which is good.

Yet *Good Omens* challenges the coherency of this association from its opening scene, a challenge repeated throughout the 2019 Amazon Prime miniseries adaptation of Terry Pratchett and Neil Gaiman's novel of the same name. In juxtaposing the demon Crowley's act of temptation as the means by which Adam and Eve gain their humanness against the naiveté of Aziraphale the angel handing off his flaming sword, which Adam uses almost instantly in the first act of killing, *Good Omens* not only connects to and presents an alternative reading of the Garden scene, but also exposes the function and limitations of the good/evil narrative. Can angels commit evil actions, as Aziraphale sits concerned? Is Crowley's act good as he himself poses?

Mirrored in the very material lives of and relationship between Crowley and Aziraphale, *Good Omens* suggests that the binary between good and evil is fluid, a tool used to justify conduct or control humans whose context, histories, and access to power make the absolute divide between that which is good, and that which is evil, impossible to delineate. From debates over the moral coherency of Noah's Flood, to the matter of fact claim by Aziraphale that guns are uniformly bad unless used by the righteous ("Episode 2: The Book)," it is angels and demons alike who seek war and destruction, not simply out of bloodlust, but to fulfill their respective and entwined destinies within a religious narrative that culminates with an apocalyptic battle. They do so also, however, simply to survive, a dynamic we see repeated throughout Christian history as believers invoke God to justify their existential continuation and worldly domination of others. Within such eschatological frames, good is whatever leads one to the desired result, often by any available means; evil, then, is simply oppositional ... and vice versa depending on the actor, religious allegiance, context, and constructs of right and wrong, which oscillate in relation to shifting expressions of evil actions and good results.

Analogously, Crowley and Aziraphale seek to avoid the End of Days not simply out of empathy for creation (though this is part of it), but out of love for their selfish lives, for each other, and for the human world they cherish. In this unique way, the demon Crowley emerges as the moral compass, torn between and betwixt his function, his ego, and his relationships. In a world where acts of violence become godly (and therefore goodly), it is not that he prevents destruction from happening (though there are unique moments where it is Crowley who prevents further violence), but rather accentuates the role of choice and agency, as well as the need to realize human community by fulfilling or limiting self-desires. As with Adam's rejection of Satan as his father, *Good Omens* suggests that within free will we find the spark to carry-on, not as perfect beings, but in the recognition that good and evil are no more than tools to balance a scale of justice that remains forever in flux. Once recognized, we become neither angel nor demon, but complicated beings mutually bound to experience this world, as Crowley and Aziraphale realize, with others.

Christianity, Evil, and Purification

The complicated personal relationship between Crowley and Aziraphale, as well as that between each character and their respective "place" within the sacred realm, unveils the biblical and worldly implications of predicating human nature as balanced between the forces of Godly goodness and Satanic evil. With the apocalypse representing the realization of/for redemption, Christianity necessitates the construction of good/evil paradigms that attend final moments of purification—it is through a final eradication of evil that paves the way for the Kingdom of God. Justification is found in the site of evil, which often becomes, as with Adam and Satan, the source propelling the need for purification. Yet more than a commentary on the reification of the good versus evil divide, *Good Omens* intervenes within hegemonic discourses that emerge out of Christendom—this is not a story of or about Christ, the Antichrist, or the apocalypse, but the mechanisms by which human agency and morality exist within a mutually-sustaining dance that ultimately locates the "good" as the means for validating both one's own "evil" conduct, often as the means simply to survive, as well as that which is externally labeled "evil" and thus requiring of purification.

In this distinct way, *Good Omens* highlights the functional role of evil, the means by which normative standards are constantly negotiated and, which thereafter, create the conditions to legitimate violence as a "just" response to eradicate the externalized site of "evil." In being externalized, the presence of evil veils over the reality of the responding conduct. In other words, to establish the good, evil emerges as both the site of purification and the means by which norms are developed and maintained. Such a discourse simultaneously advances and complicates classic theological arguments regarding the presence of evil within a world constructed by a perceived to be all-good God, as well as the relative nature that allows ostensibly "evil" acts to be considered "good," and acts of "goodness" considered "evil" when undertaken by the wrong agent.

Crowley and Aziraphale explore this very dynamic in the opening scenes of "Episode 1: In the Beginning (1.01)." Discussing the tempting of Adam and Eve, Crowley and Aziraphale debate the merits of their action, with Crowley questioning the value of differentiating between good and evil. For Aziraphale, being a demon makes any action by Crowley ipso facto evil. Speaking to a reified distinction that makes angels "good" and demons "evil," both cannot comprehend the totality of this moment, nor the implications of their actions. In giving away his flaming sword to Adam and Eve once they find themselves expelled from Eden, Aziraphale's concern that he made the wrong decision (e.g., an evil act) is mirrored in Crowley's own worry that in tempting Eve and Adam to eat the forbidden apple, he actually made the right choice. Unable to reconcile this notion with their respective places as demon and angel, Crowley and Aziraphale's opening actions and conversation identify how right and wrong, good and evil, are neither wholly contingent, nor mutually exclusive. Rather than universals dictums, *Good Omens* suggests that morality itself is relative, relied upon or acted against to fulfill roles, expectations, and plans, often without the agents responsible for acting understanding the cause, purpose, or aim. Given this, if Christianity identifies God as the foundation for the good, how do we explain evil, both among humans and within religious actions? If goodness is a universal attribute of God, how do we explain both divine figures that act out of vengeance against evil and the existence of evil among humans?

This problem of theodicy finds a unique answer in *Good Omens*, one that distances itself from the restorative function of evil to highlight how the human condition simply mirrors the self-interest and mutual dependence of the divine realm, of God and of Satan. Rather than will away evil as distinct from the godly, *Good Omens* illustrates the Janus-faced nature of both concepts, the ways in which the categorization of evil works to fortify difference or justify conduct as good, while also creating norms by which righteousness does not equate with goodness and evil does not inevitably produce wrongs. Derived from the Greek words Θεός *theos* (god) and δίκη *dike* (trial, judgment, or justice), theodicy signifies efforts to vindicate God as just and good in the presence of evil and suffering. To borrow from the theological work of St. Augustine (354–430 CE), a central theologian and philosopher who delineated core Christian ideas such as original sin, given the goodness connected to God, "where is evil then, and whence, and how crept it in hither? What is its root, and what its seed? Or hath it no being" (124)?

As a salvific religion, the very promise of Christianity is one of redemption, of cleansing humanity from the presence of and tendency toward sin. While we can describe and ascribe evil and goodness in human terms (anthropodicy), within religion we encounter an almost ubiquitous presence of and justification for evil, which is commonly positioned as either the effects experienced by the righteous or the conduct of the wicked. This is not to suggest that all religious systems share the same binary standard of morality; in fact, as *Good Omens* demonstrates, the opposite is true (what is good for God is not good for Satan, and vice versa). It is not a normative definition of evil (or good) that is shared between God and Satan, angels and demons, but rather a functional discourse that helps standardize behavior (which may include punishing/damning those accused of being hosts of evil) or legitimate worldly conditions and basic human desires. Designation of that which is "evil" functions to legitimate power over and violence against; it is often the base accusation that justifies projects of purification that range from persecution to terrorism to genocide. In practice, the application of evil fluctuates, dependent more on the agent acting in relation to a universalizing sense of the good rather than a universal source of evil. In playing with this condition, *Good Omens* signifies the banality of evil and the goodness of violence.

We encounter this throughout "Episode 1," which sets the standard by which good and evil will be measured in the remaining episodes. Against the backdrop of Crowley and Aziraphale negotiating their proper role within the apocalypse, morality emerges as contingent, divorced from established categories of right and wrong, good and evil, in favor of purpose. Purpose, Aziraphale explains, remains obscured, for God's "Divine Plan" is "ineffable" (1.01). Unable to be spoken or justified in traditional moral categorization, the truth, as *Good Omens* develops, is that while the "Divine Plan" may be unspeakable, it can be and often is acted on, upon, and on behalf of. Indeed, when the angels Gabriel and Sandalphon visit Aziraphale in his book shop during "Episode 2: The Book (1.02)," Gabriel provides an update on the Antichrist, noting how all's good as it relates to God's Plan.

Yet the "good" that Gabriel gleefully celebrates is the upcoming apocalypse, the war to end all wars—this is not a result of humanity's failures, but rather, as Gabriel stresses, part and parcel to the "Divine Plan." The violence subsumed within this "Plan" is unveiled in Aziraphale's description of Sandalphon. He recalls, to Sandalphon's delight, how it was hard for Aziraphale to forget him as he was responsible for the death and destruction at Sodom and Gomorrah. Aziraphale's comments, when juxtaposed to Gabriel's report, illustrate the malleability and relative nature of moral actions. What emerges as right and good in this moment is the realization of a sanctified trajectory sprinting willingly (and joyfully except for Crowley and Aziraphale) toward destruction.

In enacting their respective roles, angels and demons alike forgo universals in favor of context and perspective, a condition reflected in Episode 2's portrayal of witches and witch-finders, both of whom see their collective actions as directed against the forces of darkness. Just as Anathema Device, the descendant of witch Agnes Nutter, understands her role as a witch is to locate and abolish evil, so too does Newton Pulsifer, the descendant of Thou-Shalt-Not-Commit-Adultery Pulsifer who led the burning of Agnes Nutter in 1656, understand his calling to be directed against evil when he accepts Witchfinder Sergeant Shadwell's newspaper ad to aid in his mission to defend against the "forces of darkness" (1.02). As with Crowley and Aziraphale's mirrored paths, *Good Omens* situates the witch and witch-hunter as two sides of the same coin, each directed against the same forces of "darkness" yet trapped by the capacity to see only from their perspective. Connected not only by their ancestors' violent crossing, Anathema's and Newton's purposes are entwined, both at the exoteric level of their designated roles as witch and witch-hunter, as well as at the esoteric level through the shared sense of darkness that becomes distinctive depending only on which side of the coin we land upon.

Each is out to destroy ostensibly the same evil (Satan), yet the witch-hunter identifies the site of Satan's worldly expressions with witches who, in the frames of *Good Omens*, represent an essential element in the battle against Satan Itself. In this case, the evil remains consistent— it is simply that the site of evil, as well as the notion of what counteraction represents the good (killing witches or preventing Satan), exist in a never-ending cycle of contradiction. Importantly, Crowley and Aziraphale demonstrate how this condition is not the result of humanity's fallibility, but rather is a direct reflection of the divine and of humanity created in the "image" of God.

The second scene in "Episode 3: Hard Times (1.03)" finds Crowley and Aziraphale at the foot of Noah's Ark. Excusing God's temperament to Crowley, Aziraphale proceeds to describe the forthcoming punishment, the wiping out of an entire community—minus a few select persons— because God is simply bad-tempered and irritable. While he never tries to explain *why* this act is warranted (it is, after all, ineffable), it is Crowley who emerges as the moral compass. Aghast by the realization that children will be killed, Crowley captures the ambiguity of good and evil. In conceding how indiscriminate killing aligns more with his "lot," Crowley identifies that morality, if it exists at all, can never include the genocide of people, a punishment Aziraphale seems to accept and legitimate by explaining how God will follow the flood with a rainbow to signal his promise never to drown humanity again. Crowley responds sardonically with "how kind" (1.03). Given the fluidity of that which operates to secure/ realize the good, when the reality of God's violence is mitigated through a rainbow, evil becomes a mechanism for self-interest and a means to secure community through the exclusion of those who are evil. It also demonstrates the reciprocal recognition that evil calls forth destructive violence in the name of securing the good; in this rendering, the horror of a flood— of death and permanency—finds balance in the ephemeral beauty of a rainbow.

Rather than categorical imperatives, the good/evil dichotomy morphs to fulfill descriptive and proscriptive needs. It adapts to situate expressions of right versus wrong, moral versus immoral, as relative states of being. The good/evil dichotomy thus operates to both dispel conduct not conducive to one's role or place, as well as legitimate immoral action as a consequence of securing or maintaining the good. It becomes a tool to legitimate right and wrong not as absolutes, but as everchanging means. In this unique way, when Crowley seeks to prevent Armageddon by working with Aziraphale to reduce his evil influence on the Antichrist, his act would be considered "good" in a traditional moral sense of valuing the sanctity of life, but "wrong" in relation to his designated role in paving the way for Satan. Similarly, when Aziraphale justifies violence, his conduct and understanding would be considered "evil" in a traditional moral sense, but "good" in relation to his designated role as ensuring God's Kingdom. Although his actions, like Crowley's, would be considered "good" in a traditional moral sense of valuing the sanctity of life, when he works with Crowley to influence the Antichrist toward the "light" side, he is acting evilly against God's "Divine Plan."

Good Omens pushes this cosmological and human dynamic even further in relation to the base instinct towards survival. Rather than an obligation to do what is morally right, what ultimately compels the actions of Aziraphale and Crowley is concern for their livelihood, which is predicated entirely on their affinity for human culture as opposed to their "place" within a sacred battle or in balancing the scales of good and evil. Following the opening Garden of Eden scene in Episode 1, we encounter two demons, Duke of Hell Ligur and Duke of Hell Hastur, waiting in a cemetery for Crowley. According to Hastur, Crowley cannot be trusted as he has "gone native" (1.01), indulging too much in the fineries and delicacies of human culture. Pulling up in his fancy car and designer clothes, Crowley proceeds to complain about traffic, only to become truly upset when Ligur and Hastur deliver the news: Crowley bears the responsibility of helping bring the Antichrist into the world to begin the process that will culminate eleven years later with Armageddon. Shocked and evidently saddened by this news, Crowley's unease at the very thought of Armageddon is apparent. Intoxicated by the joys of human culture, Crowley's response illustrates, as we encounter throughout the miniseries, how he holds no qualms working in "general terms" to bring about Armageddon, but it is "quite another for it to actually happen" (1.01). Distinctly, *Good Omens* does not suggest that selfishness and egoism are the consequence of being a demon, of being "evil," but rather express a root condition connected to creation and the aims of living, including the primal urge to survive.

Echoing Crowley's affinity for human material culture, the very next scene finds Aziraphale marveling over a plate of sushi, only to be interrupted by Gabriel who asks, with an air of superiority and godliness, why Aziraphale consumes "gross matter" for he is an angel. Shocked by this dismissal of sushi, Aziraphale challenges Gabriel, calling sushi "nice" because, as Aziraphale makes clear, it is distinctly human (1.01). Mirroring the cemetery scene among demons, this moment of debating the merits of humanness shifts to the Antichrist, with Gabriel informing Aziraphale of Crowley's role. As with Crowley, we instantly see the anguish on Aziraphale's face as he realizes that while indicating the culmination of the "Divine Plan" and his role within it, his place on earth, where he has been since the very beginning, is coming quickly to an end. From Crowley's passion for fancy objects to Aziraphale's obsession with books or fine food, both exist within the carnal joys of humanness, a condition that will not survive the apocalypse.

Crowley accentuates this exact point when he and Aziraphale meet to discuss the forthcoming Armageddon. Believing the coming destruction to be "rather lovely" (1.01), Aziraphale celebrates the news because it is a sign of God's victory, demonstrating, as we will explore in the next section, the conditional state of good and evil—after all, what is "lovely" about war and death? Crowley, however, laments the news, attacking Aziraphale's logic not by recalling universal truisms of good and evil, but by speaking directly to their respective carnality and base desires. These include Aziraphale's affection for famous composers, whose music will be replaced exclusively with the (repetitive) sound of angels following the apocalypse, and his penchant for fine dining and love of books that will both cease to exist (1.01). In other words, their respective roles as agents of "good" and "evil" prove to be both relative to time and context, as well as in relation to what each perceive and accept as right or wrong for their circumstances, which directly reflect the eschatological challenges facing humanity itself.

In juxtaposing ethical hypocrisies with the desire to simply survive, *Good Omens* deconstructs the normalization of moral standards, demonstrating how neither good and evil, nor right and wrong, speak to innate qualities. Importantly, this stripping away occurs at both the sacred and profane levels. In this unique way, both Crowley the demon and Aziraphale the angel legitimate evil actions when it is conducive for their positions within their divine plans, and act against the good of both Satan and God when it threatens their agency or the human world they participate in. That is, they act on behalf of "good" and "evil" in relation to their divine roles and individual desire for survival, which are often at direct odds. What becomes good and evil is thus relative to either the aim of their divine missions or their historical contexts and subjective needs. More than another the ends justify the means retelling, *Good Omens* offers an intervention on the good/evil dichotomy in order to ultimately illustrate the root humanness calling forth and endlessly complicating religious morality.

Indeed, as God reminds us when narrating the scene at the convent of Satanic nuns responsible for switching out the Antichrist baby: the "great triumphs and tragedies of history are caused not by people being fundamentally good or fundamentally evil, but by people being fundamentally people" (1.01). Such a sentiment finds roots in the corresponding lives of Crowley and Aziraphale who are neither good nor evil but remain trapped between their roles as divine agents acting on behalf of Satan and God and their own agency, which connects them to the human world that comes to hold more value than manifesting the End of Days.

The Function of Evil and the Role of Free Will

A theme found throughout Christianity's New Testament, evil represents a position of deficiency, of being "less than." It neither signals God's fallibility nor does it even represent a "thing." Rather, from a theological perspective as St. Augustine describes it, evil is the "perversion of the will, turned aside from … God … towards these lower things" (137). This perversion of will, when one chooses to move away from sacrality to lesser things, manifests in the mirrored paths of Crowley and Aziraphale—both act against the authors of their divine role (the "greater" thing) by following their own will (the "lesser" thing). Perversion is not, then, simply a way to describe a type of action, but rather is found in the moment of choice, in the very expression of free will directed away from or against the dominion of God or Satan. It is not their conduct alone that is evil, but the various moments of acting in accordance with their respective free will and contextual sense of conscience represent the "lesser thing" in relation to their sacred roles. Designed to be obedient, neither Crowley nor Aziraphale can escape the humanness of their historic relationships— to each other and the various individuals they interact with on behalf of God or Satan—and of agential choice, of choosing what they thought was "right" or "good" according to their specific circumstances and admiration for the creativity and hedonism of human society, of creation itself.

Through this dynamic, *Good Omens* pushes us beyond strictly theological concerns and discourses to arrive at the functional heart of the good versus evil dichotomy. It suggests that the realm of religion functions on behalf of basic human needs and to assuage feelings of inadequacy in light of a universe beyond human control. Through othering, evil legitimates privilege by justifying one's own conduct as undertaken for the "good." In his study of evil and religion, James Aho stresses how:

> [E]ven if it appears at first glance to be crazy, human evil is always "reasonable." It can always be rationalized, excused and/or justified…. Excuses admit to an evil but deny responsibility for it; this, by claiming that it was "caused" by passions outside (*ex*) the evil doer's control. Justifications admit responsibility for the evil but either deny its harmfulness or relativize its damage by situating it in the context of a presumably higher good [205].

Reflecting the classic theory of religion posed by sociologist Emile Durkheim (1858–1917), Aho, himself a professor of sociology, outlines the way evil functions to combat anomie, what Durkheim described as a state of normlessness, or the disorientation and disorder resulting from clashes between individual desires and social needs and standards (Durkheim 8–11). For Durkheim, evil is normative because it serves specific and necessary functions. Concerned with the viability of society, Durkheim identifies a sacred/profane divide that requires the imposition of evil to make claims against anomie efficacious by demarcating what does and does not constitute morality and the good in the name of social cohesion (*The Elementary Forms of Religious Life*).

To manage anomie, evil simultaneously isolates the realm needing purification (the profane world) and identifies the good (the sacred), thereafter solidifying social bonds by normalizing a standard of goodness. Such measurable standards of the good further fortify cohesion and convinces those within the social order that their position, privilege, and conduct is warranted and thus "right"—even if, as *Good Omens* repeatedly poses, it would be considered evil within the moral mapping of Christianity. In other words, what is right may not be morally good; and what is evil might not be wrong but "right" for the agent(s) acting.

Good Omens unveils the consequences of this relative state in its various references to war and violence by highlighting the way in which intentional violence finds moral legitimacy when situated exclusively in the good versus evil paradigm. Without any defined boundaries, the relative applications of good and evil become symbolic references, a means to legitimate conduct that, on the surface, would be considered immoral. Bypassing what is morally right (e.g., killing is wrong) versus what is religiously good (e.g., survival, power, or privilege), *Good Omens* demonstrates the way in which religious narratives become malleable—for both humans and sacred beings—in order to legitimate action and fulfill the needs of a specific moment or desired end. The identification of evil is often accompanied by claims that the agents of evil pollute or distort, making protective—and often preemptive—action necessary for essential survival. To identify something or someone as evil is to allow for purificatory action or defensive counter-violence; it provides the necessary justification to "remove" the pollutant. It is this essential orientation that explains Christian Just War Theory, or the religious justification for war, a theme *Good Omens* explores at both the cosmological level and within human history.

Drawing from the original rationalizations offered by St. Augustine, it is St. Thomas Aquinas (1225–1274 CE), an immensely influential priest, theologian, and philosopher within Christianity, who outlines most clearly the basis by which Christians are called to and justify war. Considering when warfare or military defense becomes necessary for Christians, Aquinas recognizes that while all war appears sinful, a "just war," as Aquinas concludes by citing Augustine, must be about the "advancement of good, or the avoidance of evil ... true religion looks upon as peaceful those wars that are waged not for motives of aggrandizement, or cruelty, but with the object of securing peace, of punishing evil-doers, and of uplifting the good" (43). Aquinas bases the realization of peace with good conquering evil through violence—to avoid evil, it must be both manifestly present and consistently destroyed. The very acts of "securing peace" and "uplifting the good" are thus based on identifying the site of evil and eradicating its manifestations.

A "just war," then, signals a preemptive moment of violence necessary to realize God's "Divine Plan"—or, to state this more in line with *Good Omens*, the good becomes the measure by which evil is relied on to actualize the good. In this scenario, the violence of war paves the road to heaven. This root message undergirds the foundational Christian narrative adopted at the heart of *Good Omens*; the Kingdom of God follows the violent battle between the forces of God and the minions of Satan. This is not a moral condition, nor an issue of universal rights or wrongs, but rather the privilege to claim exclusive access to advance one's perception of the good by asserting absolute control over the site of evil, which must be overcome.

Distinctly, this sense of totalizing war and destruction as the mechanism to realize the good is presented most consistently through the lens of angels, who are most commonly positioned within Christian lore and popular consciousness alike as the ideal of divine compassion. After agreeing to help Crowley influence the Antichrist to the light in Episode 1, Aziraphale reports on his efforts, believing—more for himself and his continued place on earth—that such intervention represents the will of God by fulfilling his divine mission to thwart the influence of Crowley/evil. However, as he waits for the other angels to commend his actions as right and good, Gabriel, Uriel, the Archangel Michael, and Sandalphon respond in chorus, stressing that such efforts can never succeed exactly because God's "Divine Plan" necessitates a final moment of reckoning that culminates in death and destruction. Indeed, as the Archangel Michael emphasizes, wars are conducted to identify—and empower—winners and cannot, as Uriel adds, be "avoided" (1.01). God's agents understand the good as expressed and achieved through war, as destroying the site of evil through actions that, traditionally, would be considered morally wrong.

Episode 2 extends this through the personification of War. War's emergence as the first of the Four Horsemen of the apocalypse begins with a scene, as the narrator describes it, in which "sometimes, despite everything, peace breaks out" (1.02). The caveat, "despite everything," demonstrates the intentionality of both God's and Satan's plans, and the way each are predicated on maintaining an instability that can only be resolved in a final totalizing moment of violently starting anew. Yet despite the best efforts of God and Satan, humans still find peace—however, the very emergence of War signals not a validation of peace but a message from God to return to and carry on through violence. War's role is not to fortify peace to prevent mass death and destruction, but rather to prevent peace from being realized. Rather than sending an agent of God to secure a potential peace accord, War surfaces, her presence physically symbolizing the antagonisms, selfishness, and hubris that transforms a scene of reconciliation into a mass killing, with all three sides of the peace accord turning on the other as War walks off to join the other Horsemen of the apocalypse.

Within this scenario, any clearly demarcated line between good and evil becomes secondary to the desired end of securing—through violence—God's Kingdom or the fall sought by Satan. In navigating this changing landscape of moral contingencies, the miniseries highlights the various ways that the good promised by God is secured through ostensibly evil and violent conduct. Within the context of war, we find an expression of violence based in discourses of good and evil—although war results inevitably in death, each side will always see their cause as just, righteous, and good, with their opposition as wrong, the site of evil that needs overcoming. War, as with good and evil, is thus relative and contingent, a condition that makes the value of life secondary to individual (or group) survival. It allows for the demons of Satan to celebrate their fallen status within an upcoming war just as the angels of God smile and laugh at the thought of the Four Horsemen fulfilling the horrific (and horrifying) conditions represented by their names: Death, Pollution, Famine, and War.

This orientation lies at the heart of Aziraphale's conclusion regarding guns. When used by the wrong agents, guns represent evil and wanton destruction; but when used by the righteous, guns enforce and justify moral codes (1.02). Aziraphale's logic is important here as he directly connects morality not to universal conditions, such as the oft-cited Christian ethics of "do unto others" or "love thy neighbor," but rather to relative constructs of right and wrong, which mirror ever-shifting narratives of evil motives or good (just) causes. It is not that Aziraphale does not see the evil results of war and violence, but positions both within the frames of his specified role as an agent of God—if directed against the site of evil, morality itself is expressed through sanctified violence.

This, of course, is Crowley's response to Aziraphale's claim. Visiting the location of Adam's birth at a convent in Tadfield, England during

116   The Theology of *Good Omens*

Episode 2, Crowley and Aziraphale do not encounter the Satanic nuns who accidentally misplaced the Antichrist, but rather a handful of paintball players in the now converted-to paintball facility. After graciously removing a paintball stain from Aziraphale's jacket in an act of kindness, Crowley proceeds to turn the paintball guns into real guns to help participants fulfill their true desire: to murder coworkers. Horrified by his actions, Crowley responds to Aziraphale by simply using Aziraphale's claim regarding the connection between guns and moral weight against him, as well as by pointing to the basic incongruity between absolute free will, "including the right to murder" (1.02), and moral imperatives to not kill or act with love. Rather than uniquely human, this incongruity, Crowley believes, directly mirrors the very relational structure of the universe, including that between God and Satan, angels and demons, humans and the divine. Crowley's justification to Aziraphale thus suggests that violence and the need to dominate reflect the divine realm more than kindness and compassion. Yet he quickly assuages Aziraphale's concern by assuring him that, miraculously, no killing will actually occur. Aziraphale celebrates this as a sign of Crowley's true virtuous nature, an accusation Crowley vehemently denies for he is a demon, but which illustrates how neither see the cruelty and implications of this moment of fun. Presented with the option in a game of paintball among co-workers between play and real, the scene devolves into willful acts of "war" (1.02), as one participant declares, before being shot and miraculously saved. Although Aziraphale contends that these miracles of continued life granted by Crowley indicate his goodness, Crowley highlights the truth of the moment. Him saving the paintball players does not negate the base fact that each participant, without prodding, accepted and chose to act on their newfound ability—and now perceived right—to murder.

As *Good Omens* ultimately suggests, there is no moral standard regarding right/wrong or good/evil. This truism is presented to the audience most directly when, rather nonchalantly during Episode 1, neither Crowley nor Aziraphale can recall whether angels or demons inspired the Reign of Terror, but Aziraphale, with a delightful smile, can remember what they ate: crepes (1.01). Within this play of circularity, where evil can be good and acts of goodness can be labeled evil, *Good Omens* pushes even further through the intimate relationship between Crowley and Aziraphale. It is not only that good and evil are relative in relation to right and wrong, but must be as both exist for functional purposes, operating to help individuals and systems navigate selfishness and the demands of coexistence.

Good and evil thus become reflections of insecurity and immediate need, of failing to live up to divine expectations or acting in over-accordance with one's will. Evil, then, offers a way to help define and actualize the good; in turn, the good becomes hegemonic through both the application of evil (or immoral) conduct and in the opposition to evil, whether real, fictional, or, most often, a tad of both.

Conclusion: Evil, Feelings of Inadequacy, and Survival

In *Good Omens*, the realm of the sacred and its agents simply mirror—and thereby help to legitimate—the conditions and justifications driving human society towards moments of insanity and destruction, as well as friendship and empathy. Crowley and Aziraphale model this, becoming reflections of both our own humanness as viewers, as well as the moral exigencies of Christian narratives. Their own existential concerns and inadequacies address the scarcity of religious fulfillment and the relative nature of conduct and survival found within Christianity and replicated in human culture. When it comes to Aziraphale, for example, his more anxious quest to fulfill God's expectations speak to what Northwestern University Professor of English Regina Schwartz identifies as the relevance of scarcity as it relates to violence, that God's love and acceptance are not boundless, but restrictive. When perceived as scarce, the need to cling to the privilege and power God bestows only intensifies.

As Schwartz develops in her study of the violent legacy of monotheism, "scarcity is encoded in the Bible as a principle of Oneness (one land, one people, one nation) and in monotheistic thinking (one Deity), it becomes a demand of exclusive allegiance that threatens with the violence of exclusion" (xi). Within this religious discourse, evil emerges as the tool by which privilege and power are bestowed during (or as the result of) the maintenance of anomie and identification of allegiance. To see Aziraphale's choices as evil, or understand Crowley's empathy as good, misses the purpose (and point), which in both cases connects to the need to survive, to carry on. Such self-preservation allows for the designation of evil as good (and vice versa) in order to contend with their own needs and to overcome individual and collective scarcity.

Thus, when Crowley and Aziraphale agree to thwart the emergence of the Antichrist by balancing the evil influence of Crowley with the light presented by Aziraphale, both act in contradiction to their established roles. Although seeking a traditionally good end (e.g., the maintenance of life), to actively interject into the life of the Antichrist is to perform "evil" in relation to the "Divine Plan" by preventing the realization of God's Will and Satan's role. Rather than an anomaly, the Armageddon is called forth by God, who requires the very presence of Satan and the Antichrist to realize eternity, just as Satan requires God to exist and overcome. To thwart this is to reject the eternity promised by God and the overcoming sought by Satan—it is, to return to St. Augustine, an expression of evil (for Aziraphale) by turning away from the "greater" (God) to "lesser" (Satan) thing (and vice versa for Crowley).

However, more than simply turning away from God and Satan, Crowley and Aziraphale do so by seeking to help Adam become all-too-human, suggesting that survival and the maintenance of life (the lesser thing) matter more than reigning supreme. This is a moment of pure hubris and ego, of God and of Satan, as well as of Crowley and Aziraphale. Yet where the former demonstrates the relative stance of good and evil vis-à-vis their privileged positions, Crowley and Aziraphale outline a path forward based within the existential need for survival and togetherness. To prevent the emergence of the Antichrist—and thus Armageddon—is to recognize this relative state of "right" and "wrong" as the condition by which life itself is maintained, not perfectly of course, but through ongoing negotiations. As Crowley reflects following Aziraphale's decision to fulfill his angelic role in propagating goodness as a virtue by ostensibly going against the good sought by God, if "we do it right, he won't be evil. Or good. He'll just be normal" (1.01).

In the end, where both Crowley and Aziraphale seek the freedom of the exclusion Schwartz identifies, both remain fearful of the punishments that attend to the rejection of their place within the scarcity of Satan's rebellion and of God's salvation. Armageddon, for Crowley and Aziraphale, represents a totalizing end, one that dispels their ongoing roles and severs their ties to one another and the human world they both revere. Through the lens of Crowley and Aziraphale's complicated relationships, we, as viewers, encounter the root challenges, horrors, and joys of human existence, realizing, as Terry Pratchett and Neil Gaiman write in *Good Omens*, that where we "go wrong, of course, is in assuming that the wretched road is evil simply because of the incredible carnage and frustration it engenders every day" (13). For Crowley, as with Aziraphale, joy is found both in moments of obedience, which often entail explicit expressions of violence, as well as in rebellion, when they find their "good" by rejecting simultaneously the "wrong-ness" of Satan's plan and the "right-ness" of God's salvation to live in the immediacy of their mutual conditions and human circumstances.

Works Cited

Adams, Marilyn McCord. *Horrendous Evils and the Goodness of God*. Cornell University Press, 1999.

Aho, James. "The Religious Problem of Evil." *The Oxford Handbook of Religion and Violence*, edited by Mark Juergensmeyer and Margo Kitts. Oxford University Press, 2013.

Aquinas, Thomas. "Whether It Is Always Sinful to Wage War? *Summa Theologica.*" *Princeton Readings in Religion and Violence*, edited by Mark Juergensmeyer and Margo Kitts. Princeton University Press, 2011.
Durkheim, Emile. *The Division of Labor in Society.* Free Press, 2014.
Durkheim, Emile. *The Elementary Forms of Religious Life.* Oxford University Press, 2008.
"Episode 1: In the Beginning (1.01)." *Good Omens*, written by Neil Gaiman, directed by Douglas Mackinnon, BBC Video, 2019.
"Episode 2: The Book (1.02)." *Good Omens*, written by Neil Gaiman, directed by Douglas Mackinnon, BBC Video, 2019.
"Episode 3: Hard Times (1.03)." *Good Omens*, written by Neil Gaiman, directed by Douglas Mackinnon, BBC Video, 2019.
Pratchett, Terry and Neil Gaiman. *Good Omens: The Nice and Accurate Prophecies of Agnes Nutter, Witch.* William Morrow, 2019.
St. Augustine. *The Confessions of St. Augustine.* Translated by E.B. Pusey, E.P. Dutton, 1920.
Schwartz, Regina. *The Curse of Cain: The Violent Legacy of Monotheism.* University of Chicago Press, 1997.

Sola Fide

Ineffability, Good Omens, *and the Reformation*

Philip Goldfarb Styrt

The apocalyptic climax of Neil Gaiman and Terry Pratchett's *Good Omens* hinges on whether it is possible to know what God intends: that is, on whether the divine plan as revealed in scripture, prophecy, and the practices of Heaven and Hell is a true guide to God's ineffable plan for creation. As it turns out, it isn't, and Adam the no-longer-Antichrist remakes the world so that it never was.

I argue that this emphasis on the ultimate ineffability of God's true plan reflects *Good Omens*' adoption of the Reformation emphasis on individual faith and interpretation over and against the pre- (and Counter-) Reformation belief in the significance of traditional practices and collective cultural consensus. In *Good Omens*, what individuals think about the world is more important than what prior generations have handed down as the truth. This manifests itself most strongly in the ability of Adam's own personal beliefs to literally change the world around him, no matter how outlandish the belief. But beyond Adam's powers, this sensibility is reflected in Crowley's and Aziraphale's progressive alienation from their respective supernatural sides, in Newton Pulsifer's urging Anathema Device to get on with her own life, and in The Them's triumph over the Four Horsemen through their own individual convictions. Reading *Good Omens* in this light allows us to understand the book's emphasis on the liberating power of individual belief as well as the importance of individual interpretation of both the written word (of God or otherwise) and of the divinely-created world around us. Ultimately, it produces a positive reading of God's ineffability as a necessary and valuable part of the world's design, as well as its salvation.

I further propose that several of the changes made between the book and the 2019 adaptation re-emphasize this Reformation aspect of the text. Jon Hamm's Gabriel serves as vigorous exponent of the traditional viewpoints that the series rejects, while the expansion of the history of the Crowley-Aziraphale friendship reminds us of the importance of the individual choices they each made along the way. The final switch between Aziraphale and Crowley serves a metaphor for the Reformation belief that no one truly knows what is in another's heart: the forces of Heaven and Hell are convinced that they have condemned (respectively) an angel and a demon, but their examinations are literally only skin-deep. Crowley and Aziraphale survive because their true colors are known only to God—and, perhaps, to Agnes Nutter.

A central theme of the Reformation and the Catholic responses to it was the question of how to interpret religious questions, and particularly the Bible. For the Protestants, and particularly those in what we now know as the Reformed tradition (following from Calvin as well as Luther), the answer was simple: *sola scriptura*, only Scripture. Only the word of God mattered, and no depth of tradition or authority of the church could disallow an interpretation that was rooted in the Biblical text. For Catholics, this assertion threatened to both wipe out hundreds of years of collective understanding and de-center the role of the church in the lives of its flocks. On the extremes, this meant that for Protestant reformers an individual had the right to interpret the scripture however they pleased, as long as their interpretation remained true to the text, however that was conceived, while for Catholics the weight of tradition and the collective beliefs on the church could and did determine which interpretations were valid. Not every believer held the most extreme version of their respective position, of course. Many Protestants accepted the wisdom of the church fathers, especially in the early church, where they found it convincing; many Catholics read the Bible and thought about it for themselves. Studies of the historical relationship between the Catholic and Protestant communities in Britain especially have come to emphasize the degree to which simple binaries between the two groups are insufficient (Walsham 6–27). But at its core, the dispute at question here revolved around the question of how to understand what God wanted for people and for the universe: whether a traditional, collective interpretation was the key to truth, or whether individual thoughts and beliefs played a central role.

At the time, these debates could become heated. The 1560 Scots Confession, written by the Scottish reformer John Knox and others and still in use in the Presbyterian church, explicitly disclaimed the value of "antiquity, usurped title, lineal succession, appointed place, nor the numbers of men approving an error" in interpreting scripture (19). That is to say, for Knox and his fellows, length of tradition and unanimity of agreement were not defenses for or against an accusation of error. When interpreting the meaning of God's word, in other words, "we ought not so much to ask what men have said or done before us, as what the Holy Ghost uniformly speaks within the body of the Scriptures and what Christ Jesus himself did and commanded" (20). Only the scriptures and an individual's belief in what God intended them to say matter.

A similar attitude emerges from the 1566 Second Helvetic Confession, also still in use, which explicitly claimed to "reject human traditions, even if they be adorned with high-sounding titles, as though they were divine and apostolical" (80). Rather, good interpretations of the Bible must be "gleaned from the Scriptures themselves" by individual believers (79). For the Protestants, these were pointed attacks at the Catholic church and its means of interpretation (the Scots Confession refers to Catholicism as the "horrible harlot, the False Kirk" [19]) and they were received as such by contemporary Catholics.

This divide remains a point of contention between Protestants and Catholics even today. Recent attempts to heal divides between the various branches of Christianity have emphasized that the role of tradition and church authority remains an area of disagreement (Noll and Nystrom 161–3). The Catechism of the Catholic Church still holds, following the words of Pope Paul VI, that their belief is founded on that which is "contained in the word of God written or handed down, and that the Church proposes for belief as divinely revealed." Note the emphasis on tradition, what is "handed down," and corporate authority, what "the Church proposes." Ultimately, the division is between a Protestant belief that individual readings of Scripture, if true to the word of God, are more important than the traditions and teachings of the Church, and a Catholic rejection of that belief. It is also valuable to note in this context, as several literary critics have, that *Good Omens* is of course itself an individual re-interpretation of the Biblical text (or rather, a partnered one between Gaiman and Pratchett), primarily of the Book of Revelation (Clemons 87; Haraldsdóttir 13–25).

Sola scriptura was one of three *soli* crucial to the Reformation, along with *sola gratia* (only grace, the belief that salvation was a divine gift and not earned in any way) and *sola fide* (only faith, the belief that only individual faith in God mattered, rather than acts of good works). *Sola gratia* and *sola fide* work together in Reformed theology, as historians of theology have noted, to the effect that individuals were saved only by the ineffable grace of God, and that no outside observer, sometimes not even including the individual themselves, could tell from outward works whether any individual was saved (Preston and Simpson 132). As a result, a reliance on outward behavior to determine inward truth was itself a failing (Evener 88). All three of these represented a strong shift towards an individual-centered belief in and worship of God and away from any sense of a corporate, collective, or traditional system in which other people were necessary to an individual believer's relationship to God—a system which the Catholic church retained.

The interplay between these two approaches to the word of God and the plans of God behind those words is a crucial element in *Good Omens*. One the one hand, we have the divine and angelic hordes, who stand firm in their belief in the Plan: the way the Apocalypse is supposed to happen. Now, this may—or indeed may not—be the same as God's ineffable plan for the universe. But they are all sure, and have been for centuries, that it definitely culminates in an Apocalypse whose terms are believed to be absolute. They know what is coming because of their collective tradition about it: one ironically shared between both Heaven and Hell. This is, in the sense above, a very Catholic point of view. Aziraphale and Crowley are both informed, in no uncertain terms, that their individual interpretations of what is going to happen in the Apocalypse, or what should happen in it, are not welcome (this is especially clear in the television adaptation, where Aziraphale especially gets roughed up by a gang of angels ["Saturday Morning Funtime"]). Tradition and the corporate authority (here not of the Church, but of Heaven and Hell) are dominant. Aziraphale's attempts to suggest that perhaps it would be possible to avoid the Apocalypse fall on the deaf ears of the Metatron, who tells him that Heaven wants to defeat Hell, not stop the fighting from happening (Gaiman and Pratchett 222). The way the world will end is not available for re-interpretation. This position—on the Apocalypse's inevitability, if not its victor—is also shared by the Four Horsemen of the Apocalypse, who ride out because it is written.

On the other hand, we have the individual beliefs of various characters: Aziraphale and Crowley, obviously, but also crucially Adam, the would-be Antichrist and his friends (the Them), as well as Agnes Nutter, the only prophet to be completely correct, her descendant Anathema Device, and Anathema's eventual boyfriend Newton Pulsifer. Each of these entities (I would say people, but Aziraphale and Crowley aren't) has a different take on exactly how much influence their own particular belief might have on the outcome of the Apocalypse, but they are unified in their sense that something about their own personal belief matters to that Apocalypse. This is, in the sense discussed above, a Reformed Protestant view: as long as it doesn't end up conflicting with the ineffable plan of God or the revealed word of Scripture, individual beliefs and interpretations are valid regardless of traditional understandings.

At first, *Good Omens* makes it seem as if the heavenly and infernal Apocalypse is assured. Hell instructs Crowley to deliver the Antichrist-as-baby, and sets in motion a seemingly inexorable process leading to the end of the world. However, the angelic and demonic belief in the Apocalypse runs into a rather significant snag almost immediately in the mix up of babies by the Chattering Nuns. On the one hand, the fact that the apocalypse appears to continue without interruption even with everyone looking the other way suggests that at least some of their belief in the inevitability of the Plan is justified. On the other, however, the substitution of the fairly normally raised Adam for the carefully groomed Warlock means that the Apocalypse is in the hands of someone who does not know what tradition or corporate authority say he ought to be doing. Rather, it is up to someone who has his own very idiosyncratic ideas about what he wants to do.

It turns out that while the machinery in the background of the apocalypse continues to run smoothly—the Four Horsemen ride, the Hellhound appears, the world twirls unawares towards its end—the identity of the Antichrist, and his personal beliefs about how the universe works, matter quite a lot. The Hellhound becomes an ordinary dog, compelled by urges he does not understand to bedevil not all of humanity but just the neighbor's cat—because Adam believes that is what dogs are (Gaiman and Pratchett 71–5). The immense powers of the Antichrist are put to the use of confirming the ridiculous stories Adam reads in the trashy magazines he gets from Anathema Device, because that is what he has chosen to believe (this is interspersed with other action in the book, but concentrated primarily at the end of one episode of the TV adaptation and the start of another ["Hard Times"; "Saturday Morning Funtime"]). Ultimately the Apocalypse itself is stopped by Adam's dogged certainty that it shouldn't happen (Gaiman and Pratchett 334–8). This is specifically re-emphasized in the TV adaptation by his similar insistence to Satan that he is not and never was his father ("The Very Last Day"). For all their collective traditional reliance on the Plan, the forces of heaven and hell are placed at a standstill by the individual belief of a single boy—even to the point where that boy ceases to be the Antichrist because he does not believe he is. This is explicit in the TV adaptation; but even in the book it is Adam's choice, expressed by a motion of his hand, that changes the world and unmakes the condition of the Apocalypse (Gaiman and Pratchett 343–4). Where once his Satanic father loomed, now Mr. Young drives up the lane. Adam averts the Apocalypse through the sheer belief that Mr. Young, not Satan, is his father—and if the book's ending is to be believed, he does so pretty much "forever" (Gaiman and Pratchett 369).

Adam is also the occasion for some of the most direct statements about the importance of individual interpretive power in the book. For instance, when debating with the Them about taking sides in the Apocalypse, it is he who decides that he doesn't have to choose sides after all

(Gaiman and Pratchett 292). Crowley shares an echo of this in the TV adaptation when he tells Aziraphale that doesn't really have a side anymore ("The Very Last Day"). As he decides to not take sides in the climactic battle (or perhaps more accurately, to take his own), Adam's firmest declaration of his unwillingness to trigger the end of the world is that he doesn't see the point of "what is written," at least "when it's about people" (Gaiman and Pratchett 337). For Adam, people's own interpretations of what's happening trump anything else. Even at the moment of the actual Apocalypse, when Satan himself is coming to chastise Adam, the book reminds us that he is inevitably "on his own ground" (Gaiman and Pratchett 343). This is a reference to his status as Antichrist, theoretically king of the world, but it is also a reminder that ultimately it does not matter where he is standing—it is his decision and belief that matters, not his location, and not what he is supposed to be doing.

Though it may not matter to his power where Adam is standing, I would also suggest that Tadfield is the perfect place for this kind of Apocalypse. Compare Tadfield with the (angelically- and demonically-) intended location on the plains of Megiddo. Tadfield is, in a paradox, bombastically quiet. It is a place where the radio show is about gardening (Gaiman and Pratchett 257). The Plains of Megiddo, by contrast, are themselves inherently apocalyptic: Armageddon has to come from somewhere. It feels like the sort of place where destiny happens—as is dramatized quite effectively by the lingering shots of the plains in the television series. It is, as everyone knows, the proper place for this kind of thing: Pollution complains that they ought to be in somewhere more interesting: either Megiddo or at least a major metropolitan area (Gaiman and Pratchett 310). Even Aziraphale wants to bring in a little of the Meggido energy to the Apocalypse, asking Shadwell about the "Golden Dagger of Megiddo" (Gaiman and Pratchett 275). On the other hand, letting Tadfield, or a Tadfieldian at any rate, decide the fate of the universe is appropriate to a world in which it is every believer's decisions and beliefs that matter, not the traditional and proper way of doing things. In this sense Tadfield stands in for all the other quiet places in the world, where people are busy every day living their lives and believing their beliefs. If the Apocalypse can almost happen in Tadfield, it can happen anywhere, at any time—not just in the place that everyone has come over the years to expect. As Death puts it "IF ARMAGEDDON IS ANYWHERE, IT IS EVERYWHERE" (Gaiman and Pratchett 311, capitals in the original). But while he means that to imply the destruction of the entire world, it also serves to suggest that all the preparations that everyone has done at Megiddo are entirely meaningless.

Apparently less meaningless are the predictions of one Agnes Nutter, witch, who has managed to predict the events of the future up to the

Apocalypse with unnerving accuracy. If there is an argument against the idea of individual choice being meaningful in *Good Omens*, it lies in Agnes Nutter's predictions. But, just like scripture, the meaning of Agnes's writing lies in the interpreter: mostly, in this case, her descendant Anathema Device. When Anathema picks card 3001, she points out that her family thought it had already been solved but at that moment she finds that it might actually refer to a literal event right in front of her (Gaiman and Pratchett 298). It is the act of individual interpretation that makes the meaning from Agnes's prophecies, and as long as the interpretation is valid, it doesn't matter what earlier interpreters (say, Anathema's parents) have said. A similar moment crops up in the footnotes of the book when Crowley drives through the M25: we find out that Agnes did predict this, but that most of the family had connected it to a completely different situation (Gaiman and Pratchett 285). Again, the value of earlier interpretations agreed to by generations of interpreters is minimized in favor of a contemporary reading that takes into account new information. Just like a *sola scriptura* reading of the Bible, the age or collective nature of interpretation is no grounds for authority.

And just like the Biblical prophecies on which the angels and demons rely, Agnes's too are undone by Adam's act of belief: in her case, literally as the book of prophecies burns (Gaiman and Pratchett 253). There is, of course, a sequel, which is delivered to Anathema and her boyfriend, Newt Pulsifer, but which goes unread (Gaiman and Pratchett 358). The book version of the story is little ambiguous about what exactly happens to the new prophetic book (Gaiman and Pratchett 358, 368). The TV adaptation, by contrast, quite clearly shows them turning this book too into charcoal as part of a nice picnic ("The Very Last Day"). The ultimate interpretive choice, after all, is to no longer choose to interpret at all, and to let the ineffable divine plan simply happen.

It is not only Adam, Agnes, or Anathema whose beliefs and decisions matter. The Four Horsemen, those immense and powerful instantiations of humanity's greatest fears and threats, are defeated by Adam's friends, the Them, through the same power of belief that gives Adam the ability to undo the Apocalypse more generally. In the book this is implied to be done by individual combat between a Horseman and a member of the Them in which the Them win at a single stroke (Gaiman and Pratchett 327–8). It is made more explicitly a matter of *belief* in the TV adaptation, which specifically calls out the power of their individual beliefs as the motivating factor behind their victory. Each of the Them gets a specific claim of belief to counter the power of their respective Horseman: Pepper's "I believe in peace, bitch" to War, Brian's "I believe in a clean world" to Pollution, and Wensleydale's "I believe in food, and a healthy lunch" to Famine, while

Death just walks away ("The Very Last Day"). This marks for us that it is not only Adam, or only the supernatural beings, who can change the (end of the) world through their beliefs. The Them's beliefs and understanding of the way the world ought to work matter in a very important sense.

The Them's belief in Adam is also significant, as their abandonment of him is what triggers his own change of heart to turn against the power on offer from Hell. In that moment, Adam tries to eliminate the Them's right or ability to choose. In the book, he responds to their unwillingness to play along by telling them that he could force them to play along and it is the very act of saying that which breaks the spell the apocalypse holds over him (Gaiman and Pratchett 286–7). In the TV adaptation this is physically represented by special effects: Adam tells his friends to shut up and their mouths are wiped away; he tells them to smile and suddenly they have forced grins; then they flee him, and that brings about his release ("The Doomsday Option"). This moment is critical to the plot, because it begins the turn away from the expected apocalyptic narrative, but it is also critical to the narratives of choice and interpretation in the book. It shows us how important the Them's own choices are, both because even the Antichrist feels the need to threaten them out of their choices and because it is ultimately their choice to defy Adam-as-Antichrist that spurs his rejection of his traditional role. At the same time, it also gives us insight into Adam and the power of his choices and beliefs. Adam may be supposed to be an inexorable machine leading the world on to its doom, but he is also a young boy who wants friends—and so their opinion of him matters, even if it shouldn't according to the traditional Plan. But it matters not because their collective belief is more important than his, but because he chooses to let it matter: because his view of the way the world works includes his friends.

We see another literal extension of belief into the world in the demon Crowley's use of his car. The car should, by all rights, have collapsed into embers when he drove it through the burning barrier of the demonic sigil that used to be the M25 (Gaiman and Pratchett 284–5). But it does not, because Crowley believes it will not (Gaiman and Pratchett 287). His conviction carries the day: proof that individual belief matters rather more than ordinary physics in the world of *Good Omens*. The same is true of his own literal survival: not only the car but Crowley himself should have been destroyed (or in his case, discorporated) by crossing the M25. But Crowley believes that he will pass through with the Bentley, and so he does. The demon Hastur has no such faith, and suffers the appropriate discorporation as a consequence.

Crowley's relationship with the angel Aziraphale also presents us with a story about choice and belief, culminating (in the television version) in a physically realized metaphor of the idea of *sola fide*. Each begins their journey believing in the traditional position of their kind: that there is a Plan that must be followed. But each quickly begins deviating from that Plan according to their own, personal code. Aziraphale gives away the flaming sword to Adam and Eve because it didn't seem right not to, while Crowley finds himself much less enamored than he ought to be of the idea of evil—ideas visible in the book and made much more explicit in the twenty-minute cold open to the third episode of the TV adaptation ("Hard Times"). Over time their friendship grows—by implication in the book, onscreen in the television series—through accumulated individual choices that blur the lines between them. After all, they reason, if the end result is that Crowley's wiles will all be thwarted by Aziraphale's efforts, why put too much effort into them in the first place instead of just having a nice pint? But this eminently logical step puts them out of favor with their fellow celestial and infernal beings (though it takes Crowley's bunch longer to notice) and starts them down the slippery slope that culminates in the two of them standing with Adam against the rest of the heavenly and infernal hosts and their vision of Apocalypse.

And yet they win. Not only does Adam undo the Apocalypse, but Crowley and Aziraphale don't actually suffer any significant consequences for standing for their own belief in the value of Earth. In the television series, we see that they were intended to suffer those consequences: each is threatened with destruction by their respective sides using the power of the other (a confirmation, as if any was needed, that the powers of tradition are joined at the hip despite their apparent divide). But Crowley and Aziraphale, thanks to a timely tip, have switched bodily appearances, and their respective superiors cannot tell the difference. As a result, each of them shockingly survives their intended torment, precisely because heaven and hell are unable to see their souls through their outsides. Only God knows that under the face of Crowley beats the heart of Aziraphale and vice-versa—even the audience is kept in the dark until after the ordeals. This is a visual confirmation of the Calvinist doctrine that we cannot know another's moral state from the outside, as well as of *Good Omens*' own insistence that heaven and hell don't really know what they're going on about.

The book also contains a hint of this element of spiritual interchangeability between the two. At the end, when they expect to die in the Apocalypse, they exchange almost-final words, each emphasizing the importance of what is "deep down inside" the other: just enough good in Crowley and just enough bastardy in Aziraphale (Gaiman and Pratchett 342). Again, this affirms the crucial idea that it is the internal state that counts, and that for all they look like an angel and a demon, they could not be more similar (although, of course, as both book and show remind us, angels and demons come from the exact same stock, there is also a marked difference between the two in their described [or viewed] appearance). This same exchange appears in the show as well, but there it comes after their successful switch of bodies ("The Very Last Day"). In both contexts, the exchange serves to confirm what the audience probably has already guessed: that Aziraphale and Crowley are fundamentally the same under the surface. But in the book this is our primary acknowledgment of that fact while the televised adaptation has already depicted their connection much more explicitly.

The larger demonic and angelic forces, on the other hand, are certain of the power and accuracy of their traditional and collective understanding of Revelation. The television adaptation emphasizes this by the introduction of a cadre of Aziraphale's angelic superiors, led by Gabriel (played by a smarmy Jon Hamm). They repeatedly reaffirm the idea, which the Metatron introduces in the book, that Heaven is invested in the realization of the Apocalypse, not in preventing it. Initially they do so while allowing Aziraphale to do as he pleases to try to avert the end: as the Archangel Michael tells him "we will be most understanding when you fail. After all, wars are meant to be won, not avoided" ("In the Beginning"). As the series goes on, they repeatedly (and frustratingly) remind Aziraphale that it is not their or his duty to avert the Apocalypse, but to participate. This reveals to us that their goal is not to foil the works of evil, but to win. They also repeatedly tell him that whatever he might do with the Antichrist "wouldn't change anything, Aziraphale" and express in frustration that "the Earth isn't going to just end itself, you know" ("Hard Times"). This figures as an attempt to deny Aziraphale his own individual interpretation of his role (or perhaps more accurately, the one he shares with Crowley) that if "you see a [demonic] wile, you thwart" ("In the Beginning"). The angels want Aziraphale not to think for himself about the dictates of God, but to think *like them*. And what they want him to think is that the old ways are best—even if they permit the work of the demons to go forward. In a sense, indeed, the angels and demons are working together against the world, trying to bring about and then win the Apocalypse.

The alliance between the forces of Hell and Heaven at the end of the television adaptation—the exchange of holy water for hellfire that is intended to deal with Crowley and Aziraphale once and for all—reemphasizes their common ground against humanity. This in turn gives added force to Crowley's observation at the end of both book and show that the ultimate battle will not be good versus evil but the angels and demons against humanity (Gaiman and Pratchett 359; "The Very Last Day"). Because ultimately, in *Good Omens*, the opposition is between those who believe in the importance of individual interpretation of the world, the word of God, and prophecy, and those who do not.

There is no doubt that there is some kind of divine plan in *Good Omens*. The book opens by telling us that instead of Einstein's famous quip about quantum mechanics playing dice with the universe, God "plays an ineffable game of His own devising" (Gaiman and Pratchett 11). Perhaps that should be her own devising in the series, where God serves as narrator and is played by Frances McDormand, but the concept is the same. There is assuredly, therefore, some kind of not-entirely-random purpose to the universe; this quote invokes Einstein's argument against unpredictability, and suggests instead that there is some kind of non-random game going on, which God has planned. In this sense, then, the angels and demons are right that there is a plan for the universe.

But the rest of the quote immediately pivots to deny the central claim of the angels and demons: that they know what the plan is, and it is the traditional one to which they have pledged allegiance. We are told that the game is incredibly complex and nigh-impossible for the players to understand (Gaiman and Pratchett 11–2). In case it wasn't clear enough that no one but God can know what is going on here, a footnote assures us this difficulty applies to "everyone" (Gaiman and Pratchett 12). That means humanity, of course, but in the context of the book it also means angels, demons, and any other category of being. This is very much a *sola gratia* universe then: only God's ineffable grace can save you, because you can't know anything more than whatever God decides to let you know. As such, there is a plan for the universe, but each of us must guess at it for ourselves, because God is definitely not providing any clues—except maybe the prophecies of Agnes Nutter. Here I disagree with the critic Daniel Scott, who interprets the book's emphasis on ineffability to suggest that "the existence of a divine plan becomes ever more unlikely" as the story goes on (79). Rather, I suggest that the book insists *both* on the divine plan's existence and on its inaccessibility to ordinary mortals (and even immortals).

There is a strong suggestion in the story that despite the beliefs of Heaven and Hell, there is a lot going on that they don't have as much control over as they think. This is particularly explicit in the TV adaptation. Organized human religion evidently has some real role to play in this world: church holy water is just as potent as the stuff that Aziraphale sources from Heaven, and Crowley has to hot-foot it across consecrated ground ("Hard Times"). This implies that what people do and believe matters in a way that neither Heaven nor Hell would necessarily approve of. More substantially, both the French Revolution and the Nazis are identified for us as emphatically *not* the work of demons or angels, though Crowley got a "commendation" from his superiors for the former despite doing nothing ("Hard Times"). This points to a world in which—just as we might expect—there is an grand overarching plan, but it is not visible to the angelic or demonic hierarchy. That is, after all, the meaning of ineffability.

We are reminded of the ineffability of God's plan at the climax of the attempted Apocalypse. The angels and demons harp on their reliance on "the Great Plan" (Gaiman and Pratchett 336). Aziraphale and Crowley, however, note that this plan is not actually the same as God's ineffable plan, and that while, as Beelzebub declares, "It izz written," that doesn't mean it couldn't be "written differently somewhere else" (Gaiman and Pratchett 337). Metatron complains that "God does not play games"—but at this we might well note, as Crowley does, that Metatron is clearly wrong (Gaiman and Pratchett 337). Crowley knows this from experience; we do too, but we also know it because the book told us so from the very start. God does play games, with everyone, and at the heart of those games is the ineffable plan that no one else can comprehend.

This produces, I suggest, a much more positive reading of God's ineffability than other scholars have found in the text (Clemons 98; Haraldsdóttir 28–36; Scott 80). Ineffability is, in this reading, not a problem to be solved but a virtue to be celebrated. God's ineffability allows a space in which Adam and the rest can act, and without which the world would be destroyed. If there were no ineffability to the plan, then the Great Plan of the angels and demons would succeed and the apocalypse would inevitably come. But God is not nearly that predictable—and this is a good thing for the world.

Of course, in that way God has something in common with Adam and, since Adam is "*human* incarnate," with all humanity (Gaiman and Pratchett 338). Just as the angels and demons cannot understand the ineffable plan of God, Adam's way of thinking is difficult for others to follow (Gaiman and Pratchett 335). He, like God, thinks for himself and makes his own decisions in a manner that does not reference others' expectations—and *Good Omens* marks this for us as a distinctively human and divine (but not angelic or demonic) attribute. This suggests that it is actual individual, not collective, human interpretations of God's will that might come closest to understanding the truth behind God's plans for the world: a Reformed thought if there ever was one.

Works Cited

Catechism of the Catholic Church. 1993. Libreria Editrice Vaticana, 2003, https://www.vatican.va/archive/ENG0015/_INDEX.HTM.

Clemons, Amy Lea. "Adapting *Revelation*: *Good Omens* as Comic Corrective." *Journal of the Fantastic in the Arts*, vol. 28, no. 1, 2018, pp. 86–101.

"The Doomsday Option." *Good Omens*, episode 5, BBC, 2019. DVD.
Evener, Vincent Matthew. *"Enemies of the Cross": Suffering, Salvation, and Truth in Sixteenth-century Religious Controversy*. Ph.D. dissertation, University of Chicago, 2014.
Gaiman, Neil, and Terry Pratchett. *Good Omens: The Nice and Accurate Prophecies of Agnes Nutter, Witch*. William Morrow, 2006, first published 1990.
Haraldsdóttir, Erla Filipía. *Religion in* Good Omens: *A Study of the Usage and Effect of Religion in the Comedic Fantasy Novel* Good Omens. BA Thesis, University of Iceland, 2014.
"Hard Times." *Good Omens*, episode 3, BBC, 2019. DVD.
"In the Beginning." *Good Omens*, episode 1, BBC, 2019. DVD.
Noll, Mark, and Carolyn Nystrom. *Is the Reformation Over?: An Evangelical Assessment of Contemporary Roman Catholicism*. Baker Academic, 2005.
Paul VI. "Solemni Hac Liturgia." *The Holy See*, 30 June 1968. http://www.vatican.va/content/paul-vi/en/motu_proprio/documents/hf_p-vi_motu-proprio_19680630_credo.html.
Preston, Aaron, and David B. Simpson. "Luther's Psychology of Love." *Journal of Psychology and Christianity*, vol. 31, no. 2, pp. 130–143.
"Saturday Morning Funtime." *Good Omens*, episode 4, BBC, 2019. DVD.
"The Scots Confession." *The Constitution of the Presbyterian Church (USA)*. The Office of the General Assembly, Presbyterian Church (USA), 2016, pp. 9–26, https://www.pcusa.org/site_media/media/uploads/oga/pdf/boc2016.pdf.
Scott, Daniel. *"And the World Continues to Spin...:* Secularism and Demystification in *Good Omens." Terry Pratchett's Narrative Worlds: From Giant Turtles to Small Gods*, edited by Marion Rana, Critical Approaches to Children's Literature, Palgrave MacMillan, 2018, pp. 73–91.
"The Second Helvetic Confession." *The Constitution of the Presbyterian Church (USA)*. The Office of the General Assembly, Presbyterian Church (USA), 2016, pp. 75–143, https://www.pcusa.org/site_media/media/uploads/oga/pdf/boc2016.pdf.
"The Very Last Day of the Rest of Their Lives." *Good Omens*, episode 6, BBC, 2019. DVD.
Walsham, Alexandra. *Catholic Reformation in Protestant Britain*. Routledge, 2014.

"This Angel, who is now become a Devil, is my particular friend"

Romantic Satanism and Loving Opposition in Good Omens (2019)

Alex Tankard

In the last years of the Cold War, Neil Gaiman and Terry Pratchett wrote a buddy-comedy about two disillusioned field agents putting humanity before their respective sides to avert nuclear Armageddon. Gaiman's 2019 television adaptation of *Good Omens* updated its setting to the present day—a questionable decision in the light of how successfully *Ashes to Ashes* (2008–2010), *Stranger Things* (2016–), and *The Americans* (2013–2018) demonstrated the stylistic and dramatic potential of blending a variety of genres in Cold War settings. More importantly, while the adaptation kept brief scenes of secret agents meeting in St James Park, they were unrooted from their Cold War context, discarding the novel's effective (and affective) shorthand for friendship between enemies in the shadow of mutually-assured destruction.

In his DVD commentary, Gaiman spoke of "having to write this [screenplay] as a love story. And part of the joy of writing a love story is the breakup" ("Hard Times" 51:58–52:12). For the necessary emotional tension, the adaptation found an imaginative framework in the novel's literary ancestry: Romantic Satanism. With their partnership as gentleman-spies stripped away, the adaptation exposed, at the core of Crowley and Aziraphale's relationship, the paradoxical opposition and fluidity of angels and devils found in British Romantic-Satanic literature, like William Blake's illustrated *Marriage of Heaven and Hell* (1790). The adaptation even adds scenes in which Crowley displays real Satanic frustration with Aziraphale's determination to excuse God's cruelty, recalling the devastating moral and intellectual gulf that Lord Byron's play *Cain* (1820) finds between the Fallen and the Faithful; regarding the obedient angels who praise God:

> LUCIFER: They say—what they must sing and say, on pain
> Of being that which I am—and thou art—
> Of spirits and of men.
> CAIN: And what is that?
> LUCIFER: Souls who dare use their immortality—
> Souls who dare look the Omnipotent tyrant in
> His everlasting face, and tell him, that
> His evil is not good! [I. 134–40]

Unfortunately, while there may be a superficial resemblance to the dynamics of Cold War agents, the theological, moral, and intellectual debates inherent in Romantic Satanism have very specific affective qualities: the gloating defiance of devils who overthrow God's control over the minds of His creations, even as they writhe in torment; the panicked outrage of the faithful angels when their slavery to a tyrant God is exposed; the devils' ugly scorn, in turn, towards the enslaved. The novel's externalized conflict between distant superpowers becomes, in the adaptation's surrender to Romantic Satanism, an intensely personal conflict *between* friends and, most painfully, *within* the characters themselves.

So far, so devastating. Yet recreating *Good Omens* as a love story makes an intriguing contribution to the British Romantic-Satanic tradition—which is, by its nature, a tradition of transformative works reimagining biblical stories and characters from different perspectives. This chapter argues that, by prioritizing the affective qualities Romantic Satanism invests in theological paradoxes, the love story drives agonizing conflicts towards resolution, and demands answers to a question that Byron and Blake often abandoned as unresolvable: how can the Fallen and the Faithful learn to love one another without losing their distinctive qualities? Additional scenes allow demon and angel to play out those arguments again and again over six thousand years—but, like Blake's unique hand-colored prints, they replay with crucial variations, in different cultures, contexts, and gender presentations, experimenting with each other's viewpoints—until, at the very end, they find a perfect Marriage of Heaven and Hell.

The Enemy ... a Sort of Friend

The Cold War—in fact and fiction—provided early readers with a clear pattern for Crowley and Aziraphale's relationship. The novel compares their Arrangement to cover each other's jobs to that of enemy agents who, posted far from their respective allies, find comradeship with each other in the field (45).

The angel can perform temptations and the demon can perform miracles because their makeup is fundamentally the same (46)—but, instead of swapping sides, Crowley and Aziraphale shift their primary loyalties to each other and to Earth (232). Their concern for the real-world fallout of empty ideological posturing would be familiar to viewers of cynical Cold War thrillers like *The Spy Who Came in From the Cold* (1965), in which Alec Leamas insists "I don't believe in God, or Karl Marx. I don't believe in anything that rocks the world" (1:05:25). The pragmatic collaboration and convergence of enemies, too, had its Cold War resonances: both Crowley and Aziraphale consider seeking refuge with each other's side (85), early readers could grasp this theological dilemma through recent high-profile cases of defecting Soviet agents granted asylum by the West, and U.S. agents defecting to the Soviets ("Soviets"; "Considered").

More pertinently, the shift to Great War after six millennia of Cold War (295) crystallizes their understanding that their oppositional roles have always been arbitrary; Aziraphale "sometimes suspected that they had far more in common with one another than with their respective superiors" (232). That Aziraphale only "sometimes suspected" their symmetry implies that their friendship has remained largely unexamined but, like the human spies who share tea and buns and squabble over café receipts instead of assassinating their opponent (69), their arbitrary opposition cannot withstand everyday proximity with an enemy who has become "a sort of friend" (41).

This "sort of" does not signify emotional reserve: the novel celebrates many peculiar "sorts of" love in difficult circumstances, from the Rajits' affection for racist Shadwell (176), to Madame Tracy and Shadwell deciding to retire together (376). Thus, despite significant differences in taste and temperament, "you grew accustomed to the only other face that had been around more or less consistently for six millennia" (45). The novel's gentle mockery does not quite conceal the pathos of two creatures otherwise utterly friendless; Aziraphale has difficulties communicating with his superiors (232), and Crowley is actively bullied by his (272). For all its satire on human(shaped) folly, the novel evinces wholehearted sympathy for a "sort of" love born of habit and simple loneliness—in this case, not only the loneliness of immortals among mortals, but also of "enemy" agents largely abandoned by their own sides.

The Cold War novel therefore positioned all conflict *outside* their relationship, making Aziraphale and Crowley an untroubled oasis of affection in a collapsing world. However, when the adaptation removed that historical setting, it also replaced that stability and externalized conflict with a traumatic Romantic-Satanic conflict between Faithful and Fallen—and, worse still, internalized *within* each individual.

Better to Reign in Hell

At the dawn of the French Revolution, and in its disappointing aftermath, several British Romantic writers undertook a subversive reimagining of John Milton's seventeenth-century epic representation of the Fall of Lucifer and of Man (Schock). Byron's work in particular reflects upon "the paradoxical Calvinist insistence on the idea that reprobation—damnation—is both predestined by the will of God *and* brought about by man exercising his free will" (Rawes 133), and upon the resulting schism between those souls God selected for grace, and those He engineered for damnation (Pauw 161). Confronted by a world of suffering, Byron's Lucifer also engages with the traditional argument from skeptical philosophers (Empiricus; Hume) that "Goodness would not make/ Evil; and what else hath [God] made?" (*Cain* I, l. 146–47). This moral and theological turn finds expression in specific patterns of characterization and affect.

Although *Paradise Lost* professes "to justify the ways of God to men" (I. 26), Romantic Satanism typically overturns this intention and reads Milton's God as a tedious, self-righteous tyrant, while Satan becomes a tragic antihero who is justified in declaring "Better to reign in Hell than serve in Heaven" (I. 263). So charismatic is this characterization of Satan that, in Blake's *Marriage*, the Voice of the Devil remarks that "The reason Milton wrote in fetters when he wrote of Angels & God, and at liberty when of Devils & Hell, is because he was a true Poet and of the Devil's party without knowing it" (plate 6). In 1821, another major Romantic poet and associate of Byron, Percy Bysshe Shelley wrote "Nothing can exceed the energy and magnificence of the character of Satan as expressed in *Paradise Lost*. It is a mistake to suppose that he could ever have been intended for the popular personification of evil" ("Defence" 1191).

By contrast, the Faithful who insist on God's goodness despite all evidence are pitied as "panic-stricken slaves in the presence of a jealous and suspicious despot" (Shelley 386), or condemned as willing tools of tyranny. This creates a moral and intellectual conflict in Romantic-Satanic texts between the submissive Faithful and enlightened Fallen. *The Marriage* declares there are two "portion[s] of being" that "are always upon earth, & they should be enemies; whoever tries to reconcile them seeks to destroy existence" (plates 16–17), and in Byron's *Cain*:

> ADAH: I have heard it said,
> The seraphs *love* [God] most—the cherubim *know* most—
> And [Lucifer] should be a cherub, since he loves not.
> LUCIFER: And if the higher knowledge quenches love,
> What can [God] *be* you cannot love when known? [I. 419–23]

The gulf between these two categories of being—those who worship only in ignorance, and those who, knowing God, reject Him and rebel through enlightenment—is as narrow as a hair, but it is absolute; as Lucifer exclaims, "He who bows not to [God] has bow'd to me!" (*Cain* I. 317). To Fall is to become gods "as one of us, to know good and evil" (*KJV*, Genesis 3: 22), and yet this state of enlightenment is also one of alienation and eternal suffering.

The 1990 novel carried British Romantic Satanism in its literary DNA, opening with Crowley, like Byron's Lucifer (*Cain* I. 200–05), interrogating God's intentions for man to Fall (9–10), and the narrator characterizing God as an inscrutable trickster who plays games with our lives (17). The narrator also observes that the grotesque murder of call-center workers had some benign consequences—"So that was all right" (298)—with the same flippancy and bitterness in which Byron's Cain remarked "Strange good, that must arise from out/ Its deadly opposite" (II. 288–89). While Crowley lacks the "energy and magnificence" of Milton's Satan, this amiable serpent is certainly no "personification of evil"; rather, like Satan in Byron's poem "Vision of Judgement" (6. 41–48), Crowley despairs at human depravity (40–41).

Perhaps the novel's most fruitful engagement with Romantic Satanism—and one that would find its fullest expression in the adaptation—is its insistence that "Hell wasn't a major reservoir of evil, any more than Heaven, in Crowley's opinion, was a fountain of goodness" (84; also 245) and, "Contrary to popular belief," angels and demons are essentially the same creatures, with the same wings, although the demons' are "often better groomed" (358; also 46 and 248). The correction of "popular belief" confirms the novel's self-conscious alignment with Romantic-Satanic subversions of the "popular personification of evil" ("Defence" 1191)—with a touch of bathos to further destabilize the traditional binary. This is not to say that the demonic and the angelic are identical forces; rather, that they represent symmetrical "contraries" without moral implications. Blake's *Marriage* insists:

> Without Contraries is no progression. Attraction and Repulsion, Reason and Energy, Love and Hate, are necessary to Human existence.
> From these contraries sprang what the religious call Good & Evil. Good is the passive that obeys Reason. Evil is the active springing from Energy [plate 3].

Crowley and Blake agree that Good and Evil are "names for sides" (59), rather than moral positions. However, in *Good Omens* and *Marriage* alike, human flourishing depends on both contraries striving in perpetual opposition. Crowley reflects that if Armageddon reaches its ultimate end: "No more world" (26). The final triumph of either side means sterility and spiritual death; life, in its most expansive sense, depends on a relationship *between* contraries, and on their embodiment *within* the human heart, exemplified by Adam Young (353; 383), and in the ending's tender/awkward "marriage" of witch with witchfinder, and demon with angel.

The novel embraced Romantic Satanism's delight in the energy of perpetual opposition but, relying on the camaraderie offered by their characterization as Cold War agents, shrugged off "ineffable," abstract intellectual paradoxes as largely irrelevant to the mundane love between angel and demon. The adaptation, however, pursued the peculiar affective qualities of theological conflict inherent in the Romantic-Satanic tradition.

Archangel Ruined

This intensified conflict requires a truly satanic devil. In the novel, Crowley "did not so much Fall as Saunter Vaguely Downwards" (13), and "just hung around with the wrong people" (26), suggesting he lacks conviction in either direction. His opinion on whether his acts of temptation are truly adversarial or, like those of Job's Satan (Page 465; Job 1–2), enacting God's plan through him indirectly, shifts depending on whether he is teasing or appeasing Aziraphale (55–58). Indeed, Aziraphale regards Crowley as one of "God's creatures" (232). Crowley is a humble, humanized demon, whose powers are channeled into petty annoyances merely "because that was his job" (40).

In contrast, the TV adaptation recalls Romantic (and therefore Miltonic) characterizations of Satan, whose "form had yet not lost/ All her original brightness, nor appeared/ Less than Archangel ruined" (*Paradise Lost* I. 591–93). When screen–Crowley slithers up to Aziraphale on the wall of Eden, he transforms into a radiant Pre-Raphaelite angel immediately ("In the Beginning" 3:30), rather than continuing the conversation as a comical talking snake, as he does in the novel. Crowley also reveals his role in building the cosmos ("Saturday Morning Funtime" 8:52), elevating the demon closer to Lucifer who, in Act II of *Cain*, initiates the protagonist and audience into the mysteries of the cosmos. Still not Miltonically "magnificent," screen–Crowley is more tragic "Archangel ruined" than demonic drone.

This new emphasis on his pre-Fall angelic nature also renders his relationship with God/ Heaven far more antagonistic; in addition to repeating the novel's comical explanations of his Fall, the adaptation has him recall (amidst disorientating, choppy editing) his horrific plunge into the flaming pit of Hell (11:30), and he cries out to God:

Crowley: I only ever asked questions. That's all it took to be a demon in the old days. Great Plan? Lord—you listening? Show me a Great Plan! Ok, I know: you're testing [humanity]. [...] But you shouldn't test them to destruction ["Saturday Morning Funtime" 8:58–9:26].

Unlike novel-Crowley, he recognizes his Fall as a violent, traumatic punishment for questioning God's malevolence. Indeed, in episode three, Aziraphale prays for Crowley to be forgiven for cursing God's Great Plan, but Crowley rejects forgiveness ("Hard Times" 51:10–30). As Byron's Lucifer puts it: "If the blessedness/ Consists in slavery—no" (*Cain* I. 418–19).

Most importantly, the adaptation adds scenes in which Crowley makes precisely the moral points made by Byron's Cain and Lucifer. In the novel, too, he professed concern for animals suffering unjustly for the Fall of Man (54–55; compare *Cain* II. 152–53), but now he is also dismayed by God murdering innocents in the Flood ("Hard Times" 1:59–2:28; compare *Cain* II. 79–83), and by the agonizing crucifixion at Golgotha ("Hard Times" 2:58–3:10; compare *Cain* I. 164–66). Crowley's resentment sharpens over two consecutive scenes: at the Flood in 3004 BC, he is still naïve enough to be shocked at God's destruction of the innocent, but, in 33 AD, he immediately accuses the angel of coming to Golgotha to enjoy the fruits of his cruel labor ("Hard Times" 2:58–3:10). Like Byron's sly Preface to *Cain* (181–83), he is scrupulous in directing this criticism at Heavenly atrocities corroborated by scripture.

The novel's civil compromise between gentlemen-enemies becomes impossible for the Satanic Crowley on screen—and the resulting conflict is presented with terrible pathos that transforms the adaptation's characterization of Aziraphale, too.

Choose Betwixt Love and Knowledge

In establishing a relationship between devil and angel, Romantic Satanism might, at first glance, seem an ideal literary substitute for the specific historical context of 1990. After all, Byron's "The Vision of Judgement" has its Cold War moment when:

> ...[Michael] address'd himself to Satan: "Why—
> My good old friend, for such I deem you, though
> Our different parties make us fight so shy,
> I ne'er mistake you for a *personal* foe;
> Our difference is *political*, and I
> Trust that, whatever may occur below,
> You know my great respect for you; and this
> Makes me regret whate'er you do amiss—" [62. 489–96; italics in original]

However, while this looks like the same civility between enemy agents, Byron's satire hints that the external conflict has tainted the personal in a way that the Cold War does *not* taint Crowley and Aziraphale's friendship in the novel: an awareness of having once been closer, a "regret" for the beloved enemy's faults—and, therefore, a painful sense that the enemy *is* truly "amiss," although truly loved. Even with the most comical texts of Romantic Satanism one is often, like Newt regarding Shadwell's murky emotional life, "aware of skidding around the lip of some deep unpleasant pit" of despair (*Good Omens* 180).

Like other Romantic-Satanic texts, the *Good Omens* adaptation reflects upon the phenomenological and emotional texture of theological conflicts: how does it feel to be damned? How does it feel to watch your beloved submit to spiritual mutilation at the feet of a malevolent God? Preoccupied with that Calvinist paradox of damnation both predestined and chosen by free will (Rawes 133), Byron's *Cain* pursues the heartbreaking division between those who submit to tyranny and:

> Souls who dare look the Omnipotent tyrant in
> His everlasting face, and tell him, that
> His evil is not good! [I. 134–40]

Falling is characterized, simultaneously, as a willful expression of intellectual defiance and as an involuntary, essential trait, like the difference between cherubim created to know God and seraphim created for ignorant adoration (I. 419–23):

> Lucifer: …I scorn all
> That bows to [God], who made things but to bend
> Before his sullen, sole eternity;
> But we, who see the truth, must speak it [I. 237–40].

Although Lucifer declares that we must "Choose betwixt love and knowledge" (I. 429), this choice is characterized repeatedly as an urgent compulsion at the core of one's being: we "must speak." Clearly, the priority for Romantic writers is not so much resolving this theological (il)logic but illuminating the way in which obedience/ rebellion are *experienced* simultaneously as free choices and as essential, contrary compulsions of nature that cannot be changed by reason or argument.

While the novel used Cold War gentleman-spies as a model for friendship, the *Good Omens* adaptation depicts a far more emotionally-fraught ideological conflict where, to the Fallen, the Faithful are both incomprehensible as wretched "things" "made […] but to bend," *and* deserving of "scorn" for choosing submission. This frustration finds peculiar expression when the narrator of Blake's *Marriage* tries to enlighten a stubborn angel who snaps:

> thy phantasy has imposed upon me & thou oughtest to be ashamed.
> I answer'd: we impose on one another, & it is but lost time to converse with you whose works are only Analytics.
> Opposition is true Friendship [plate 20].

The statement that it is impossible to engage in meaningful debate with the Faithful seems to be contradicted by "Opposition is true Friendship." But Romantic literature scholar Fred Parker explains that "in six of the surviving nine copies of the *Marriage*, Blake has deleted that sentence by coloring, obliterating it beneath the dark waters from which his leviathan emerges, as if to withdraw the faith it expresses" (77–78). The *Good Omens* adaptation addresses precisely this dilemma when Crowley is compelled to "impose" enlightenment on Aziraphale—and it is just as unclear whether such imposition constitutes "true Friendship" or a futile, unkind expression of Satanic scorn for servile "things" created to be incapable of understanding:

> AZIRAPHALE: Crowley, you're being ridiculous. L-look I'm [...] going to have a word with the Almighty, and then the Almighty can fix it.
> CROWLEY: That won't happen! You're so clever! How can somebody as clever as you be so stupid?
> AZIRAPHALE: [stunned, quietly] I forgive you.
> ["Saturday Morning Funtime" 33:52–34:30].

Writhing in exasperation, Crowley announces his intention to abandon Aziraphael and flee to another galaxy. Byron's Lucifer might ask the obedient angels "How can somebody as clever as you be so stupid?"; Byron's Cain might ask it of Abel. The familiar differences between Crowley's direct, choppy statements and Aziraphale's cautious sentences now reinforce their mutual incomprehension, as does the blunt dismissal as "ridiculous," and the abrupt non-sequitur of unasked-for, unwelcome forgiveness. This is not a dialogue, but a clash of discordant declarations driving them galaxies apart.

Just as the adaptation reimagines Crowley's character as more Byronic-Satanic, so too does it strip Aziraphale of his worldly pragmatism (*Good Omens* 85) to make him willfully naïve—and his spiritual anguish all the more terrible. Crowley's increased bitterness forces Aziraphale to reject him in terms that range from their professional opposition ("In the Beginning" 29:50) to a profoundly hurtful assertion of personal dislike ("Hard Times" 52:28). Michael Sheen's performance as Aziraphale emphasizes that, far from being playful debates on "ineffability," their disagreements are in fact traumatic and painful: facing the Flood ("Hard Times" 1:59–2:28), he cries out in exasperation at Crowley's audacity in judging God and, far from smirking at the Crucifixion ("Hard Times" 2:58–3.10), as Crowley accuses him of doing, he grimaces and denies involvement in the decision. His obligation to choose Heaven over Crowley at the bandstand leaves Sheen's Aziraphale on the brink of tears ("Hard Times").

The insertion of a brutal angelic family for Aziraphale enables the adaptation, like *Cain*, to dramatize religious authoritarianism as a very immediate form of violence, and not merely an abstract intellectual debate; Aziraphale's misery interacting with other angels in Heaven—being alternately repelled and crushed under their contempt—is conveyed by the camera shifting queasily between shots far too close and too wide ("Hard Times" 38:55–41:30). Indeed, that Aziraphale clings to faith in Heaven for so long poses a question raised by religious philosopher Nathan Hilberg:

> could it plausibly be said that Abraham, the exemplar of faith, was in an abusive relationship with God? That is, did God manipulate Abraham, causing him harm by the psychologically and emotionally taxing situation he put Abraham in, commanding him to sacrifice his son Isaac? As the story goes, Abraham tolerated the cognitive dissonance this situation would have caused in that he acted on the mandate given by the God he revered to kill the son he loved [99].

Forced into a similar dilemma in both novel and adaptation—to call Heaven good despite its obvious evil—Aziraphale tolerates this cognitive dissonance by labelling contradictions "ineffable," and yet the adaptation takes a far darker tone by focusing abstract questions of theodicy through specific incidents of emotional, physical, and intellectual abuse not present in the novel: in "Saturday Morning Funtime," Gabriel shames Aziraphale for his humanly soft body (5:11), and Sandalphon punches him (41:20); later, the Heavenly quartermaster humiliates him in front of the Host ("The Doomsday Option" 7:36). In short, the adaptation follows *Cain* in allowing religious authoritarianism to infect interpersonal relationships, making it increasingly clear that Aziraphale has been turning on his beloved Crowley, like Abraham on Isaac, to placate his abusers.

The Marriage of Heaven and Hell

Gaiman declared that "part of the joy of writing a love story is the breakup" ("Hard Times" 51:58–52:12). Most of the adaptation's romance is conveyed not by the script but by gentle, whimsical music (for example, the lullaby theme used in the Blitz scene, "Hard Times" 23:55, or "A Nightingale Sang in Berkeley Square" in the series' closing scene), and by Sheen's facial expressions and tone of speech. The breakup in episode three, however, is clearly scripted as such in Crowley's insistence that "we're on our side," and Aziraphale's reply "There is no 'our side'!" ("Hard

Times" 52:42–50)—that is, no interaction between "contraries" that does not end in annihilation. Thus, the adaptation's romance maneuvers them into the most wretched intellectual and emotional stalemate of Romantic Satanism.

This stalemate has been eroded, however, by episode six, when Crowley invites Aziraphale to move in with him and, obviously touched, Aziraphale stammers that "my side" would disapprove; Crowley replies with a gentleness absent from previous arguments: "You don't have a side anymore. Neither of us do. We're on our own side" ("The Very Last Day of the Rest of Their Lives" 26:35–57). In contrast with their earlier discord, the soft tone and echoing of each other's language suggests a dialogue spiraling gently around a new understanding. Clearly, the only way out of immovable conflict is for the devil to forgo Satanic "scorn," and the angel to cease resisting painful knowledge.

The adaptation is not entirely original in this realization. Having shown the impossibility of conversing with stubborn angels in one "Memorable Fancy," Blake's *Marriage* introduces another "Memorable Fancy" on plates 22–24: "Once I saw a Devil in a flame of fire, who arose before an Angel that sat on a cloud"; the Devil makes the Angel "almost blue" with rage by offering unorthodox (but highly moral and humane) interpretations of the Gospels; however:

> When [the Devil] had so spoken: I beheld the Angel who stretched out his arms embracing the flame of fire, & he was consumed and arose as Elijah.
>
> Note. This Angel, who is now become a Devil, is my particular friend; we often read the Bible together in its infernal or diabolical sense [plates 22–24].

Characteristically cryptic, Blake seems to suggest that, once the angel finally allows himself to listen to the devil, he is convinced to embrace his flaming enemy—a transcendent, transformative experience leading to further enlightenment.

Good Omens cannot follow this precise pattern, as Aziraphale Falling might imply the triumph of Hell and the erasure of essential contraries. Instead, the adaptation allows its representative angel and devil to experiment with performing each other's roles, first intellectually, and then physically. Immediately after Crowley expresses Byronic scorn for Aziraphale's cognitive dissonance, Aziraphale struggles valiantly to negotiate that dissonance when confronted by the Heavenly Host, and an angel demands he chooses a side: Aziraphale suggests that his role in God's plan is to maintain the world and provide opportunities for *humans* to choose good over evil, rather than to destroy all of Creation and enforce the dominance of Heaven ("Saturday Morning Funtime" 40:49–42:00). Sheen's performance shows Aziraphale visibly and audibly terrified by this dawning realization, but his argument has been permeated by Crowley's Satanic questioning. Like Blake's *Marriage* (plate 3) Aziraphale realizes, much as novel–Crowley did, that angels (and, we may infer, their demonic counterparts) exist to facilitate human moral agency, rather than as moral forces in their own right (*Good Omens* 55). By the time the adaptation reaches its climactic confrontation with the Devil in the final episode, the Satanic argument has shifted from Crowley to Aziraphale entirely, as Aziraphale speaks for (and as) them both when he demonstrates to Adam his absolute acceptance of their shared function to stand on each side of humanity ("The Very Last Day of the Rest of Their Lives" 22:06–21).

The adaptation also goes further than the novel's Arrangement in pursuing the Romantic paradox of the Faithful and Fallen being absolute contraries and, simultaneously, part of the same Creation under different names. In episode three Aziraphale almost tempts Crowley to try oysters, before recoiling from stepping into his enemy's role as tempter ("Hard Times" 5:25). By contrast, in episode five, another angel tells Aziraphale he cannot possess a human body and Aziraphale exclaims "demons can!" ("The Doomsday Option" 8:31), and does, implying that he has finally overcome Heaven's propaganda, or his own stubbornness, which attempted to deny the true fluidity of angel/ demon nature (*Good Omens* 248). He now embraces the fact that an angel can behave demonically—even though he and Crowley still refuse to share the same body ("The Doomsday Option" 13:07).

These additional scenes foreshadow an entirely new sequence in episode six, in which Aziraphale and Crowley take the Arrangement to its ultimate conclusion and impersonate each other to evade execution. Again, their natures remain distinct, as evinced by their continuing immunity to holy water or hellfire—and yet the impersonation illuminates or liberates hitherto unseen aspects of their characters: confronting Aziraphale's abusers in Heaven, Crowley-as-Aziraphale exudes scornful politeness of almost Luciferian "magnificence" and menace ("The Very Last Day of the Rest of Their Lives," 43:50; "Defence" 1191). Meanwhile, Aziraphale-as-Crowley frolics about Hell in his underwear and insults the Archangel Michael; the screen frames him comfortably now ("The Very Last Day of the Rest of Their Lives" 44:9), in contrast with the queasy shifts in framing that characterized his visits to Heaven. Even when he resumes his usual form, Aziraphale squirms with glee recounting his defiance ("The Very Last Day of the Rest of Their Lives" 49:39). The transformation demonstrates not a bland merging of contraries but, rather, the most complete acceptance of each other's contrary nature—holding hands ("The Very Last Day of the Rest of Their Lives" 49:08) and experimenting with *becoming* their opposing counterpart. Fans have described their impersonations as "a love letter to each other by bringing forth the qualities they recognise as being so intrinsically important" ("Good Omens Round Table" 1:10:23–40). This wholehearted immersion in, and love of the enemy's distinctive nature, then, is the true Marriage of Heaven and Hell. In their final scene lunching at the Ritz, Aziraphale suggests that they were able to save the world because, by his demonic nature, Crowley is "just a little bit a good person," and Crowley agrees that Aziraphale is "just enough of a bastard to be worth knowing." ("The Very Last Day of the Rest of Their Lives" 50:57–51:27). The dialogue has changed slightly from the novel. Crowley no longer replies "bitterly" to this praise, but alas he loses that evocative "spark of goodness" he possessed in the novel (*Good Omens* 357). However, it is important that his goodness remains a distinct "little bit," rather than blurring his devilish nature and, although "enough of a bastard to be worth liking" becomes "knowing," we may recall that, in the Romantic-Satanic tradition, knowing is perhaps the more testing relationship. Byron's Lucifer insisted that one must "Choose betwixt love and knowledge" (*Cain* I. 429) but, in the end, Aziraphale and Crowley know and love the contraries within each other simultaneously.

Conclusion: Opposition Is True Friendship

Abandoning *Good Omens*' Cold-War setting meant sacrificing its sweet "sort of" friendship between enemies (41) for a Romantic-Satanic conflict which invests Crowley with a new Satanic energy and drives him and Aziraphale to the brink of tragedy. The playful debates shrugged off lightly as "ineffable" are rewritten as a bitter intellectual and moral conflict—and yet it is the intensity of this pain that demands its own resolution: the agonizing gulf between them *must* be bridged. This risky strategy hangs not only upon the hope that angels may eventually embrace enlightenment, but also on the hope that the devil, compelled by doubt, cynicism, and disloyalty to their Creator may, ironically, be an exemplar of unwavering fidelity to their beloved enemy.

The adaptation diverges again from the novel to foreground their Marriage of Heaven and Hell as *the* happy ending: the final scene is no longer Adam stealing apples, but demon and angel dining at the Ritz while "A Nightingale Sang in Berkeley Square." Even this restructuring reconnects with Romantic Satanism's literary ancestry in Crowley's announcement "Time to leave the garden" ("The Very Last Day of the Rest of Their Lives" 50:14), followed by that final toast "To the world"; thus, as *Paradise Lost* concluded

> The world was all before them, where to choose
> Their place of rest, and Providence their guide;
> They, hand in hand, with wandering steps and slow,
> Through Eden took their solitary way [XII. 645–69].

The most final ending, and the most hopeful beginning, Aziraphale and Crowley's "solitary way" of Marriage between contraries was as unthinkable to Aziraphale in episode three, when he cried "there is no 'our side'!," as it would be unthinkable to Byron's Lucifer. Indeed, in six of the nine surviving copies of Blake's *Marriage of Heaven and Hell*, the narrator's attempt to share his vision with a stubborn angel ends in frustration—"it is but lost time to converse with you" (plate 20)—and an image of the raging Leviathan.

However, in three of the nine copies of *Marriage*, the confrontation ends with the assertion that "Opposition is true Friendship." Parker argues that the variation suggests "equivocation" (78). Yet the variation might also indicate that dialogue between the Faithful and the Fallen is *usually* impossible, but *sometimes* this dialogue is love, enlightenment, and salvation. The *Good Omens* adaptation's peculiar contribution to the English Romantic-Satanic tradition, then, is that its devil persists in this dialogue, again and again, in the face of rejection, until he and Aziraphale reach that version of the *Marriage* where Opposition is an expression of steadfast love.

Works Cited

"Ace August: *Good Omens* Round Table." *Three Patch Podcast*, episode 95. 1 August 2019. https://three-patch.com/2019/08/01/episode-95/. Accessed 27 June 2020.

The Bible. Authorized King James Version, Collins.

Blake, William. *The Marriage of Heaven and Hell*, 1790, Dover, 1994.

Byron, Lord George Gordon. *Cain*, 1820. *The Major Works*, edited by Jerome J. McGann, Oxford University Press, 2000, pp. 881–983.

Byron, Lord George Gordon. "The Vision of Judgement," 1822. *The Major Works*, edited by Jerome J. McGann, Oxford University Press, 2000, pp. 939–68.

"Considered Major Catch Soviet Agent Defects," *Globe & Mail* [Toronto, Canada], 21 February 1986, p.10. *Gale OneFile: News*, https://link.gale.com/apps/doc/A165495964/STND?u=chesterc&sid=STND&xid=83af96e3. Accessed 27 December 2019.

"The Doomsday Option." *Good Omens*, written by Neil Gaiman, directed by Douglas Mackinnon. BBC/ Amazon Prime Original, 2019.

Empiricus, Sextus. *Outlines of Pyrrhonism*, III.3. *The Skeptic Way: Sextus Empiricus's Outlines of Pyrrhonism*, translated by Benson Mates, Oxford UP, 1996, pp. 173–5. *The Problem of Evil: A Reader*, edited by Mark Larrimore, Blackwell, 2001, pp. 35–7.

Gaiman, Neil. Commentary in "Hard Times" (episode 3). *Good Omens*. BBC, 2019. DVD.

"Hard Times." *Good Omens*, written by Neil Gaiman, directed by Douglas Mackinnon, BBC/ Amazon Prime Original, 2019.

Hilberg, Nathan. "Cognitive Dissonance and 'The Will to Believe.'" *Fudan Journal of the Humanities and Social Sciences*, vol. 10, no. 1, 2017, pp. 87–102. *Springer Journals*. DOI: 10.1007/s40647-016-0130-2. Accessed 29 August 2019.

Hume, David. *Dialogues Concerning Natural Religion*, edited by Richard H. Popkin, Hackett, 1980, pp. 58–66, 74–6. *The Problem of Evil: A Reader*, edited by Mark Larrimore, Blackwell, 2001, pp. 216–23.
"In the Beginning." *Good Omens*, written by Neil Gaiman, directed by Douglas Mackinnon. BBC/Amazon Prime Original, 2019.
McGann, Jerome. *Byron and Romanticism*, edited by James Soderholm, Cambridge University Press, 2002.
Milton, John. *Paradise Lost*, 1667 edition. Penguin, 1996.
Page, Sydney H.T. "Satan: God's Servant." *Journal of the Evangelical Theological Society*, vol. 50, no. 3, 2007, pp. 449–65, *ProQuest*, https://search.proquest.com/docview/211186194?accountid=14620. Accessed 28 January 2020.
Parker, Fred. *Devil as Muse: Blake, Byron, and the Adversary*, E-book, Baylor University Press, 2011.
Pauw, Amy Plantinga. "Election," *The Cambridge Dictionary of Christian Theology*, E-book, edited by Ian A. McFarland et al., Cambridge University Press, 2011, pp. 160–62.
Pratchett, Terry, and Neil Gaiman. *Good Omens: The Nice and Accurate Prophecies of Agnes Nutter, Witch*. Corgi, 1991.
Rawes, Alan. "Byron's Romantic Calvinism." *Byron Journal*, vol. 40, no. 2, 2012, pp. 129–141. doi:10.3828/bj.2012.16. Accessed 8 June 2020.
"Saturday Morning Funtime." *Good Omens*, written by Neil Gaiman, directed by Douglas Mackinnon. BBC/Amazon Prime Original, 2019.
Schock, Peter A. "'The Marriage of Heaven and Hell': Blake's Myth of Satan and Its Cultural Matrix." *ELH*, vol. 60, no. 2, 1993, pp. 441. *Gale General OneFile*, https://link.gale.com/apps/doc/A14362365/ITOF?u=chesterc&sid=ITOF&xid=92c0e6c2. Accessed 24 January 2020.
Shelley, Percy Bysshe. "A Defence of Poetry," composed 1821, *Romanticism: An Anthology, Third Edition*, edited by Duncan Wu. Blackwell, 2006, pp. 1184–99.
Shelley, Percy Bysshe. "On the Devil and Devils." *The Prose Works of Percy Bysshe Shelley, Second Edition*, vol. II, edited by Harry Buxton Forman, Reeves and Turner, 1880, pp. 381–406. www.en.wikisource.org/wiki/The_Prose_Works_of_Percy_Bysshe_Shelley/On_the_Devil,_and_Devils. Accessed 30 May 2020.
"Soviets Take in Renegade CIA Agent." *UPI Archive: International*, 7 August 1986. *Gale OneFile: News*, https://link.gale.com/apps/doc/A446386387/STND?u=chesterc&sid=STND&xid=db925f07. Accessed 27 December 2019.
The Spy Who Came In from the Cold. Directed by Martin Ritt, performances by Richard Burton and Claire Bloom, Salem Films/Paramount, 1965.
"The Very Last Day of the Rest of Their Lives." *Good Omens*, written by Neil Gaiman, directed by Douglas Mackinnon. Amazon Video, BBC/Prime Original, 2019.

Naming, Artifacts, and Texts in *Good Omens*

Adam's Task
Naming and Sub-creation in Good Omens
Janet Brennan Croft

Names are, in one sense, the outward indication of a power negotiation. The *namer*, the one who bestows a new name or uses an already-given name, reveals, through the choice of name they give or use, their relationship to that which they *name*. The act may indicate a more or less equal relationship; it may represent an attempt to exert power over someone or something by imposing a name on it or by using a name that will influence those who hear it; or it may be an act of submission and ingratiation, using a name to flatter or placate someone or something more powerful. One's personal name is a nexus for many deeply important concepts and feelings about being a person and having a place in the world in relation to other people, to a family, and to that which is ineffable.

Naming may also be performed as a magical act, as a form of *logizomai*—that is, bestowing a name in order to pronounce something to be equivalent to, or encourage something to become, what the namer desires. This kind of naming may be self-reflexive: a person may rename him- or herself out of a desire for anonymity or a new identity, to indicate an alliance with someone or something else, or out of pride, hubris, or even shame. Names, as a special category of powerful (and, in a very real sense, embodied) language, are vitally significant, and naming is a primary and primal speech act. In Genesis 2, naming is the first officially delegated *sub-creational* task, for God does not name the animals, but brings them before Adam to see what he will call them.

Sub-creation is fantasy author and theorist J.R.R. Tolkien's term for a human being's right, need, and divinely sanctioned, even *appointed*, task to create, not *ex nihilo*, but as a being created in the image of a Creator. Sub-creation positions Art as the link between the Imagination and its realized result ("On Fairy-stories" [OFS] 59), and as a writer and a philologist Tolkien sees that artistic power first manifesting in language, in narrative art (61), in "combining nouns and redistributing adjectives" (64). Like the animals, "[T]rees are not 'trees,' until so named and seen—/ and never were so named" until named by Man, the "sub-creator, the refracted light" ("Mythopoeia"). In the beginning was the Word; and we name, as language-makers, as our first sub-creative task.

Terry Pratchett and Neil Gaiman, working individually, both take pleasure in names and have a keen understanding of how they work in story. In their sole collaborative work, names fizz and pop and delight. *Good Omens* (book, 1990; television series, 2019)[1] concerns itself with the last days of the world, from the birth of the Antichrist through several days after his eleventh birthday, the day he comes into his power. At its heart are the demon Crowley (David Tennant) and the angel Aziraphale (Michael Sheen), who, due to their long posting on Earth among humanity and their frequent interactions with each other, have forged a sort of working arrangement, and a fond attachment to the comforts and delights of the twentieth century (and to each other). They would rather Apocalypse *not* take place, thank you, and work together to derail what all the rest of the forces of Heaven and Hell look forward to with such anticipation.

As Pratchett was dealing with the terminal stages of his early-onset Alzheimer's in 2014, he asked Gaiman, as the only person who had the same "passion, love and understanding" for the book as he did, to commit to finishing the script and seeing it filmed (Whyman 13).[2] In creating the six-part television series script, Gaiman drew on their early–1990s attempts to write a screenplay, incorporating some of the new characters and situations they developed at that time and later (Whyman 10–11).

Good Omens, book and show alike, is rife with significant acts of naming by both humans and other sentient beings, from Crawly[3] renaming himself Crowley to the constantly changing self-claimed sobriquets of the Four Other Horsemen. While all humans have the power to name, to rename, to take a new name, to give a nickname, to deny a name, to deadname,[4] and so on, Adam Young (Sam Taylor Buck) has this power in spades. Reality bends to his will, and his acts of naming *stick* and change what he names. While other name stories will be examined in this chapter, the naming acts I will concentrate on will be the naming of Adam himself, Adam's naming of his hell-hound as he comes into his power, and his climactic act (in the show) of naming Satan to be *not* his father, and thereby making it so, retrospectively and eternally.

Powers and Principalities

Let us start at the level closest to the Ineffable, as the book does. It is not just humans who have the power of naming in this fictional world; supernatural beings also name, rename, self-name, and nick-name. Self-naming in fact shows up on the very first page of the text: the Serpent, introduced as Crawly, has decided the name doesn't fit his self-image and is thinking of changing it (*Good Omens* 5). When he reappears in the next chapter, set in contemporary times, he has a new name (15).

The television script draws attention to this when the demon Ligur (Ariyon Bakare) asks what name the Serpent is calling himself now and Hastur (Ned Dennehy) uses the new name (*Script Book* 16). In a scene added for the third episode, Crowley says his old name Crawley was uncomfortably "squirming at your feet-ish" (*Script Book* 173). The script also establishes Aziraphale's modern alias as A.Z. Fell much sooner than the book (9). In the modern era, his counterpart goes by Anthony J. Crowley, a name Aziraphale says will take getting used to, and what does the J stand for, anyway (194)?

The cluster of names and naming activities around the Four Horsemen of the Apocalypse, or Apocalyptic Horsepersons, as they are called in the *Dramatis Personae,* is particularly interesting. Death (Brian Cox), War (Mireille Enos), and Famine (Yusuf Gatewood) retain their traditional names, but Pestilence has retired and been replaced by Pollution (Lourdes Faberes). Three of them also have aliases under which they operate in the human sphere. War is first encountered as an arms dealer called Scarlett (*Good Omens* 54), then becomes a war correspondent whose byline is Carmine "Red" Zuigiber (112).[5] Famine is known as Raven Sable and appears as a best-selling diet-book author (59) who later runs a food conglomerate called Newtrition (145).[6] Pollution, more variable (male in the book, but appropriately cast as non-binary[7] in the show), goes by a variety of names like White, Chalky, or Snowy (61), always playing a minor role in environmental disasters or the sort of research that creates things like plastics and petroleum byproducts and radioactive waste, and then moving on. Death, of course, is always Death; his only concession to disguise being a set of motorcycle leathers with HELL'S ANGELS on the back of the jacket.

Which leads us to the *other* Four Horsemen. In the book, the roadside diner in which the Four meet is already occupied by a gang of four motorcyclists. The humans are effectively swept up in the wake of the final ride to the place of Armageddon. Elated to be included, Big Ted, Greaser, Pigbog, and Scuzz go about choosing their own aliases as the incarnations of thoroughly modern problems like Grievous Bodily Harm or Really Cool People (*Good Omens* 269). These names, including others briefly considered like No Alcohol Lager and Treading in Dogshit, use the comic ineptitude of the Other Four Horseman to conceal pointed social commentary (a standard tactic of Pratchett in particular).[8]

Humans

Venturing yet further from contact with the supernatural, we might consider the Chattering Nuns of St Beryl. A Satanic order, they invert expectations; for example, being expected to speak whatever is on their minds at all times except for a half an hour on Tuesday afternoons (*Good Omens* 25). Their names are satires on traditional virtue- or saint-connected names taken in conventional orders: Sisters Mary Loquacious, Maria Verbose, Katherine Prolix, Grace Voluble, and Theresa Garrulous are among their members (*Script Book* 31 et seq.).

The Witchfinder Army is also a font of original and humorous names. In Puritan times Witchfinder Major Thou-Shalt-Not-Commit-Adultery Pulsifer (Jack Whitehall) was the one responsible for putting Agnes Nutter (born 1600, exploded 1656; played by Josie Lawrence), author of the centrally important *Nice and Accurate Prophecies*, to the torch (*Good Omens* 188); his name is similar to others in the Army of his time. His descendant Newton Pulsifer (also Jack Whitehall) and Agnes's descendant Anathema Device (Adria Arjona) become romantically involved and help save the world. The modern head of the much-reduced army, Witchfinder Sergeant Shadwell (Michael McKean), is a namer par excellence, padding the pay ledger (which both Aziraphale and Crowley bankroll, unbeknownst to each other), with Witchfinder officers named Jackson, Robinson, Smith and all its variations, household items once he ran out of names, and then some five hundred lower ranks, also mostly named Smith (*Good Omens* 176), as well as insultingly nick-naming his long-suffering neighbor Madame Tracy with a variety of vaguely Biblical epithets.

To return to Anathema Device: she has, oddly, two contradictory naming stories in the book, given on the same page. One is that her mother (Gabriella Cirillo) just thought *Anathema* was a lovely-sounding name (*Good Omens* 35), but this does not entirely make sense, because she is written about by name in Agnes Nutter's prophecies, handed down in her family for generations, and in the script her mother emphasizes that Agnes had made predictions specifically about her (*Script Book* 112). So while the name *Anathema* was predestined for her, a more conventional naming-story might be told to outsiders, like the baffled Immigration Clerk at Heathrow (*Script Book* 118).

Adam Young, the child Antichrist (more of him anon) is the focus of a great deal of naming energy, as a child to be named and as a powerful namer himself, once he comes into his full power. He and his friends constitute a gang darkly referred to in Lower Tadfield as the Them (*Good Omens* 121), a tight-knit group of four in thematic and symbolic opposition to the Four Horsepersons of the Apocalypse, each with a naming story of their own: Wensleydale [Alfie Taylor], whose parents don't even use his proper first name Jeremy but always call him Youngster (*Script Book* 132); Pepper (Amma Ris), who was christened Pippin Galadriel Moonchild but was Pepper to everyone but her mother upon pain of suffering her considerable fury (*Good Omens* 123); and Brian (Ilan Galkoff), whose name seems almost to be a position title, like the Janets in the TV show *The Good Place* (2016–2020): always the somewhat grubby supportive friend willing to go along with all of Adam's ideas (*Script Book* 133).

In the depiction of the imaginative play of the Them, there is a great deal of fun with names and words. They role-play the British (formerly Spanish) Inquisition, sprinkling their speech with bits of fake Spanish and Latin and referencing Torturemada in place of Torquemada (*Good Omens* 133). Adam confuses *occultist* with *oculist* (137), and uses *nucular* for *nuclear* (139), is excited about the *Aquarium* Age (151), talks about *Atlantisans* rather than Atlanteans (152), and references Madame *Blatvatatatsky* (161) and the secret city of *Shambala* and tunnels under the *Goby* Desert (157) which are inhabited by the Secret Master *Tibetters* (162). As Adam's powers start to grow and the wildly jumbled contents of his imagination start to become real, it is perhaps for the best that he never gets the names quite exactly right.

Adam Young, an Antichrist

Adam's personal name-story begins with the Chattering Nuns of St. Beryl, at their birthing hospital where, in the best tradition of the classic horror movie trope, the infant Antichrist is to be switched for the newborn child of the American cultural attaché's wife. The presence of local resident Dierdre Young (Sian Brooke), showing up to give birth at the same time, results in a mix-up where her baby winds up with the Americans, the American baby is adopted elsewhere,[9] and Mr. and Mrs. Young go home to Lower Tadfield with the little Antichrist.

But before the children can go home, they must be named. "The proper name," as literary scholar Michael Ragussis reminds us, "exerts the power of a magical wish which expresses the will of the family" (7), and in this case, the nuns attempt to influence the earthly parents of the Antichrist to express the will of Satan, reinforcing Ragussis' observation that "what is at stake in the naming process is no less than an act of possession" (7). Sister Mary Loquacious (Nina Sosanya), thinking that Arthur Young (Daniel Mays) is the American attaché, which he isn't, and the baby is the Antichrist, which he is, suggests Wormwood or Damien, referencing classic horror movies (*Good Omens* 33–34), but when she suggests Adam, Mr. Young looks down at the blond curls of the incarnation of "the Adversary, Destroyer of Kings, Angel of the Bottomless Pit, Great Beast that is called Dragon," and so on, and observes that he looks like the name Adam would suit him perfectly (40).

The adaptation adds a scene showing the parallel naming of the other child: Mother Superior (Susan Brown), more persuasive than Sister Mary, also suggests Damien to Harriet Dowling (Jill Winternitz), thinking *she* has the baby Antichrist, but Harriet settles on Warlock—perhaps in part to spite her husband (Nick Offerman), across the ocean in America rather than at her side, and fully expecting his son to be named Thaddeus Dowling III (*Script Book* 44).

Adam is a wonderfully ambiguous name, full of potential for good or evil, implying a state of prelapsarian balance and innocence, a fresh beginning, a child who could be as much God's as Satan's. In meaning, it derives from the Hebrew "adama," meaning earth or soil; whatever Adam's parentage, he is also of the earth, in a human body, and develops a deep human love of the landscape of his own little corner of the world.

"What Adam believed was true was beginning to happen in reality"

Up until the eleventh birthday of the three children, we spend time only with Warlock (Samson Marraccino), whom Aziraphale and Crowley believe to be the Antichrist. But when a certain event does NOT happen at Warlock's eleventh birthday party, they realize they have been on the wrong track all along. Crowley has told Aziraphale that the forces of Hell are sending the boy a hell-hound for his birthday to be his companion and protect him, and which Adam is supposed to name. Crowley expects it to be some bloodthirsty name like Killer. "If he *does* name it, we've lost." The Antichrist will come into his full power and Armageddon will be inevitable (*Good Omens* 66–67).

The hell-hound materializes in Lower Tadfield rather than at Warlock's party in London, and homes in on the voice it had been built to find and follow (*Good Omens* 75). Subverting all the expectations of Hell, Adam's rock-solid declaration that the dog he fully expects to get for his birthday will be a funny little mongrel with an inside-out ear, the right size to go down rabbit holes (78), transforms the hell-hound itself from a terrifying beast into Dog, immediately possessed by unlimited devotion to Adam and an overwhelming desire to jump up on people and wag his tail (80).

Adam's act—saying "I'll call him Dog" (*Good Omens* 80)—is his first major act as he comes into his powers on his birthday. As with the original Adam in the Garden of Eden, it is a sub-creative act of naming. Dog here is as "freshly named" as the animals in the garden (7); in the words of poet John Hollander's "Adam's Task," he "came for the name [Adam] had to give [...] in a fire of becoming," and for Adam Young as well as the biblical Adam, this work is "as serious as play."

Animal trainer and philosopher Vicki Hearne places a mystical importance on the naming of animals; it is when animals "learn their names" that they become capable of a reciprocal relationship with a human, and in the act of training, the "name becomes larger" and eventually the animal "and his name become near enough to being the same size" (Hearne 167). "Without a name and someone to call [him] by name," Hearne insists, the animal can't "enter the moral life" (168). As Katherine Mershon observed in her review of Hearne's work, this "relational redemption [...] allows for the restoration of a prelapsarian language between humans and animals" (Mershon 2); the name "give[s] the soul room for expansion" but also allows us, the humans in the equation, to "return to Adam's divine condition" where a name is the invocation of a unique individual rather than a mere generic label (Hearne 170).[10] The process of training creates "a new language between an individual human and dog that radically changes the two of them"; "the dog and the human being are [thus] transformed together through the work of training" (Mershon 11–12).

The choice of the name Dog doesn't just save time; it re-creates the hell-hound as what Adam considers the Platonic ideal of dog-ness, and even more specifically, a certain type of dog-ness in relation to a certain kind of human-ness. Adam, the quintessential eleven-year-old boy, wants a dog he can have fun with (78). Mr. Young notes that they look at each other like they were meant to be together (*Script Book* 157). In a voiceover in the script, God ruminates on nature and genetics in a way that implies that that Dog had been rewritten down to the level of his DNA by Adam's naming (*Script Book* 203). In a nicely ambiguous passage, Adam notes that he is working assiduously to teach Dog to mind him, since his *father* has said he can only keep Dog if he trains him properly. Dog learns to obey his Master's voice, and his hellish origins fade ever further away (*Good Omens* 137).

It is all the more poignant, then, when, at the height of Adam's demonic temptation to remake the world, when his friends have turned away from him in horror and revulsion, Dog also rejects him, siding with the Them. "Give me back my dog," howls Adam, and Pepper reminds him that Dog is his own creature and free to make his own decisions, including rejecting a Master who's lost his moral compass. But Dog is the first to realize when Adam has overcome his temptation, licking the boy's face in joyful reunion (*Script Book* 367–368). Through naming and training, Dog has developed a moral life of his own, and even plays a role in the apocalyptic showdown with the Four Horsepersons. The closing scene of the book[11] overlays imagery of the tarot Fool card over the unfallen Edenic play of a boy and his dog among the apple trees of late summer in rural England.

"Adam rarely did what his father wanted"

The entire reason the Antichrist, the offspring of Satan, exists is to bring about Armageddon, the culmination of the Great Plan, the final battle between good and evil to determine the ultimate fate of the world—or as Adam cannily observes, to see who's got the more dominant gang (*Good Omens* 342). Adam and the Them defeat the Four Horsemen of the Apocalypse as a team, but Crowley at least knows that's not the end of it; Adam still has a solo task to face.

Gabriel (Jon Hamm)[12] and Beelzebub, both mightily desiring Armageddon as the proper conclusion of the Great Plan, each alternately threaten and cajole Adam, perhaps the least effective tactic that can possibly be used with a stubborn and intelligent eleven-year-old boy—especially one who has already faced temptation and come out the other side with a very clear idea of what he is *not* going to do with his powers. In the show, Gabriel chastises Adam and suggests someone should tell his (unearthly) father, and Beelzebub makes sure that happens (*Script Book* 425).

It's not entirely clear *what* Adam does in the book, but there are clues. Crowley realizes that Adam's powers could bend reality—could make someone not only cease to exist, but never to have existed at all (*Good Omens* 340). Adam waves his hand, and Satan's imminent threatened appearance on the scene simply ... doesn't happen (350).

The show is less subtle about it, making it clear that there is a distinction to be made between Adam's harmless human father and his Satanic father, coming to destroy Adam for his refusal to start the battle (*Script Book* 428). As Satan (Benedict Cumberbatch) erupts through the pavement of the deserted airfield, Crowley urgently explains to Adam that right now, he has the ability to alter reality (429). When Satan demands that his rebelling son come before him, Adam rejects him as a deadbeat father, only turning up now because Adam's come into his power, and with no right to discipline him after being absent for eleven years. And then, the clincher that bends reality to Adam's will, that sub-creates a new reality: "You're not my dad. You never were." At that point, it is true and always has been true; solid and comfortingly concerned Mr. Young *is* his dad, approaching through the smoke haze left by the banished Satan, and Satan ... is *not*, and *never has been*, Adam's father.

Adam has effectively renamed Satan from his-father to not-his-father, eternally and retroactively, and reiterated that Mr. Young is and always has been his one and only father. Ragussis suggests that "certain novels are designed as the moral trial of the child," concerned with a "battle to possess" and "struggle to indoctrinate" the child (35), where "two adversary camps seek the power to name the child" (39). Here the child claims the power to cross out the name of the father who has tried to possess and indoctrinate him.

Jungian analyst Jean Shinoda Bolen, in speaking of the major Greek gods, points out that these powerful figures exemplified the "dark side of the patriarchy" and were often "hostile towards their children, especially towards sons, whom they feared would challenge their authority" (18). Such a "destructive father" (18) will insist that his children "not differ from him or deviate from his plans for them" (22). He will "consume" his son's life, whether that son "lives out his father's ambitions" or "the son's own bent differs from the position his father expects him to play" (26); this father's fear is that "unless he is swallowed up in some way a son will someday be in a position to challenge his father's power and overthrow his authority" (29).

But Adam did not grow up with Satan present in his life; as Crowley points out, neither side had a representative there to influence him. He's neither the incarnation of Good nor Evil: "he's just ... a *human* incarnate" (*Good Omens* 245).[13] Instead he grew up with Arthur Young, stereotypical suburban dad with a pipe and a mustache and a perfectly-maintained car and a comfortable soul; the sort who thinks confining Adam to the house and stopping his pocket money for two weeks is a strict punishment (*Script Book* 437), though Adam knows it will all be forgotten by tomorrow (460).

In a scene not included in the final episode, Arthur tells a nosy neighbor he's proud of his son (439). Arthur is not the father as Evil Incarnate or Good Incarnate, but loving, decent, solid, and simply human incarnate. One can hardly picture Arthur and Dierdre Young having any other names,[14] or their solidity changing one bit. They are such fixed points for Adam, representing "stability, the epitome of goodness" (Sian Brooke, quoted in Whyman 187), that even at the height of Adam's temptation to remake the world, when he says he will make his friends new parents to replace the old—he seems to imply this will not apply to himself (*Script Book* 300), since all he wants is Tadfield, his own personal vision of paradise (365).

Conclusion

The sudden burst of playful naming creativity on the part of the hitherto unimaginative Other Four Horsemen points us in the direction of a hypothesis compatible with Tolkien's concept of sub-creation in "On Fairy-stories": increasing closeness or receptiveness to the supernatural, to fantasy and imagination, seems to heighten the individual's sub-creative power and hence their power to name. A fizzing fecundity of sub-creative power seems to increase as beings originate closer to, or draw nearer to, or open up to, the Ineffable source of creation. Human children at play, occultists, Satanist nuns, and Witchfinders are more open to this influence than the average London pedestrian who *knows* that ancient Bentleys can't do 90 mph in the heart of the city and therefore they did *not* actually see it happen—the sort of person who, in Tolkien's formulation, "dislike[s] any meddling with the primary World, or such small glimpses of it as are familiar to them" (OFS 60). This applies to supernatural beings as well; powers and principalities who are closer to God (or Satan), or more flexible in their habits of mind, appear to have more power to name.

Adam's power is far more than human, and given his supernatural parentage, rivals all but the power of the Creator itself. Tolkien might characterize the conundrum facing Adam as the conflict between Enchantment, which, as we see in the games the Them play, "produces a Secondary World into which both designer and spectator can enter, to the satisfaction of their senses when they are inside"—and Magic, which Tolkien distinguishes as the operation of "*power* in this world, domination of things and wills" (OFS 64). Adam has the wisdom to know his limits, and postulate potential actions to their unforeseen conclusions, as he does in refusing to bring the whales back—knowing full well that wouldn't stop humans from killing them (*Good Omens* 346). He could bring them back, but he can't change human nature without doing enormous harm to the balance of the world. Enchantment and art are our appropriate *métier* as human sub-creators—not the desire for power, which Tolkien calls "the mark of the mere Magician" (OFS 64).

"We make," Tolkien declares, "in our measure and in our derivative mode, because we are made: and not only made, but made in the image and likeness of a Maker" (OFS 66). Naming is, in this Biblical and mythological sense, our first and greatest sub-creative power as humans and not to be taken lightly, but approached, as Adam does his powers, with a sense of responsibility (*Good Omens* 346). We may, as Pratchett and Gaiman have done, fill "all the crannies of the world" with not-so-evil demons and slightly tarnished angels and perfectly human Antichrists. It is our right to sub-create: "The right has not decayed. / We make still by the law in which we're made" (Tolkien, "Mythopoeia").

Notes

1. The original book will be cited as Good Omens, the filmed miniseries by the episode title, and the script book (which does not match the filmed series dialogue and settings precisely) as *Script Book*.
2. I heard Neil Gaiman speak on 30 May 2019, the day the series was released, at Rutgers University in New Jersey, and many of us in the audience had already seen at least the first episode. Gaiman's recounting of his collaboration with the late Sir Terry Pratchett and his intent to honor his memory in the adaptation was quite moving.
3. The original book has *Crawly*; the script book spells it *Crawley*.
4. "Deadnaming" is the act of referring to someone by a previously held name against their will; it is a particularly disrespectful tactic used frequently, but not exclusively, against transgender individuals.
5. *Zuigiber* was a typo for *Zingiber*, which Neil Gaiman says he and Pratchett liked and therefore kept (@neilhimself). *Zingiber* is the genus name for the ginger plant. The name gets changed back to *Zingiber* in the script book (101).
6. Sable, in this position, makes use of his own power to name, naming products with no actual food content whatsoever CHOW™ and SNACKS™ and MEALS™ (*Good Omens* 146).
7. In the show, deliberate genderfluid and genderblind casting for the supernatural characters, while keeping their names unchanged, emphasizes their quintessential lack of gender: God is voiced by Francis McDormand; Beelzebub (Anna Maxwell Martin), Dagon, Lord of the Files (Elizabeth Berrington), Uriel (Gloria Obianyo), and Michael (Doon Mackichan) are all played by female actors, and Crowley is twice depicted as female, while Aziraphale shares Madame Tracy's (Miranda Richardson's) body and voice for several hours (see Casillas for the significance of these casting and writing choices).
8. The Other Four Horsemen sequence was scripted and cast for the television series, but unfortunately never filmed. In this version Death's coat has, picked out in rhinestones on the back, the iconic bat-winged hourglass used as a printer's dingbat throughout the original book (*Script Book* 472).
9. Gaiman and Pratchett do tidy away this loose end properly (*Good Omens* 122n, 373–374).
10. In the terms devised by Owen Barfield, an Inkling and a strong influence on Tolkien's thoughts on language, the name-as-invocation might be thought to belong to the *metaphoric* stage of language, where there is an "identity of word and thing, word and will" (Croft 82) and there is "potential magic in any use of words" (Frye, qtd. in Croft 82). The name-as-label belongs more to the *demotic* phase of language, where "subject and object are clearly separated" (Croft 83) and "the word has no power to be anything but a word" (Frye, qtd. in Croft 83).
11. The televised series changes its placement and ends with Aziraphale and Crowley dining at the Ritz instead ("The Very Last Day of the Rest of Their Lives"), the focus of the show having shifted to emphasize their relationship.
12. This role goes to the Metatron in the book.
13. Compare this to how Warlock grew up. In an effort to achieve exactly this balanced

result, Crowley and Aziraphale took roles as gardener, nanny, and tutors in Warlock's household, attempting to influence the child equally in the directions of good and evil nearly from birth. Adam arrives at the same place naturally.

14. Dierdre is a name of a princess who suffered many sorrows in Irish mythology, and Arthur of course references King Arthur.

Works Cited

Bolen, Jean Shinoda. *Gods in Everyman: Archetypes That Shape Men's Lives.* 25th anniversary edition. Harper, 2014.
"The Book." *Good Omens.* Dir. Neil Gaiman. Perf. David Tennant, Michael Sheen, et al. Episode 2. BBC Worldwide, 2019.
Casillas, Caspian. "'Good Omens' Radical Take on Non-Binary Representation." The Geekiary. 14 Aug. 2019. https://thegeekiary.com/good-omens-radical-take-on-non-binary-representation/68751.
Croft, Janet Brennan. "The Name of the Ring; Or, There and Back Again." *Mythlore*, vol. 35, no. 2 (#130), 2017, pp. 81–94.
"The Doomsday Option." *Good Omens,* written by Neil Gaiman, performances by David Tennant, Michael Sheen, et al, season 1, episode 5. BBC Worldwide, 2019.
Gaiman, Neil *The Quite Nice and Fairly Accurate Good Omens Script Book.* William Morrow, 2019.
"Hard Times." *Good Omens,* written by Neil Gaiman, performances by David Tennant, Michael Sheen, et al., season 1, episode 3, BBC Worldwide, 2019.
Hearne, Vicki. *Adam's Task: Calling Animals by Name.* Knopf, 1987.
Hollander, John. "Adam's Task." *Selected Poetry.* Knopf, 1993. https://www.poetryfoundation.org/poems/49110/adams-task.
"In the Beginning." *Good Omens,* written by Neil Gaiman, performances by David Tennant, Michael Sheen, et al., season 1, episode 1. BBC Worldwide, 2019.
Mershon, Katharine. "The Theology of Dog Training in Vicki Hearne's *Adam's Task.*" *Religions*, vol. 10, no. 25. 2019. www.mdpi.com/journal/religions, doi:10.3390/rel10010025.
@neilhimself (Neil Gaiman). "@Italian_Hobbit It was a typo that we liked. It was originally meant to be Zingiber." Twitter, 31 Mar. 2016, 1:28 p.m., twitter.com/neilhimself/status/715606704306720768?lang=en.
Pratchett, Terry, and Neil Gaiman. *Good Omens: The Nice and Accurate Prophecies of Agnes Nutter, Witch.* Illustrated by Paul Kidby. Limited edition. Gollancz, 2019.
Ragussis, Michael. *Acts of Naming: The Family Plot in Fiction.* Oxford University Press, 1986.
"Saturday Morning Funtime." *Good Omens,* written by Neil Gaiman, performances by David Tennant, Michael Sheen, et al., season 1, episode 4. BBC Worldwide, 2019.
Tolkien, J.R.R. "Mythopoeia." *Tree and Leaf, Including the Poem Mythopoeia*, Houghton Mifflin, 1989, pp. 97–101.
Tolkien, J.R.R. "On Fairy-stories." *Tolkien on Fairy-stories*, edited by Douglas A. Anderson and Verlyn Flieger, HarperCollins, 2008, pp. 27–84.
"The Very Last Day of the Rest of Their Lives." *Good Omens,* written by Neil Gaiman, performances by David Tennant, Michael Sheen, et al., season 1, episode 6. BBC Worldwide, 2019.
Whyman, Matt et al. *The Nice and Accurate Good Omens TV Companion: Your Guide to Armageddon and the Series Based on the Bestselling Novel by Terry Pratchett and Neil Gaiman.* HarperCollins, 2019.

The Book as Character
Tracing Textual Elements of Good Omens Across the Novel and Miniseries

TARA PRESCOTT-JOHNSON

Terry Pratchett and Neil Gaiman's *Good Omens* (1990) has been an underappreciated text since its original publication, partly because it bears the double burden of existing in two traditionally sidelined genres: comedy and fantasy. Until recently, books in these genres were considered "light," as if the pleasure in reading them somehow made them less worthy of critical study. The biases against the novel echoed a similar problem each of its individual authors faced early in their careers. As Gaiman noted about his co-author, Pratchett "exists in a blind spot, with two strikes against him: he writes funny books, in a world in which funny is synonymous with trivial, and they are fantasies" ("Neil Gaiman on Terry Pratchett" 387). This tendency to disregard "escapist" or enjoyable genres, Gaiman has noted, implies that "the only fiction that is worthy, for adults or for children, is mimetic fiction" ("Why Our Future" 9). Even within the fantasy worlds of its co-authors, *Good Omens* has often taken a backseat to its more famous half-siblings *The Color of Magic* (1983) and *Sandman* (1989–present). However, with the celebrated reception of the 2019 miniseries adaptation, a co-production between Amazon and the BBC starring David Tennant as Crowley and Michael Sheen as Aziraphale, *Good Omens* is now back in the spotlight where it belongs.

The Problems (or Side-Effects) of Adaptation

Following in the path of other recently-adapted Gaiman novels, such as *Coraline* (2009) and *American Gods* (STARZ 2017–2021), *Good Omens* is bringing renewed attention to its source material and inviting new generations of viewers and readers into the fandom. Many viewers have noted the strengths that the television series brings to the source material, including an opportunity to modify dated jokes to make them more appropriate for a twenty-first-century audience. It is easy to see all of the ways that the television series capitalizes upon and celebrates the opportunities of its medium, including choice of casting, special effects, music, and costumes, but also in the opportunity to reshape a story informed by nearly 30 years of social progress.

Yet one curious byproduct of the television adaptation is that, in doing such a good job playing to the strengths of its medium, the adaptation actually calls attention to the "bookness" of the original. It is this quality that helps *Good Omens* the television series also exist as a celebration of the book and print, despite being a live action streaming production. Just as *Good Omens* seeks to break apart the simplistic dichotomy of good and evil, these two iterations of the *Good Omens* story resist the unnecessary "book vs movie" argument, and instead celebrate the endurance and unique allure of print, one of the oldest technologies, well into the digital age.

Alan Moore and Adapting *Watchmen*

In thinking about these two versions of *Good Omens,* it is helpful to consider another recent fantasy novel adaptation by Gaiman and Pratchett's contemporary, Alan Moore. The adaptation process for Moore's graphic novel, *Watchmen,* began with a 2009 film which suffered from its fidelity to the original. Screenwriters David Hayter and Alex Tse and director Zack Snyder selected and reproduced scenes and dialogue from the text, practically cutting and pasting them to the screen, often at the expense of "filmic" qualities. The end result was a film that was often relentlessly faithful to the original text, yet regarded by many viewers as a failure as entertainment. This is in stark contrast to the 2019 critically acclaimed *Watchmen* television series created by Damon Lindelof for HBO, which is not a direct graphic novel adaptation but rather an extension of the original material. Although Moore is famously critical of adaptations of his work, Gaiman has been more willing to give his blessing, often participating in the process to great effect (Josie). His promise to Pratchett that *Good Omens* would be made sealed the deal and shortly after Pratchett's death, Gaiman started the first draft of the script (Dawn).

Neil Gaiman and *Good Omens*

If the range of adaptation is imagined as a spectrum, with absolute devotion and fidelity to the source material on one end and complete abandonment of the original text on the other, then the *Good Omens* television adaptation, released in the same year as HBO's *Watchmen*, hits the sweet spot: it builds upon the best of literary storytelling while also introducing new elements from the world of visual and performative arts. That Neil Gaiman finally received artistic control over the scripts for the Amazon version of *Good Omens* is no doubt why the series follows the original so faithfully. Gaiman wrote all six 1-hour episodes. "I've never show-run anything before," he admits, "But I knew what I needed to be able to make this thing was to cast it, to choose the director and just be able to say no when people wanted to cut the wrong bits" (Zemler).

The need to condense the story, highlighting the parts that work best in a visual medium, also necessitates editing. According to *New York Times* critic Mike Hale, "in streamlining the book—which was a digressive, more-is-more exercise in the tradition of *A Hitchhiker's Guide to the Galaxy*—[Gaiman's] made the wisest possible choice." Yet in the process of making the narrative "more straightforward," Hale adds, "Many fans of the book may be disappointed by what's been de-emphasized." One critical "character" that is nearly erased is the *Nice and Accurate Prophecies of Agnes Nutter, Witch* itself. Although the book appears and is referenced in the name of the second episode ("The Book"), in the miniseries the *Nice and Accurate Prophecies* is a plot point rather than a central part of the viewing experience. This is a large departure from the book's place in the source material.

The Power of Books in Good Omens

A chunk of the novel's humor is predicated on its physical, textual nature. The materiality of *Good Omens* is part of the experience of reading it. One of the fun aspects is that it is a text *about* texts—primarily the Hebrew Bible, the Book of Revelation, and *The Nice and Accurate Prophecies*, but also the *Buggre Alle This Bible* (44), the *New Aquarian Digest* (135), *The Tadfield Advertiser*, the *Boy's Own Book of Practical Electronics, Including a Hundred and One Safe and Educational Things to Do with Electricity* (37), comics with "a lot of exclamation marks in the title" (147), women's liberation self-help books, *Just Seventeen* "under plain covers" (147), and *Poultry World* (152).

It's also surprising how many texts and periodicals drive the plot: Newt Pulsifer becomes a Witchfinder through responding to an ad in the *Gazette* (and is hired to scour daily newspapers); the Antichrist Adam unwittingly brings UFOs, Atlantis, and tunneling Tibetan monks into existence as the result of reading the *New Aquarian Digest*, which also compels him towards bringing about Armageddon; and Anathema's sole purpose as a "professional descendant" is the care and study of Agnes's bound prophecies.

But the character most driven by books is the angel Aziraphale, who dutifully follows God, but "worship[s] books" (106). He is the consummate "book moth" (to borrow a term from Gaiman's *The Ocean at the End of the Lane*), a bibliophile who has a second-hand bookshop as an excuse to hoard books for his own collection. Aziraphale would nearly resort to "actual physical violence to prevent customers from making a purchase" (43). When Crowley wants to force his friend to admit that perhaps Heaven winning isn't what's best for life on earth, he hits Aziraphale where it hurts: "No *Daily Telegraph* crosswords. No small antique shops. No bookshops, either. No interesting old editions" (41). *Good Omens*, in many ways, is a book for book lovers, with extended inside jokes about religious interpretation and Biblical editions.

From the title page formatting of the novel as a play with a cast of characters to the self-referential moments where the narration directly addresses the reader, just as Agnes addresses her descendants, *Good Omens* often feels like a thinly veiled *Nice and Accurate Prophecies*. (And frankly has pretty on-the-nose predictions about climate change and the human species' tendency to destroy itself.) Agnes's book, though an inanimate object, clearly "speaks" and is very much a character in its own right. *The Nice and Accurate Prophecies,* perhaps like the TARDIS, is a silent, prescient object that faithfully accompanies different (re)generations of the same main character.

As a celebration of print and books, in all their forms, *Good Omens* frequently calls attention to its own print-based nature. For example, the excessively long footnotes "of an Educational Nature" that eat up half of the printed page draw their humor from the worst tendencies in academia, medicine, and fiction. Some contain tangents that take on a life of their own in the vein of David Foster Wallace. Others' conspicuous brevity supplies a humorous beat in the narration.

Perhaps the best example of this is the footnote for the diet food CHOW™. In the main body of the narrative, readers learn that if someone consumed CHOW™, "It didn't matter how much you ate, you lost weight" (142). There is a caveat, however. Just as modern pharmaceutical ads attempt to deemphasize side effects in a condensed section of quick speech or fine print, CHOW™ sinister undertones appear at the bottom of the page, in the footnote. People who eat it lose weight, "*And hair. And skin tone. And, if you ate enough of it long enough, vital signs" (142). Footnotes, like characters' internal dialogue, don't translate very easily to screen, and the most common workaround, voiceover narration, has limited use before becoming tedious.

This is just one of the "bookish" aspects of the text that Gaiman sacrificed in order to successfully translate the story to screen. Another delicious example, fit for a collector like Aziraphale himself, is the use of illuminated capitals. The Workman first edition of *Good Omens*, published in 1990 (and, later, the 1991 British Corgi edition), begins each chapter with ornately decorated capital letters created by children's book illustrator David Frampton. These woodcuts tie the novel to the tradition of Medieval illuminated manuscripts. Where the Book of Kells might feature a horned beast entwined with its own tail, *Good Omens* offers a snake in sunglasses coiled around the opening letter of "It was a nice day," a witch blithely burning at the stake (also appropriately serving as the first letter of Anathema's name), and the Angel Aziraphale absorbed in a book.

The capitals in fact directly match the description of the first page of "The Book" Anathema reads: "It did have a rather good eighteenth-century woodcut of Agnes Nutter being burned at the stake and looking rather cheerful about it" (38). By starting each chapter with the woodcuts, and indeed, one of the very same woodcuts that begins *The Nice and Accurate Prophecies*, this edition gives the reader an approximation of what it might be like to sit in a Special Collections room, holding an ancient text, perhaps the *Prophecies* themselves. The woodblock capitals serve as another opportunity for puns and jokes about elements from the Biblical world injected into contemporary culture.

The table of contents, frontispiece, marginalia, and back matter are all part of the apparatus of printed books that don't easily make the translation to screen, stage, or audio. They are funny because they are nearly obsolete yet defining features of books and they recreate the experience of reading older texts. The reader encounters *Good Omens* the way Aziraphale and Anathema encounter *The Nice and Accurate Prophecies* (although of course at a much less intensive level). Anathema must study Agnes's passages in order to determine what they mean, and when these same passages are reproduced in *Good Omens,* imaginary–Old-English-and-all, the reader must parse them alongside her.

Good Omens *as Textual Experience*

Good Omens is a text about texts, and invites readers to interpret the humor of Pratchett and Gaiman just as Anathema works to interpret Agnes. As Jessica Walker, has argued, "In the case of Agnes's text, the burden of contextualization and interpretation shifts from the author to the reader—the generations of Devices who bear the responsibility of making sense of her obscure, nonlinear style" (249–50). Maria K. Alberto uses the term "ergodic enterprise" to describe *Good Omens'* nonlinear, embellished style that forces readers to be especially active in their engagement with the text. The aspects of the print version that play a role in the metanarrative include the marginalia, the extended footnotes and textual asides, the play formatting, typesetting, the illuminated capitals (in certain editions), and the front and backmatter, including the authors' photograph.

These are all aspects understandably missing from the television miniseries (which must play to its own medium's strengths). In many ways, viewing the *Good Omens* series changes the way fans have thought about the original text itself, since the "readerly" aspects that are easy to take for granted paradoxically become more apparent through their omission. Unexpectedly, the textual elements of *Good Omens* receive a new kind of importance in the filmed series, which in turn generated new editions such as *The Illustrated Good Omens* and the *Script Book* which offer reflections of the film which offers reflections of the text.

These small features of the novel, while hardly necessary, are nonetheless hallmarks of the two authors. The extraneous, tangential details sometimes give more texture to a scene or description, but mostly, they seem to exist simply for the fun of it. In describing the tendency to insert these tidbits, Gaiman reveals:

> When Terry Pratchett and I were working on *Good Omens*, we needed shorthand ways to communicate with each other. And what I loved about talking with Terry was that he would come up with terms for things that there were not terms for, in ways to write comedy.... A "figgin" was a term that he had started using in Discworld ... initially you think it's something terrible like a body part ... and later you discover a figgin is a small raisin-filled pastry ... a little joke that becomes a running joke. But a running joke that then will pay off in some way toward the end. And they were distinguished from something that we built in *Good Omens* which Terry called "sherbet lemons" ... because there's a moment in the text where Adam the 11-year-old Antichrist has fallen asleep eating sherbet lemons ... and a nuclear power station discovers their reactor has gone missing ... and when they go and inspect the enormous room where the reactor used to be, the only thing they find is a sherbet lemon. So Terry would start using "sherbet lemons" to mean little things you'd throw into the text to make someone smile.... As opposed to a "figgin" ... which you would think is just a sherbet lemon, but then it would pay off ["Neil Gaiman Teaches..."].

The figgins and the sherbet lemons in *Good Omens* abound; so numerous, in fact, that on an initial read-through many people are puzzled as to which details to pay attention to and which to laugh at and leave aside in order to follow the main plotline.

Although the condensed form of a television miniseries has less room for extraneous material that doesn't directly serve the plot, some of Gaiman's favorites still make cameos, and they can also be preserved in the "special features" or "bonus scenes," and indeed, in the screenplay itself. Gaiman warns his readers as much in the introduction to the published screenplay, noting, "If any of you are hoping to learn anything about scriptwriting from this book, I should warn you that there are jokes in the stage directions, and there shouldn't be" (xii). The screenplay contains enough sherbet lemons for a meringue.

The Various Versions of Good Omens

Different versions of *Good Omens* include the figgins and sherbet lemons to different degrees, even among the print editions. For example, both the 1990 Workman first edition and the 1991 Corgi edition include a particularly playful take on the ubiquitous "author photo" genre, which is normally an overly serious black and white headshot that indicates that the work is by A Serious Writer. Author photos are a piece of marketing material and are not normally meant to be "read" as commentary on the text itself—except in the case of *Good Omens*.

A dual author photo appears in the first edition Workman hardback (in color) and the Corgi edition (cropped and in black and white). The image depicts Gaiman and Pratchett, full-length, relaxing outside an open stone doorway in Kensal Green Cemetery in London, with vines trailing down the weathered exterior (Campbell 64). Gaiman is dressed, as he often is, completely in black, wearing dark sunglasses, dark denim, and a black leather jacket beneath his signature mop of black unruly hair. It's only when viewing him alongside his co-author that Gaiman's aesthetic takes on a new resonance: where Gaiman is all in black, Pratchett is all in pristine white, from his crisp fedora and white turtleneck down to the cuffs of his white pants. His hands are neatly clasped, whereas Gaiman is comfortably sprawled on a ledge of the building.

These details clearly present Pratchett as the composed, genteel angel Aziraphale alongside Gaiman's casual demon Crowley. "I'm wearing white," Pratchett said at the time the photo was taken, "That way, when they come after us for writing a blasphemous book, they'll know I'm the nice one" (Campbell 64). By cosplaying as their own characters, Pratchett and Gaiman invite speculation of what a book coauthored by Aziraphale and Crowley might be (one expects Aziraphale would be stuck with all the revising). The author photo is so delightfully connected to the text that one review of the book actually references it. According to *The Times*, *Good Omens* is "Not quite as sinister as the authors' photo."

In aligning the creators with the two main characters of the book, the authors' photo invites the reader to imagine that the authors are actually the angel and demon, that if, after thwarting the apocalypse and perhaps taking in a dinner at the Ritz, Aziraphale and Crowley paired up to write their story. It's also pleasant to imagine each author divvying up the text by character and writing their half—although of course, that isn't the way Gaiman and Pratchett wrote the novel.

Subsequent editions of *Good Omens* dropped the authors' photograph, but the playfulness of representing the angel and the demon took new forms, such as alternative colors (black for Crowley, white for Aziraphale), alternating which author is listed first (Pratchett in UK editions, Gaiman in the U.S.), and embellishing cover fonts with haloes and pointed tails. Rather than encouraging readers to imagine the protagonists as versions of the authors, the most recent miniseries tie-in mass paperbacks, as well Paul Kidby's 2019 illustrated edition, offer actors David Tennant and Michael Sheen as stand-ins for Crowley and Aziraphale instead.

Like many of Gaiman's and Pratchett's later single-authored works, *Good Omens* gained cult status and was frequently shared from friend to friend. Gaiman has noted that this volume in particular shows up at book signings in dire straits, especially prone to near-death experiences in bathtubs. Through asking either or both authors to autograph their copies, fans added a new layer to the discourse in the physical copies. Just as *The Nice and Accurate Prophecies* accrued comments from generations of readers, so too do copies of *Good Omens*. Gaiman and Pratchett frequently signed their books in character, treating the book as if it were the *Nice and Accurate Prophecies* itself, advising fans to "BURN THIS BOOK!!" and offering helpful directions such as "apply hot match here" (see figure 1). (Luckily *Good Omens* books aren't hiding gunpowder and roofing nails between their pages.) Pratchett signed books confessing, "We made the Devil do it," with Gaiman adding the footnote, "*But we kept all the money" (Campbell 65). Appropriately enough, even the authors' autographs in *Good Omens* get footnotes.

The joking about book-burning and blasphemy of course was prophetic as well—the novel offended some religious conservatives who didn't even read it (and Gaiman and Pratchett fielded humorously oblivious questions from people who didn't realize the book was fiction). This escalated to new, ludicrous heights with the release of the miniseries, which inspired even larger misinformed censorship efforts, culminating in a 20,000 signature petition sent to Netflix demanding that *Good Omens* not be released (Ross). The only problem was that Netflix had nothing to do with the Amazon Prime series. The "negative" publicity backfired as fans gleefully circulated Netflix's sarcastic response: "ok we promise not to make any more" (@NetflixUK).

Readers often pick up on the "bookish" humor of the novel, such as the cross-referencing system that Agnes' descendants developed to decode her prophecies. Part card-catalog entry, part 3×5 recipe card, these entries are visually striking in the novel and serve as little puzzles for the reader as well. In 2017, *Good Omens*' fan and UCLA undergraduate Eddie Torres chose to create his own *Nice and Accurate* "prophecies" based on contemporary events such as the election of President Donald Trump (see figure 2).

This sort of engagement with the text is not possible in the television miniseries. Of course, the miniseries offers wonderful new additions to the original next, and in several important ways, improves upon the original—particularly in omitting misogynist and homophobic jokes. The miniseries turns the sustained jokes about

Figure 1. An autographed copy of *Good Omens*.

2017: Beware the manne of syckly orange skynne wyth hair of scragly hay, for he wyll dyvide hys lande turne many awaye from hym; he spreds hate and scorne across the worlde for many that live in hys owne realm, hys power wyll be one to fear as the ignorante do not cuestion his wordes.

perhaps some form of troll?... one of the Horsemen perhaps Famine or Pestilence? [Dr. Thos. Device, 1833]
refers to the rise of dictator in Germany?.. the appearance does not quite match [Edgar Device, 1943]
based on how this election is going, I think Agnes may have been warning against someone else, good luck America! [2016]

Figure 2. Eddie Torres's "prophecies" inspired by the *Nice and Accurate* notecards.

Aziraphale's gender presentation and instead plays them straight (for lack of a better term), taking the bond that exists between the two characters and turning it from a gag into the emotional core of the story. And it is important to note that some of the most intimate moments for Aziraphale and Crowley in the miniseries are built around books.

"The Book" (1.02) begins, appropriately enough, in Aziraphale's maroon corner bookshop in Soho. Inside, there are stacks of rich, jewel-toned embossed hardbacks clinging to every surface, the sort of curated chaos that is the hallmark of a one-of-a-kind book paradise. As the archangels enter in search of Aziraphale, they make a pathetic attempt at blending in as humans. Their ignorance about books underscores their lack of understanding of, and empathy with, humanity:

> GABRIEL: (*loudly*) I would like to purchase one of your material objects.
> SANDALPHON *corrects him.*
> SANDALPHON: Books.
> GABRIEL: Books. Let us discuss my purchase in a private place. Because I am buying, er....
> SANDALPHON: Pornography?
> GABRIEL: (*proudly and loudly*) Pornography.
> He picks up an (*obviously not pornographic*) vintage book [93–94].

The humor in the scene comes from Gabriel's cocky and completely obtuse performance. The human customers raise their eyebrows at the announcement of purchasing porn, but the two angels are oblivious. "Pornography" as a cover for buying *Mrs. Beeton's Book of Household Management* makes sense to them—if you don't understand what books are, you certainly don't know their genres. They are clearly out of touch with what porn is, what books are, and why humans—much less, a principality—would waste time with them. But the book is Aziraphale's holy object and the bookshop, his sanctuary.

Books and Love (Stories)

As literature scholar Raven Johnston notes, the bookshop symbolizes Aziraphale's humanity. His attitude towards selling books is unfitting for an angel, and his bookshop gets destroyed as soon as he gets discorporated. In discussing the filming of the miniseries, Gaiman noted, "The people who are making *Good Omens* are building a glorious edifice, a huge and unlikely place, part temple and part nightclub and a great deal of it is bookshop" (ix–x). To understand the story, to understand humanity, one must understand the bookshop. The archangels cannot ever understand Aziraphale because they fundamentally cannot comprehend the appeal of people or of books—which is in stark contrast to Aziraphale's friend of 6,000 years, Crowley.

In "Hard Times," Crowley demonstrates his affection for his friend through saving a stack of books. In a flashback from the London Blitz in 1941, Aziraphale meets Nazi spies in a church, bringing a stack of books of prophecy that Hitler wants. His plan is to use the books as bait to capture the spies, but then he himself is double-crossed. Crowley arrives, gingerly walking across the consecrated ground, to warn his friend that his "demonic intervention" has sent a bomb coming for the church—and it will require a miracle for them to avoid discorporation:

> *Boom—Huge Explosion. Fire And Light And Things Being Blown Around.*
> *So Cool An Explosion That I Am Typing In Capitals.*
> *They look up and the screen goes black.*
> Ext. The Rubble—Night—1941
> *Smoke and dust blow away, to reveal ... we're outside, because the walls of the church have gone. There is dust in the air. Crowley polishes his dark glasses with a handkerchief and puts them back on.*
> AZIRAPHALE: That was very kind of you.
> CROWLEY: Shut up.
> AZIRAPHALE: Well, it was. No paperwork, for a start. The books! I forgot all the books!
> They'll have been blown to....
> *Crowley reaches down, removes the leather bag from Harmony's dead hand, sticking out from the rubble. Hands it to Aziraphale.*
> CROWLEY: Little demonic miracle of my own. Lift home? [195–6]

In this scene, Crowley downplays (as always) the great lengths he has gone to in order to help his friend. He burns the soles of his feet, risks discorporation from the holy water in the church, and orchestrates the bomb to fall to save Aziraphale from the Nazis. But the coup de grace is saving the *books*, which he's miracled into a protective bag on site. In acting impeccably casual about his gift to Aziraphale, immediately changing the subject to "Lift home?" and walking away with barely a beat, Crowley reveals how deeply he cares about his friend, even though he is too proud to admit it. The camera closes in on Aziraphale's face as the magnitude of Crowley's actions dawns on him. Crowley has risked his life in order to save a pile of books because these are books that matter to *him*. The way to Aziraphale's heart is through books (with a side of sushi). In the next time jump, we see the characters in 1967 Soho, when Aziraphale meets Crowley in the car, this time with his own gift in return, a Thermos of holy water. This is the scene in the series where Aziraphale most openly bares his heart ("You go too fast for me, Crowley") and it notably comes immediately after the miracle books scene.

There are many ways to interpret the bond between Crowley and Aziraphale, and the other chapters in this volume argue for various definitions, but regardless of whether the audience sees them as platonic, ace/asexual, gay, friends in love, or something ineffable, this scene with the book shows how strong their bond is, and how much it means to both characters. And the miniseries makes it much more explicit than the source material. As Gaiman tweeted, "Whatever Crowley and Aziraphale are, it's a love story."

A parallel love story in the novel, between Newt and Anathema, is also predicated on (and predicted by) a book. When the follow-up volume to the *Nice and Accurate Prophecies* arrives at Jasmine Cottage at the end of the novel, Anathema must decide if she will read it, continuing her work as a "professional descendant," or leave it closed and let the future unfold in real time. The book ends without revealing her choice. "That the answer lies beyond the scope of *Good Omens* is perhaps the entire point," notes Walker, "The issue will always remain ambiguous and undefined, with no text left to guide us" (259). In the miniseries, however, her choice is clear: Anathema burns the sequel. Despite Anathema's choices in the novel and the miniseries, the work survives, both in the titles of the tales and the impact it has on the characters and the audiences.

Conclusion

In moving from a text-based to image-based sign system, the *Good Omens* miniseries sacrifices the over-the-top literary play of the novel and downplays *The Nice and Accurate Prophecies*' status from tacit character to secondary point that moves the narrative. Although the constraints of film reduce these areas of "bookishness," the miniseries highlights the importance of books in the narrative in other ways. And just as the original success of the novel led to television adaptation thirty years later, the resulting success of the miniseries is returning the favor, encouraging viewers to read the original novel. The latest iteration of the story is also able to engage in intertextual and metatextual commentary, much like the original, but now through fan-created animatics and fanfiction on sites like Archive of Their Own.

As *Good Omens* goes into its second season (which follows events that take place after the end of the novel) and is joined by other television adaptations in "the Gaimanverse," including *Sandman* and *Anansi Boys*, fans will have much to watch, read, and delightfully discuss ("An Evening with Neil Gaiman"). The editions and interpretations are multiplying, like Aziraphales dancing on a pinhead, and bibliophiles and cinephiles alike eagerly anticipate the iterations to come.

Works Cited

Alberto, Maria. "*Good Omens* (2019) and Adaptation as Ergodic Enterprise." Southwest Popular/American Culture Association Conference, February 20, 2020.
Campbell, Hayley. *The Art of Neil Gaiman*. Harper, 2014.
Coraline. Directed by Henry Selick, performances by Dakota Fanning, Teri Hatcher, and Jennifer Saunders, Universal Studios Home Entertainment, 2009.
Dawn, Randee. "Q&A: Neil Gaiman Promised a Dying Friend He'd Carry *Good Omens* Forward." *The Los Angeles Times*. June 18, 2019.
Fuller, Bryan, and Michael Green, creators. *American Gods*, Living Dead Guy, The Blank Corporation, and Starz Originals, 2021.
Gaiman, Neil. "An Evening with Neil Gaiman." Ace Hotel, Los Angeles. May 23, 2022.
Gaiman, Neil. *The Quite Nice and Fairly Accurate Good Omens Script Book*. William Morrow, 2019.
Gaiman, Neil. "Why Our Future Depends on Libraries, Reading, and Daydreaming: The Reading Agency Lecture, 2013." *The View from the Cheap Seats: Neil Gaiman*. William Morrow, 2016.
Gaiman, Neil, creator. *Good Omens*. Amazon Studios and BBC Studios, 2019.
Gaiman, Neil and Terry Pratchett. *Good Omens*. Corgi, 1991.
Gaiman, Neil and Terry Pratchett. *Good Omens*. Workman, 1990.
Hale, Mike. "Review: In 'Good Omens,' Angel and Demon Try to Save the World: Critic's Pick." *New York Times*. May 31, 2019.
Johnston, Raven. "Bibliophilia and Book Worship in *Good Omens*." Southwest Popular/American Culture Association Conference, February 20, 2020.
Josie, Bailey Joe. "Every Movie Adapted from an Alan Moore Story (& What He Said About Each)." CBR.com. July 5, 2021.
Kidby, Paul (illustrations). *The Illustrated Good Omens*. Terry Pratchett and Neil Gaiman. Gollancz, 2019.
Lindelof, Damon, creator. *Watchmen*, White Rabbit, Paramount Television, DC Entertainment, Warner Brothers Television, 2019.
"Neil Gaiman Teaches the Art of Storytelling." MasterClass, 2019, https://www.masterclass.com/classes/neil-gaiman-teaches-the-art-of-storytelling.
@neilhimself. "I wouldn't exclude the ideas that they are ace, or aromantic, or trans…they are an angel and a demon, not as make humans, per the book. Occult/ethereal beings don't have sexes, something we tried to reflect in the casting. Whatever Crowley and Aziraphale are, it's a love story." *Twitter*. June 8, 2019, 7:46 a.m., https://twitter.com/neilhimself/status/1137370226931228672
@NetflixUK. "ok we promise not to make any more." *Twitter*. June 20, 2019, 1:19 p.m., https://twitter.com/NetflixUK/status/1141787587390201862
Nicosia, Laura. "The Apocalypse and Other Silly Bits: *Good Omens*, Collaboration, and Authorial One-Upmanship." *Critical Insights: Neil Gaiman*, edited by Joseph Michael Sommers. Salem Press, 2016, pp. 166–177.
Ross, Charley. "Good Omens: Thousands of Christians Sign Petition Urging Netflix to Ban Amazon Prime Show for 'Mocking God's Wisdom.'" *The Independent*. June 21, 2019.
Walker, Jessica. "'Anathema Liked to Read About Herself': Preserving the Female Line in *Good Omens*." *Feminism in the Worlds of Neil Gaiman*, edited by Tara Prescott and Aaron Drucker. McFarland, 2012, pp. 246–260.
Watchmen. Directed by Zack Snyder, performance by Billy Crudup, Matthew Goode, and Jackie Earle Haley, Warner Home Media, 2009.
Zemler, Emily. "Nothing but 'Good Omens' as Neil Gaiman's Series Finally Hits TV." *Los Angeles Times*. June 5, 2019.

"Welcome to the end times"
A Conclusion

Amanda Taylor *and* Erin Giannini

Regardless of the medium, *Good Omens* is both apocalyptic catharsis and lesson manual. Coupled with an incessant loop of R.E.M. and one's beverage of choice, *Good Omens* offers an often absurd but still poignant journey of belief, doubt, wordplay, and contemplations of mortality, love, and friendship. As is often the case, it is up to the reader or viewer to take from the text what they will. Indeed, as this collection demonstrates, there is much to explore in any iteration of *Good Omens*. The Amazon Prime adaptation breathed new life into the novel, introducing fans of one medium to the other and providing new avenues of interpretation, analysis, and fan creation. Personally, we were thrilled to see the adaptation happen and to see Neil Gaiman so directly involved, though we wish Terry Pratchett had been able to contribute fully as intended.

As highlighted in this collection, Pratchett's absence was present, and Gaiman's mourning is visible in the love-filled negotiation of Crowley and Aziraphale's relationship. The implications of the story's refocus on this relationship have been well-covered in this volume. However, there is still space to parse the effects that David Tennant's and Michael Sheen's performances have on the novel's characterizations. As actors bring prior roles with them to every new character consciously or not, it will be interesting to (re)consider past and future performances in relation to *Good Omens*. We can see the dangerous fury and reluctant humanization of a Time Lord, the mercurial nature of Barty Crouch, Jr., and, of course, Tennant's Shakespeare acumen in Crowley. We can see the vexing and sometimes subtle mixture of propriety, wanton sensuality, and physicality of Sheen's past roles in the humanized angel Aziraphale. More than likely, we can see ourselves and relationships we've had in those we see between Crowley and Aziraphale, Adam and the Them, Shadwell and Newt, Newt and

Anathema, or any of the others in the texts. There is much left to explore in *Good Omens*, especially as a second season approaches. We hope that this volume encourages renewed scholarly attention to the novel, television adaptation, and fan works.

Gaiman and Pratchett's spirit of collaboration drove the genesis of this collection. We live approximately 750 miles apart and rely on instant messaging, social media, and text messages for communication. Five minutes into the first episode, Mandy sent Erin a message saying in part, "I already have ideas for SWPACA [Southwest Popular Culture/American Culture Association] projects. Such an incurable academic." Twenty minutes later, after another exchange of possible projects, Erin offered up the ultimate academic temptation: "Maybe you and I should consider an edited collection on it."

Temptation accomplished.

About the Contributors

Melissa D. **Aaron** is a professor of English at Cal Poly Pomona. She has two specialties—Renaissance drama and young adult fantasy literature—and teaches courses in Shakespeare and Harry Potter. She is the author of *Global Economics: A History of the Theater Business, the Chamberlain's/King's Men, and Their Plays, 1599–1642* (2005), and "'It's Just Lucky I Put Mr. Tibbles on the Case': The Spy Cats of Harry Potter" (2019).

Cait **Coker** is an associate professor and curator of rare books and manuscripts at the University of Illinois at Urbana–Champaign. Her research takes place at the intersections of gender, genre, and publishing history. She is the editor of *The Global Vampire: Essays on the Undead in Popular Culture Around the World* (McFarland, 2020) and the forthcoming *Sex and Supernatural: Critical Essays*.

Janet Brennan **Croft** (ORCiD 0001-0001-2691-3586) is an Associate University Librarian for Content Delivery at the University of Northern Iowa. She is the author of *War in the Works of J.R.R. Tolkien* and has written on the Whedonverse, *Orphan Black*, Terry Pratchett, Lois McMaster Bujold, and many other authors, TV shows, and movies, and is editor or coeditor of many collections of literary essays, including *Loremasters and Libraries in Fantasy and Science Fiction*. She edits the scholarly journal *Mythlore* and is assistant editor of *Slayage*.

Erin **Giannini**, PhD, is an independent scholar. She served as an editor and contributor at PopMatters and has written numerous articles about topics from corporate culture in genre television to production-level shifts and their effects on television texts. She is also the author of *Supernatural; A History of Television's Unearthly Road Trip* (2021) and *The Good Place* (TV Milestones), and coeditor of the book series B-TV: Television Under the Critical Radar.

Philip **Goldfarb Styrt** is an assistant professor of English at St. Ambrose University in Davenport, Iowa His work focuses on early modern literature and religious and political culture. He has also written extensively on the role of Reformation resistance theory in early modern literature, and its use of both Catholic and Reformed theology to question authority. In addition, he teaches frequently on fantasy and young adult literature, particularly in relation to how these texts recycle past concerns and attitudes into the present and future.

Mary **Ingram-Waters**, PhD, is an honors faculty fellow and principal lecturer at Barrett, the Honors College, Arizona State University, where she serves the

About the Contributors

honors community as its assistant dean. Her teaching and research addresses gender, sexuality, and popular culture. Her work has been published in *Transformative Works and Cultures*, *Sexualities*, *Public Understanding of Science*, and many edited volumes on fans and fandoms.

Pavan **Mano** received his PhD in English literature and cultural studies from King's College London and is presently Research Fellow in the Sarah Parker Remond Centre for the Study of Racism and Racialisation at University College London. He is a cultural theorist working around the intersections of contemporary literature, popular culture and affiliated intellectual fields. He regularly writes and speaks on topics related to nationalism, anticolonialism, decolonization, race, gender and sexuality.

Julia Vanessa **Pauss** is a doctoral student of Anglistics and American studies at Paris Lodron University of Salzburg. Her master's thesis "Straight outta Mordor: Race as the Monstrous Other in Contemporary Fantasy Film" received the Fulbright Award for American Studies. She is interested in literature, film, games studies, and popular culture studies and is working on her dissertation, which focuses on the representation of race in rewriting, remaking, and adaptation in the U.S.–American media landscape.

Tara **Prescott-Johnson**, PhD, is a continuing lecturer in writing programs and a distinguished teacher at UCLA, where she teaches an honors seminar on the works of Neil Gaiman. She is the editor of *Neil Gaiman in the 21st Century* and coeditor of *Feminism in the Worlds of Neil Gaiman*. She has also served as a consultant for "Neil Gaiman Teaches the Art of Storytelling" for MasterClass and wrote "Diving into the Ocean" for the official program for the National Theatre's stage adaptation of Gaiman's *The Ocean at the End of the Lane*.

Morgan **Shipley**, PhD is the Inaugural Foglio Endowed Chair of Spirituality and an associate professor of religious studies at Michigan State University. He is the author of *Psychedelic Mysticism: Transforming Consciousness, Religious Experiences, and Voluntary Peasants in Postwar America* and coeditor of *The Silence of Fallout: Nuclear Criticism in a Post-Cold War World*, and his research explores spirituality and heterodox religious inflections in the United States through an interdisciplinary perspective.

Alex **Tankard**, PhD, is a senior lecturer in English literature at the University of Chester, UK. They found *Good Omens* in the school library back in the '90s and was immediately corrupted. They have published on tuberculosis in nineteenth-century literature and eugenics in the Captain America movies. Their research interests include unusual representations of asexuality in literature and television.

Amanda [Mandy] **Taylor** is an instructional designer and former English lecturer at California State University, San Bernardino. She has an MS in instructional design and technology and an MA in English composition and literature. She has a variety of research interests across several fields. Her publications include work on *The Walking Dead*, *Supernatural*, and the Apollo space program. She is working on her Doctor of Education (EdD) in educational technology at Boise State University.

Rhian **Waller** holds a PhD in creative and critical writing. She teaches in the journalism BA and MA programs at the University of Chester. Her publications appear in *Mobile Culture Studies, Short Film Studies,* and the *Journal of Mental Health* and she has forthcoming work on ecofeminism, fantasy literature, and journalism. Her interests include written journalism and literature, and she also writes poetry and fiction.

Index

"Adam bomb" 19
adaptation 2–3, 11–29, 30–45, 48–49, 75–76, 163–165
Amazon Prime 30, 57, 61, 87, 104, 170, 177
American Gods (novel) 11, 62
American Gods (TV series) 11 62, 163
angelology 87–88
antichrist 2, 15–16, 18–20, 48, 88, 92–93, 99–101, 106, 108, 110–111, 114, 116–118, 120, 123–125, 152, 154–156
apocalypse 11–29, 30, 33, 62–64, 67, 91–92, 106, 108, 111, 114–115, 123, 125–129, 131, 152–153, 170
Aquinas, Thomas 87, 89–90, 92, 97, 102, 113–114
Archive of Our Own 61, 77, 174
Armageddon 2, 11–12, 14, 17, 26–27, 92, 101, 109–111, 117–118, 125, 133, 137, 153, 156, 158, 166
atom bomb 19
aziraphale 2–3, 6n1, 12, 15–18, 24, 34–38, 44, 46–47, 50, 58n1, 62, 64–68, 70, 71n7, 76–80, 87–101, 102n12, 104–106, 108–112, 114–118, 120–121, 123, 125, 127–131, 133–135, 138–146, 152–154, 156, 161–163, 166–167, 169, 170, 172–177

Beelzebub 3, 33, 36, 38, 101, 131, 158, 161n7
Belphegor 63
Blake, William 133–134, 136–137, 140–141, 143–144
books 2, 61, 66, 76, 88, 91–92, 96–98, 100, 111, 163–175
Butler, Judith 53–54, 56
Byron, Lord George Gordon 133–134, 136–137, 139–141, 143, 145–147

cabalistic tradition 87, 102n9
canon 13, 67, 69, 71, 75–81, 83–84, 87, 93
Castiel 63–65, 67–70, 71n3
Catholicism 89, 121–123, 179

Chattering Nuns of St. Beryl/Satanic nuns 15, 111, 124, 154–155, 160
CHOW™ 161n6, 166
Christianity 19, 105–107, 112–113, 117, 122
climate change 13–15, 20–21, 24–27, 166
Cold War 11–27, 133–135, 138–140, 145
Corgi edition 167, 169
counter-reformation 5, 120
Crowley (*Good Omens*) 2–3, 6n1, 12, 15–18, 20, 22–24, 34–38, 44, 46–47, 50, 58n1, 62, 64–68, 70, 71n7, 76–80, 87–101, 102n14, 104–106, 108–112, 114–118, 120–121, 123, 125–131, 133–135, 137–146, 152–154, 156, 158–159, 161–163, 166, 169–170, 172–177
Crowley (*Supernatural*) 62, 64, 69, 71n5

Dearheart, John 51
Derrida, Jacques 12, 15, 46–47, 49, 53, 55
Death (character) 33, 39, 91–92, 125, 127, 138, 153, 161n8
death (concept) 14, 16, 21–22, 26, 46–49, 51–52, 54–56, 63, 65, 68–69, 71n3, 108–109, 111, 114–115, 164, 170
Device, Anathema 1, 6n1, 20, 66, 108, 120, 123–124, 126, 154, 167
De Doctrina Christiana (*Christian Doctrine*) 90
Dog (character) 124, 156–158
Dogma (film) 33, 37–38, 41, 43
Durkheim, Emile 113

ecocriticism 12–15
eco-fascism 21
Eden, Garden of 1–2, 14, 106, 110, 138, 146, 157–158
End Times/End of Days 19, 27, 105, 112, 129, 152
English literature 88, 133, 141
eschatology 5, 15, 104–118
Evil 2, 12, 17, 63, 89, 91, 98–99, 104–118, 128–129, 134

183

184 Index

faith 104, 120, 122, 127, 134–136, 140–142, 144, 146
Famine (character) 21–23, 115, 126, 153
fan desire 74–84
fan studies 76, 77–80
fandom 2, 67, 71n5, 74–78, 80, 83, 164
fanfiction 1, 61, 76–79, 84, 174
Fanon 76–79
fathers 33–34, 92, 105, 121, 124, 152, 157–159
footnotes 39–40, 126, 166, 168, 170
Four Horseman 19–23, 27, 33, 114–115, 120, 123–124, 126, 158
Four (Other) Horseman 152–153, 160, 161n8
free will 5, 64, 70, 87–90, 104–105, 112–117, 136, 140
Freud, Sigmund 40, 52–53, 56

Gabriel 3, 5, 36, 38, 62, 67, 93, 95–96, 98, 100–101, 108, 110, 114, 121, 129, 142, 158, 172
Gaiman, Neil 2–3, 11, 15, 21, 26, 30, 33, 35, 38–40, 43, 46–58, 61–67, 71n3, 74, 83–84, 87–88, 90, 104, 118, 120, 122, 133, 142, 152, 161, 163–170, 172, 174, 177–178
gender/gender fluidity 30, 33–35, 40–41, 44, 65–66, 76, 77–79, 98, 102n15, 134, 161n4, 172
ghosts 46, 48, 50, 52, 56–57
gift economy 78–80
Going Postal 51
Good 2, 12, 17, 63, 89, 91, 98–99, 104–118, 128–129, 134
Good Omens Holiday Gift Exchange 74–83
good works 107, 122
Grand Plan/Divine Plan 91–92, 101, 102n7, 108, 110–111, 114, 117, 120, 123, 126, 130–131
grief 24, 46–58

Hastur 110, 127, 153
Heywood, Thomas 89, 95
Hogfather: A Novel of Discworld 35

ineffability 35, 91, 120, 130, 131, 141
"Ineffable Husbands" 2
ineffable plan 65–67, 70, 87, 91–92, 101, 108, 120, 123, 130–131, 138

Just War 110–117

Knox, John 121
Kozloff, Sarah 31–32, 38, 40, 43
Kripke, Eric 4, 61, 64, 71n3
Kundera, Milan 55–56

Lawrence, Josie 32, 154
Ligur 110, 154

male gaze 40–44
manuscript 167
Masters, Meg 69
McDormand, Frances 4, 32–33, 35, 39, 41, 44, 130, 161n7
Megiddo, Plains of 125
Metatron (*Dogma*) 37–38
Metatron (*Good Omens*) 34, 100–101, 123, 129, 131, 161n12
Milton, John 87–102, 136–138
Mpreg (male pregnancy) 79
Mulvey, Laura 37, 40–42
mutually assured destruction (MAD) 16, 133

names/naming 6, 17, 53, 55, 56, 115, 137, 151–162, 161n7
Netflix 71n3, 170
Nice and Accurate Prophecies of Agnes Nutter, Witch 16, 97, 154, 165, 166, 167, 170, 174
nuclear anxiety 4, 13, 27
nuclear war 16, 97, 154, 165, 166, 167, 170, 174
Nutter, Agnes 1, 17, 32, 66, 108, 121, 123, 125, 130, 154, 167

opposition 24, 62, 63, 115, 117, 129, 133, 135, 137, 138, 141, 145, 146, 155
"Orgy Pants to Work" (*Lucifer*) 71n3

Paradise Lost 1, 5, 87, 88–95, 97, 98, 99, 100, 101, 102, 136, 138
Pollution (Horseman) 21, 22, 23, 26, 33, 98, 115, 125, 126, 153
Pratchett, Terry 1, 2, 3, 5, 13, 15, 38, 40, 43, 46–48, 49, 50, 52, 54, 62, 64, 71, 87, 88, 93, 133, 152, 154, 161, 163, 168, 169, 170, 171f1, 177
Protestantism 5, 93, 121, 122, 123
pseudo–Dionysius 87, 89, 102n4
Pulsifer, Newton 2, 6n1, 108, 120, 123, 154
Pulsifer, Thou-Shalt-Not-Commit-Adultery 108, 154
purification 105, 106, 107, 113

Queen (band) 12, 62
queerbaiting 71n6
queering 2, 62, 64, 65–67, 69, 70, 79

Raphael (Milton) 87, 91, 93–97, 98, 99, 100, 101, 101n2, 102n12, 101n14
Raphael (*Supernatural*) 64

Index

Reformation 5, 120–121, 122
resurrection 56, 57
Revelation, Book of 1, 14, 18, 20, 22, 91, 92, 93, 122, 129, 165
romantic Satanism 5, 133–146

St. Augustine 107, 112, 113, 114, 118
St. James' Park 16, 18, 133
Salvation 90, 118, 120, 122, 146
San Diego Comic Con 61
Satan 14, 16, 18, 41, 43, 90, 91, 94, 99, 105, 106, 107, 109, 110, 111, 112, 114, 115, 116, 117, 118, 124, 125, 136, 137, 138, 139, 152, 155, 158–159, 160
Satanism *see* romantic Satanism
screenplay 133, 152, 169
Shadwell, Sergeant 11, 15, 16, 66, 108, 125, 135, 140, 154, 177
Sheen, Michael 2, 3, 4, 61, 74, 75, 82, 83, 141, 142, 143, 152, 163, 170, 177
Shelley, Percy Bysshe 136
Shippers 71
slash fiction 76, 77, 78, 80, 81
sola fide 120, 122, 128
sola gratia 122, 130
sola scriptura 121, 122, 126
The Sound of Music 12, 100
sub-creation 6, 151, 160
Supernatural/*SPN* (TV series) 4, 61–71, 71n3, 71n5

Tadfield 1, 19, 20, 115, 125, 155, 156, 160, 165
Tennant, David 2, 3, 4, 6n2, 61, 74, 75, 83, 152, 163, 170, 177
text 1, 3, 4, 5, 6, 11, 13, 15, 20, 24, 26, 39, 44, 49, 61, 62, 65, 66, 67, 69, 70, 70n1, 76, 78, 79, 101, 101n1, 121, 122, 131, 153, 163, 164, 165, 167–168, 169, 170, 171, 174, 177
The Them 3, 19, 20, 120, 123, 124, 126, 127, 155, 158, 160, 177
theodicy 107, 142
theology 3, 5, 88, 122, 179
Tobit, Book of 93–94, 95, 96, 100, 101
Tolkien, J.R.R. 151, 152, 160, 161, 161n10
Torres, Eddie 171
transformative works 66, 75, 78, 134, 180

Uck (river) 22

voice of God 4, 31–33, 35, 37, 40, 43, 44
voiceover 4, 157, 166

War (Horseman) 21, 22, 23, 114, 115, 126, 153
warlock 34, 42, 124, 156, 161, 162
Watchmen 164, 165
Winchester, Dean 61, 63, 64, 65, 67, 68, 69, 71
Winchester, Sam 61, 63, 71

Young, Adam 1, 2, 3, 5, 6, 12, 18–21, 24, 26, 27, 35, 39, 42, 92, 105, 115, 118, 120, 123–127, 128, 131, 138, 144, 151–152, 154–162, 165, 168
Young, Arthur 156, 159, 162n14
Young, Diedre 155, 159, 162n14

"Zari, Not Zari" (*Legends of Tomorrow*) 71n3
Žižek, Slavoj 51